Leading with Wisdom

Spiritual-based Leadership in Business

Peter Pruzan and Kirsten Pruzan Mikkelsen

together with
Debra and William Miller

Epilogue
President A.P.J. Abdul Kalam of India

Advance praise for the book

Leading with Wisdom is an absolutely sensational book. I've never seen anything like it. I can't wait to share it with the leaders I meet.

Patricia Aburdene (USA): author of *Megatrends 2010: The Rise of Conscious Capitalism* and, together with John Naisbitt, of *Megatrends 2000: Re-inventing the Corporation*

I was truly surprised and in disbelief, when Peter Pruzan, a life-long source of inspiration, started lecturing about spirituality and leadership. We shared the conviction that the business of business was much more than business. But 'spirituality'? What had happened to this stringent and analytical academic? *Leading with Wisdom* provides the answers. Kirsten and Peter call it 'spirituality'; I have thought of it as decency, dignity and love of your fellow man. This discussion is not important. This book reminds us that true leadership does not exist unless you are a friend of all mankind and have that as a guiding higher principle. *Leading with Wisdom* inspires and gives you the courage to preach what you practise.

Mads Øvlisen (Denmark): Chairman of LEGO; Board member, UN Global Compact; former CEO and Chairman, Novo Nordisk

Leading with Wisdom is a fascinating attempt to capture the essence of the timeless in the tapestry of our times. The authors bring together very credible voices in corporate storytelling. The book will take the reader on a voyage of self-discovery. It may just as well provide a fundamental shift in the way we look at the very purpose of business. It is a trendsetter and a refreshing contrast to conventional success literature.

Dr Debashis Chatterjee (India): Professor and Head, Leadership Centre, Indian Institute of Management, Lucknow

Leading with Wisdom shows that one can achieve leadership positions while being spiritual but is not tempted to claim that people will be more successful in business if they are spiritual. At no point are the authors trying to 'sell' spirituality or to 'translate it into a set of tools'. Spirituality, as experienced by the leaders in this book, is their personal journey which is a source of inner strength and humility.

Dr Marjo Lips-Wiersma (New Zealand): Senior Lecturer, University of Canterbury, New Zealand; past Chair of Management, Spirituality and Religion Interest Group, American Academy of Management

Compassion, humility, love, and at times even responsibility, are rare attributes in today's corporate world. *Leading with Wisdom* shows how these attributes can lead individuals and organizations to excel. Reading it is a deeply enjoyable and enlightening journey into the potential of spiritual-based leadership. I warmly recommend it!

Elena Bonfiglioli (Belgium): Director, Corporate Citizenship, Microsoft Europe, Middle East and Africa; Chair of the Business Group, European Academy of Business in Society

Leading with Wisdom is a rare gem: a truthful, reflective, inspirational text from the front lines of business management. It is a radical interpretation of business as a mission, as a purposeful pursuit that goes to the heart of our existential quest, fulfilling humankind's ultimate reasons for being. If only this book will pave the way for such interpretation, it will have achieved a tremendously important objective.

Marcello Palazzi (Netherlands): Founder-President, Progressio Foundation; Co-founder, Spirit in Business (EU and USA)

Leading with Wisdom is a milestone in moving conventional thinking forward to a time when we will look back at the present and wonder how people could have led from any-place other than a spiritual centre. This artificial vacuum—this 'hole in the leader's soul'—has been a root cause of much pain, stress and damage done in the name of free-market capitalism. This book can help leaders become whole—to be fully alive, vital and engaged in what they do.

John Renesch (USA): Businessman-turned-Futurist; former Publisher and Editor-in-Chief of New Leaders Press; author of *Getting to the Better Future*

This book is full of eloquent stories. It profiles people who are breaking new ground and leading the way towards a more humane role for business in the world. This is a book that will appeal to your mind, your heart and your soul. It will give you the courage to live and lead and love from a more integrated place.

Dr Judi Neal (USA): President and CEO, Association for Spirit at Work; President, Judi Neal & Associates; author of *Edgewalkers*

A marvellous challenge to conventional thinking about leadership and the purpose of business in society as well as support for leaders at all levels seeking authenticity in expressing their spirituality in day-to-day decisions and actions. My one wish is that the inspiration of this journey in spiritual-based leadership will reach tomorrow's leaders, many of whom are sincerely seeking this reassurance that spirituality and leadership are mutually reinforcing.

George Starcher (France): President, European Bahá'í Business Forum; former Director, McKinsey & Co. (Paris and Milan)

I found the profiles in *Leading with Wisdom* to be absolutely fascinating. I could *feel* the identities of the leaders and their business challenges, even as I appreciated the variety of their spiritual orientations and religious traditions. What I particularly like is the book's realistic premise that 'it is enough to realize that these executives have achieved their leadership position *while* being spiritual'. This is a book for those of us who are naturally sceptical to read, ponder and possibly allow ourselves to be changed by.

Sandra J. Sucher (USA): Senior Lecturer, Harvard Business School; author of *The Moral Leader: Challenges, Tools* and *Insights* and *Teaching 'The Moral Leader'*

This inspiring book is an authentic account of spirituality in business. The Pruzans engagingly demonstrate that spirituality need not be separated from business practice. The documented examples of extraordinary business leaders show that spirituality can survive and flourish, even in large-scale business organizations.

Dr László Zsolnai (Hungary): Professor and Director, Business Ethics Center, Corvinus University of Budapest; Co-founder, European SPES Forum (Spirituality in Economics and Social Life)

Leading with Wisdom provides a wealth of intimate insights into the critical importance of our inner compasses in guiding our very purpose for providing leadership to others. Without this well-developed sensibility, no number of policies, rules or systems will provide the much-needed accountability of our leaders for their actions and impacts.

Dr Simon Zadek (UK): CEO, AccountAbility; Senior Fellow, Center for Government and Business, J.F. Kennedy School, Harvard University; author of the award-winning book, *The Civil Corporation*

This is an odd and dangerous book—and utterly delightful. Odd, because the authors, who obviously know their game, try to obfuscate things with their attempt to fit subjective ruminations of 31 astonishingly likeable business leaders into an objective scheme. Dangerous, because this book will change your mind; you'll find yourself re-weighing many pieces of your life. Delightful, in every sense of the word: brilliant, light and nimble, and shining with love. It's a great leadership book!

Dr Jack Hawley (USA): bestselling author of *Reawakening the Spirit in Work: The Power of Dharmic Management* **and** *The Bhagavad Gita: A Walkthrough for Westerners*

Leading with Wisdom shows us that it is possible to be a human being in the business world, and not be reduced to being simply a 'human doing'. It invites us to ask ourselves what kind of wisdom is needed to lead today's organizations, and how we can access this wisdom.

Dr Josep M. Lozano (Spain): Professor, ESADE Business School, Barcelona; Director, Institute for the Individual, Corporations and Society

Leading with Wisdom touched my heart as a leader. But not only did it deeply appeal to my feelings; it also heightened my conscious awareness of the roles of wisdom and love in the art of leadership.

Maria Helena Gomes (Brazil):Vice President for Latin America, AyurVida S.A.; former President, Olsten do Brazil Ltda

This book highlights the role of businesses in service to society. I truly enjoyed reading this in-depth analysis, brought to life with real-life examples.

Dr Ajay S. Mookerjee (India/USA): President, Harvard Business School, India Research Centre; Country Head, KPMG Business Advisory Services; former Managing Director for Asia, Capital One

So far no one has been able to break into the intellectual fortress: how leaders understand and relate concepts like spirituality, leadership and wisdom, and how they integrate and apply them in their daily life. But *Leading with Wisdom* pierces a big hole in its walls. A hole through which the reflective reader will be able to glimpse what one day will be the standard way to conceive of the purpose of business in society, and of what business leaders need to do to integrate the inner truths they pursue with the external responsibilities they face.

Dr Maurizio Zollo (France/Italy): Professor, INSEAD, France; from September 2007 Professor, Bocconi University, Italy and Director, Bocconi International Center for Advanced Management Studies

LEADING
WITH
WISDOM

Spiritual-based Leadership in Business

PETER PRUZAN and **KIRSTEN PRUZAN MIKKELSEN**
together with Debra and William Miller

Greenleaf
PUBLISHING

2 0 0 7

Published by Greenleaf Publishing Limited
Aizlewood's Mill
Nursery Street
Sheffield S3 8GG
UK
www.greenleaf-publishing.com

Printed and bound by CPI Group (UK) Ltd, Croydon, CR0 4YY

FSC
www.fsc.org
MIX
Paper from
responsible sources
FSC® C013604

Cover by LaliAbril.com.

British Library Cataloguing in Publication Data:
    A catalogue record for this book is available from the British Library.

ISBN-13: 978-1-874719-59-5

Contents

Foreword

The Spiritual-based Leadership
Research Programme

Have you ever heard a story, read a book or pondered upon an article that felt like 'a breath of fresh air'? Perhaps it gave you a new uplifting view of something you had been discouraged or sceptical about. Or perhaps it spoke an inspiring truth that confirmed what you already knew deep inside, but hadn't yet been able to express.

When such fresh air comes into our lives, our minds are elevated, our hearts feel a renewed peace and joy, and we naturally begin to breathe more deeply. Ultimately, this is what all the four directors of the Spiritual-based Leadership Research Programme felt as we met the executives who are profiled in this book. Each one broadened our horizons and gave us new insights and confidence about *spirituality* as the basis not only for business leadership, but for self-leadership and for living life as well.

The research reported on here started in 2002 when William Miller, an international consultant on corporate innovation, and Dr Peter Pruzan, Professor of Systems Science at the Department of Management, Politics and Philosophy at the Copenhagen Business School in Denmark, were both visiting professors at a university in India. Since the university's MBA programme was permeated by the concept of spirituality and human values, they felt strongly that there was a need for the MBA students to have access to the experiences and perspectives of executive role models who demonstrate that business leadership and spirituality can be mutually supportive. They were convinced there was a need amongst students and business leaders for ideals and academic theories as to the role of spirituality in business to be backed up by true-to-life stories of successful leaders throughout the world. Leaders, whose approach to such matters as wealth generation, ethics, responsibility, sustainability, reputation and success are founded on a firm spiritual basis.

Together they began to design an international research programme focused on spiritual-based leadership in work organizations in general, including businesses, governmental organizations, unions, NGOs, etc. Its purpose was to investigate the nature, activities and results of leading from a spiritual basis. As time went on, it became clear that their wives had significant skills and perspectives to offer as directors of the research programme: Debra Miller, a consultant, author and lecturer; and Kirsten Pruzan Mikkelsen, a senior journalist and former editor with a major national newspaper in Denmark.

Thus we joined together and focused our initial research on spirituality as the basis for *business* leadership. This was in line with our many years of personally exploring the arena of spirituality and business, and our striving to incorporate our insights into our professional lives. As of the autumn of 2006, the four of us have conducted interviews with business executives from North and South America, Africa, Asia, Australia and Europe. In addition, we have interviewed a number of leaders from fields other than business, including the President of India (whom you will meet in the Epilogue).

Based on the valuable contributions of these executives, Peter and Kirsten took on the responsibility of harvesting the wisdom of these leaders. In producing this book, they have skilfully edited and abridged these interviews into enlightening profiles—a collage of top executives who portray an emerging new culture of leadership in the world: *spiritual-based leadership*.

We have felt personally inspired and touched by each and every one of the 31 spiritual-based executives profiled in this book. From them we have learned about integrity and determination: how they strove to live up to their spiritual principles, even in the most trying of times. We have learned about courage and faith: how they drew upon their spirituality to make difficult decisions that others might not agree with. We have learned about humility: how they gained strength from their spirituality to stand up to face their mistakes.

Whether you are currently a leader or are aspiring to be one, we hope and trust that the experiences and perspectives of these business executives will stimulate and support your own growth and leadership. We feel confident that these men and women provide a fresh look at what business leadership can be—*and already is*—when we have the faith and confidence that it is possible to lead business organizations from a spiritual basis.

Debra and William Miller,
India, January 2007

Preface

This book is written for business executives and for all those women and men who want to lead with integrity from a spiritual basis. Although it presents the results of an international research project, it is also a very 'personal' book. From the very beginning of the project in 2002, it was our intention to demonstrate that business leaders can achieve success, recognition, peace of mind and happiness, while at the same time serving the needs of all those affected by their leadership, when they lead from a spiritual basis.

We have travelled, worked and lived in many parts of the world, in both developed and developing countries, over the past several decades. We have become aware of a trend that is increasingly manifest in business organizations of all kinds, no matter where they are located or what products or services they produce: Many business executives are increasingly becoming workaholic human-*doings,* longing to be full and integrated human-*beings.* They aspire to live with integrity, where their thoughts, values, words and deeds are in harmony. The problem is that they don't know how to do so in a business world that is increasingly characterized by complexity, turbulence and greed.

Leading with Wisdom provides food for thought for dealing with these challenges. It contains stories and reflections of inspiring and compassionate business leaders who care about what is truly important in life and who integrate this awareness and sensitivity into their leadership. Leaders who search for meaning, purpose and fulfilment in the external world of business and in the internal world of consciousness and conscience. Leaders whose leadership is a natural expression of their hearts, minds and souls. In other words, leaders who lead from a spiritual basis, where their external actions and their internal reflections are mutually supportive—so that spirituality and rationality can go hand in hand, rather than being each other's competitor.

Aside from some introductory commentary and conclusions, the words of wisdom you will meet will be the words of the 31 spiritual-based leaders from 15 countries and six continents that we[1] have interviewed as part of the broader research project on spiritual-based leadership. They are leaders who are able to express from their first-hand experience what it is like to lead a business from a spiritual basis. While they share certain characteristics, they are also very different individuals who live in different societal and organizational cultures. In their own unique ways, they are people who are nourished by their spirituality, which is a source within them that informs and guides them. Janiece Webb, senior vice president with Motorola Corporation, USA, exemplified this reliance on spirituality as the source of inner strength in saying:

If ever there's a time for spiritual leadership, it's now. You must earn the right to lead every day, and spirituality is necessary to do that. Spirituality means to be connected in a real way to life, with the centre, at the core. It keeps you from doing many short-term tactical actions that are often wrong for the business and the people. It also gives you immense courage to stand tall against damaging politics. Being a spiritual leader can sometimes be lonely, but you feel happy and grounded inside. You also embrace your own humanness and imperfection. And, it keeps you humble as a leader and yet still strong.

Our approach

In order to develop the profiles presented here, the research team chose to conduct first-hand interviews with business executives who have a consciously held spiritual view of life and who have led their business from that basis. At first, this task seemed daunting as we had to come to terms with questions such as:

- 'What do people mean by spirituality?' 'How will we know if a leader is spiritual?' 'How will we know if he or she is actually leading from a spiritual basis?'

- 'Where will we find executives who lead from a spiritual basis?' 'Will they allow such a deeply personal matter as their spirituality to be made public?'

---

1 In order to be able to present the profiles in as readable a fashion as possible, we write 'we' and 'us' no matter who in the research team has performed the interview. For example, we write, 'he told us . . .' also when an interview was performed by our research partners, the Millers.

Regarding the questions about 'spirituality', we knew from our travels in many cultures around the world that people have a wide variety of spiritual views, which may or may not be connected with an organized religion. Rather than using one single definition of spirituality for our Spiritual-based Leadership Research Programme, we chose to let the leaders we interviewed define this term, sometimes for the first time. In so doing we created a 'spiritual framework' that honours a wide variety of definitions and perspectives.

Within the spiritual framework that evolved, we did not consider it to be our job to judge the spiritual views of these leaders, nor to judge their 'spiritual maturity'. Rather, our task was to probe in-depth, listen, and record how they defined and understood spirituality and their spiritual views of life, and how their perspectives and actual experiences of leadership might be a reflection of those views.

We achieved this by creating an environment where the interviewees could openly and authentically share with us their perspectives and stories. We spent an average of two hours with each executive, building trust and drawing out their experiences as they could relate them. As in all such interviews, there is a risk that the interviewee has painted a picture of his or her motives and actions that others might challenge. Nevertheless, as is expanded on in Appendix A, which discusses the methodological aspects of the project, we feel secure in our decision to trust that the executives have given us an authentic picture of who they are and how they lead.

To find business leaders to interview, we looked in two directions: to executives we knew personally who were spiritually inclined; and to our network of colleagues and friends whom we trusted to refer us to executives who were spiritually inclined. In the process we discovered, much to our surprise, an abundance of business executives around the world who were not only spiritually inclined, but who were willing to speak openly with us about their spirituality and how it shaped their leadership.

Each interview was transcribed by a member of the team, and then edited and reviewed by all of us, using a template so as to be comparable with other interviews. Finally, after being approved by the interviewee, the interview was abridged into what we here refer to as a 'profile'; the length of a profile is roughly one-third the size of the transcribed and edited interview.

Appendix B provides an overview of the business topics these leaders have dealt with while the table at the end of this Preface provides an overview of the 31 spiritual-based leaders we have interviewed to show what is possible in leading a business from a spiritual basis.[2]

---

2   All data is based on the date the interview was conducted. Country refers to where the leadership was performed, not to the country of birth.

In the Epilogue you will find an example of spiritual-based leadership beyond business—the profile of the internationally known space technologist and missile scientist who is also the spiritual-based leader of a nation, the honourable President of India, A.P.J. Abdul Kalam.

In putting this book together, it has not been our intention to imply that people will be *more* successful in business (however one may define success) if they are spiritual. It is enough to realize that these executives have achieved their leadership positions *while* being spiritual—that the two do not have to be mutually exclusive.

Nor are we implying that spirituality is the royal road to the top of the corporate pyramid, or that personal success is ensured if people are spiritual. Some of the executives you will meet in this book have chosen to put their wealth at risk in order to stop harm. Others had to face the challenges provided by business failure. Just as jogging and eating organic food do not provide a guarantee of a long and healthy physical life, neither is a spiritual perspective on leadership a guarantee of a long-lived and healthy organization.

A source of scepticism we have met when presenting our research results to audiences of MBA students and business leaders is a belief that, in order to be spiritual, one must renounce the world and its material wealth. Some of the executives we have interviewed lead rather affluent lives, to put it mildly—several even live in splendid manor houses. Others live in modest dwellings with a simple lifestyle, all according to their values and aspirations. None of the leaders we interviewed indicated that wealth is an impediment to living a spiritual life or leading from a spiritual basis.

In *Leading with Wisdom*, business leaders at every level, as well as spiritually inclined working people of any profession, MBA students, professors and consultants, will discover for themselves: first-hand experiences of spiritual-based leadership in business; new insights into business practices when traditional success criteria are supplemented and reshaped by a spiritual perspective; and opportunities for spiritual growth through business leadership.

If you have been a pioneer-practitioner in this area, this book will be a powerful confirmation, validating what you have already known and practised. If you are moving in this direction, this book will give you inspiration and strength to continue your journey. If you are searching for more fulfilment in your work, this book will be a much-needed source of wisdom and guidance—also as to how to deal with the challenges that pop up when one conscientiously attempts to make spirituality the foundation for business leadership.

Having experienced the confidence of each of the leaders who have been interviewed, we know that spirituality is alive and well in the world of business, though in a subtle and often tacit way: it is not yet a part of the common business vernacular; seldom is it explicitly expressed in corporate mission statements, policies, PR and reporting; and it is taught at only a small minority of MBA programmes throughout the world. But, as the legendary American folk singer Bob Dylan proclaimed, 'The times they are a'changin' '.

Peter Pruzan and Kirsten Pruzan Mikkelsen
Denmark, January 2007

Name	Country	Organization name	Sector or industry	Position	Age	Years in leadership
Aguenza, Flordelis, F.	The Philippines	Planters Development Bank	Banking	President and COO	62	30
Behner, John R.	El Salvador	Nabisco	Food	Country Manager	66	40
Cañada, Francisco	Argentina	Errepar S.A.	Publishing	Director/Partner	47	20
Chand, Amber	USA	Eziba	Retail marketing	VP of Vision	53	9
		Amber Chand Collection	Retail marketing	Founder		
Chattopadhyay, A.K.	India	ACC Ltd, Refractories Division	Manufacture and installation, refractory	VP—Senior	50	20
Covey, Stephen R.	USA	FranklinCovey Co.	Global professional services	Co-founder and Vice Chairman	73	40
Cruz, Alvaro	Colombia	Cundinamarca	Government	State Governor	54	23
		I.C.M. Ingenieros	Building construction	Owner and CEO		
Cuneo, Federico	Peru	Bank of Boston	Banking	Corporate Director	50	20
		American Glass Products	Manufacturing and distribution	Chairman		
Daugherty, Thomas	USA	Methodist Health Care System	Health care/medical care	VP of Spiritual Care and Values Integration	61	27
Delbecq, André L.	USA	Santa Clara University School of Business	Business education	Director—Institute for Spirituality and Organizational Leadership	67	25

Name	Country	Organization name	Sector or industry	Position	Age	Years in leadership
Franklin, Carol	Switzerland	World Wide Fund for Nature (WWF)	Environmental protection	CEO	53	20
		Swiss Re	Insurance	Head of HR		
Govindan, Rajan	USA	Bankers Trust	Banking	Senior Managing Director	56	35
Jensen, Niels Due	Denmark	Grundfos Management A/S	Manufacturing, pumps	Group Chairman	60	30
Jiang, Niran	Australia	Institute of Human Excellence	Training and consulting	CEO	40	15
	USA	S.C. Johnson	Household products	Manager, Marketing		
	USA	Coca-Cola	Food	Trends Manager		
Kolind, Lars	Denmark	Oticon	Hearing aid products	CEO	54	26
Levy, Ricardo	USA	Catalytica, Inc.	Energy/pharmaceutical	Chairman/Co-founder	57	30
Maitra, Ashoke	India	Times of India Group	Publishing, NEWSPAPER	Director, HR	45	16
Merchant, Nilofer	USA	Rubicon Consultants	Marketing	President	34	8
Moitra, Deependra	India	Lucent Technologies	Telecommunications	General Manager, Engineering	32	7
Narayana, G.	India	Excel Industries Pvt. Ltd	Chemicals, biochem, agricultural	Executive Chairman	60	38
Narendran, Parantha	Czech Republic	Eurotel	Telecommunications	Strategy Director	34	3

Name	Country	Organization name	Sector or industry	Position	Age	Years in leadership
Ollé, Ramon	The Netherlands	Epson Europe B.V.	Electronic equipment and services	President	52	27
Pillai, Anand	India	HCL COMNET	Computer technology	Head, Centre for Leadership and Management	43	18
Ploix, Hélène	France	Pechel Industries Partenaires	Equity Investment	Chairman and Managing Director	62	38
Raghavan, N.S.	India	Infosys Technologies Ltd	Information technology	Joint-founder and Joint Managing Director	61	35
Raman, Ananth	USA	Graphtex, Inc.	Manufacturing—electrical and aluminium	Chairman and CEO, President	55	25
Ranganathan, V.V.	India	Ernst & Young India	Consulting, assurance and advisory services	Senior Partner	53	24
Sinclair, James	USA/Tanzania	Tan Range Exploration, Ltd	Mining	Chairman and CEO	62	41
Vrethammar, Magnus	UK	Pergo	Laminated flooring	President	52	22
	Switzerland	Finess	Consumer paper products	President, Consumer Division		
Webb, Janiece	USA	Motorola Corporation	Electronic communications	Senior Vice President	47	28
Welling, S.K.	India	HMT International Ltd (Hindustan Machine Tools)	Machine tools, watches, tractors	Executive Director	55	33

Acknowledgements

We humbly acknowledge that the real contributors to this book are the inspiring leaders we have interviewed. We extend our sincere gratitude to each and every one of them for their gifts to the emerging global culture of spiritual-based leadership. Each gave generously of their time, openly sharing reflections about spirituality and leadership and making their experiences and personal convictions available to the public. Not only have these magnanimous people enriched our knowledge about leadership and business conducted from a spiritual basis, they have also touched our lives as human beings.

We also wish to express our sincere gratitude to Debra and William Miller, our dear American friends who live in India, and our cohorts in the research project that provides the 'data' for this book. Not only have they carried out a significant share of the interviews that form the basis for the profiles presented here, they have also provided inspiration and critique that goes far beyond what one can ordinarily expect from friends and colleagues. In the process of designing and carrying out the research reported on here, our work has been transformed from an academic undertaking to a work of sincere service, love and dedication. Without the contributions by the Millers, this book would never have fructified.

You may access the computerized knowledge-base that this book draws from at the website of the not-for-profit organization, Global Dharma Center, which the Millers have founded: www.globaldharma.org. Readers who want to dig even deeper into the subject matter of this book will find a proverbial goldmine of inspiring information at this website.

Introduction

Spirituality as the basis of leadership

They do it!

A CEO, freshly recruited from a highly profitable, family-owned business, faced the stark reality that the high-tech company he now led would not survive unless a major reduction in staff was made. He made the decision that, aside from keeping the very few people whose skills were absolutely critical for the survival of the business, the first to be released would be those who could most easily find a new job. Furthermore, no one over the age of 50 would be let go. Everybody—including the company's bankers who were keeping extremely close tabs on what was going on—was deeply sceptical about the rationale behind the CEO's decisions.

When the staff reduction was to take place, instead of leaving the task to the department heads, the CEO talked personally with each employee who was to be laid off. Training and assistance was given to help them find new positions. As he told us, 'We got through this amazingly well. There was total acceptance, even though no one really understood it. But once it was done, people said "wow" and respected my decisions.' What remained was a revitalized and dedicated group of people who focused together with the CEO on creating a far-reaching purpose for the company and a revolutionary form of organization. Today, the company is a world leader in its industry.

What was the basis of Lars Kolind's decisions as he handled this crisis at Oticon, the renowned Danish manufacturer of products for the hearing-impaired? 'Later,' he said, 'I realized that this was really an expression of my spiritual theme of "love God and love your neighbour." When I see what I have done, and the decisions I have made in different situations, it is clear that spirituality has always been there; I've just become more conscious about it.'

In another part of the world, where relations between union and corporate leaders are often characterized by mutual distrust, 20 union leaders showed up one morning in the lobby of corporate headquarters for a surprise visit to the company president. They looked angry and ready for a confrontation. Security officers called the president for instructions. 'Send them up to my office,' he said—and told the office assistant to 'prepare tea and coffee for 20 plus myself.'

The union leaders did not trust the president to handle an important human resource issue—that of filling two executive vacancies—believing he would pick the Chairman's favourites over 'more qualified' candidates. When they came in, they stood, shouted and complained. Security was still edgy about what might happen.

How did S.K. Welling, Executive Director of HMT (Hindustan Machine Tools) International Ltd, in India, view the situation? 'Because of the spiritual feelings I have inside, I knew immediately that they didn't mean anything against me; they just wanted to show their strength. I knew this very well in my heart . . . since I had the inner feeling that they meant no harm to me, I had no reason to be concerned.'

Looking back to that morning, S.K. Welling reflects upon what happened. 'I told them, "I will not accept these two just because there is pressure from the Chairman. Nor will I not take these two fellows just because you are saying that I should not take them. I will apply my own mind, my own judgement, and I will only go by the merits in each case. If you think that I am going to take them based on pressure from the Chairman, I am the last one to do that; I would resign and go away instead. And I will not bow to your pressure either." Once I said this, they all calmed down. Then I invited them to sit and have coffee, and we were able to talk harmoniously.'

Perspectives on spirituality

It is well recognized in the field of organizational development that you can know the culture of an organization by the 'stories people tell'. Stories about prominent people and events have always been the vehicle for transmitting culture in societies as well, passing along the 'teachings' from generation to generation. As we listened to the stories of Lars Kolind and S.K. Welling and the other executives we interviewed, we began to see and feel the unfolding of a new global culture of business leadership—a culture that transcends national boundaries and organizational ethos.

While these executives share certain characteristics, they are also very different individuals who live in different societal and organizational cultures.

This heterogeneity naturally leads to differences in their experiences and in the stories they told us. For example, some of them had long ago begun to reflect on their spiritual views of life and had discussed it with others; in our interviews with such leaders, they could readily describe their spirituality and articulate its impact on their leadership. For others, the interview process itself helped them to draw out and express their spiritual perspectives; during our time together, they began to see more fully how their spirituality, often deeply rooted from childhood, had influenced their leadership.

Some leaders made it clear that they did not consider themselves to be 'spiritual' if spirituality were to be defined in a narrow, traditional or religious sense. However, when providing their own personal definitions of spirituality, they were quite comfortable sharing their views and experiences as business leaders. The following are some of the different perspectives about spirituality we heard from these executives:

- Spirituality is knowing the true core of being within you, and realizing it is the same core within everyone.

- Spirituality for me is the essence of being. It is the invisible place within me that yearns and speaks in many ways, through writing and poetry and conversations.

- Spirituality is our deep connection with a force greater than ourselves. It is a very individual, lived experience that includes longing and belonging, for which the fruits are love and compassion.

- Spirituality is taking the principles that are taught in most religions and living them as a natural way of life.

- Spirituality is attunement with a universal spirit. It is being so in tune with that spirit that you are not acting from a place of ego or desire or greed, but you are acting from a place that is on behalf of the welfare of the totality.

- Spirituality is man's quest into his innate divinity. It's more like a road than a state of affairs, a quest more than an arrival.

During our interviews with these leaders, we asked in-depth questions not only about their spiritual views of life, but also about their spiritual purposes and values, their approach to spiritual growth, and the history of their spiritual evolution.[1] These leaders come from a wide variety of religious backgrounds: Christianity (Catholics, Protestants, Mormons), Hinduism, Bud-

---

1 To read more about the interviewing process and the editing, see Appendix A.

dhism, Judaism and Islam. Given their wide variety of spiritual and religious traditions, one of the questions we also asked was: 'How is spirituality the same as or distinct from religion for you?' Here are some of their replies:

- Spirituality is about how you live your entire life. I see religion as something that has been handed down to you. You may choose to apply some of its values in your life, and your life might become more spiritual because of that. But religion is something external to you, whereas spirituality is something that is within you.

- To me, spirituality and religion are the same thing.

- Spirituality and religion are not the same. Religion encompasses the belief system associated with a world view, patterns of worship and ritual prayer. Spirituality, in contrast, is specific to the individual and encompasses each person's lived experience.

- All of the different religions have their own belief systems and at some point they do cross over with each other. While in spirituality there is no belief system. Spirituality talks about ultimate truth: you must realize it, you must understand it, you must feel it.

- While religion offers many beautiful things like rituals and cere- monies, to me it is not spirituality. Spirituality has no borders or restraints. It doesn't separate; it connects.

- For me religion is an organized path to spirituality.

At the end of our questions about spirituality, we asked each leader to capture all that he or she had shared into a 'spiritual theme'. This spiritual theme then became a guide throughout the remaining interview, to help us and the interviewee stay focused when sharing specific examples and giving his or her perspective on leading from a spiritual basis.

The leaders' spiritual perspectives serve as the book's organizing principle; it is built up around a number of sections, each of which contains the profiles of leaders whose spiritual perspectives have a common focus. This helped us to reap the more subtle insights from their diverse, extensive interviews. Most of these sections contain profiles of executives from at least three continents, giving them the richness of a diversity of cultures.

What's missing in the dialogue on ethics, responsibility and sustainability?

'The purpose of business organizations is to serve human needs. Period!' The internationally known authority on leadership Stephen R. Covey didn't hesitate for a moment when we asked him about the purpose of business organizations. 'Spiritual-based leaders respect others,' he added. 'They are guided by the fundamental ethic: service to others comes before serving oneself. Individuals and organizations grow when they give themselves to others and relationships improve when there is a focus on serving the other.'

Such perspectives on leadership are not yet mainstream. Greed, prestige and power appear to still be prime motivating forces for leaders of the world's larger corporations. In spite of 25 years of globalization, poverty is still devastatingly ubiquitous in many parts of the world. In striking contrast, the compensation packages of top leaders in business, particularly in the West, have skyrocketed, reaching levels that would have been considered impossible only a decade ago.

Today the people behind the once so huge energy company Enron, at the time the seventh largest corporation in the USA, might wish that they had reflected more upon respecting and serving others. What started out as a fabulous success story, with what appeared to be unprecedented growth, ended abruptly when the bubble burst with the biggest bang ever heard inside and outside any corporate boardroom in the world. Twenty-one thousand employees lost more than US$2 billion in pension savings, leaving many of them with devastating prospects for their old age. Thousands lost their jobs. The market value of Enron's shares was reduced by $60 billion—and a large number of other companies together with their employees and local communities were also seriously affected. Why? Driven by greed, the Enron executives had worshipped money as their God.

There have been many other notorious scandals in world business: for example, the collapse in 1999 of South Korea's second largest conglomerate, Daewoo, with an estimated US$80 billion in debt; and Europe's largest corporate failure, the 2006 implosion of the Parmalat dairy company in Italy, with almost $18 billion in outstanding debt. Prompted by these outrageous examples, laws have been passed with the aim of reducing the risk of such infamous behaviour. The most notable of these laws is the Sarbanes–Oxley bill in the USA, which holds leaders criminally responsible if their company's accounting is faulty; indirectly, this law has also had a profound affect on the governance of companies all over the world.

But increasing the demands as to the quantity and quality of accounting information provided by corporations is only a superficial solution to the problem. Business scandals have taken place throughout the history of commerce and appear to be increasing in frequency and impact even as legal and accounting control procedures are becoming ever more inclusive. No tightening of laws and threats of punishment will end the amoral and immoral behaviour by business leaders that characterize such scandals. A 'solution' cannot and will not be found by focusing solely on rules, regulations and punishment. There are always new loopholes to be found by highly creative leaders, lawyers and accountants in increasingly complex and globalized business environments.

What is clearly needed is a change in the mind-set, values and principles of our leaders, as well as of those who finance our enterprises, and of those who teach and mentor our future leaders. At the very minimum, what is needed is an expansion of the concept of 'success' so that it transcends the prevailing myopic focus on short-term financial gains. Greed appears to be insatiable— a CEO in larger American corporations now earns roughly 700 times as much as an average worker, with leaders in other parts of the world trying to follow suit. Greed is also increasingly considered by many influential business leaders, economists and politicians to be a virtue as it is believed to be the motivating force that keeps the wheels of economic growth moving in a world where success is perceived as identical to the accumulation of wealth.

It can be argued that this rampant greed is gradually being tamed, not just by laws, but also by social and ethical norms. In the last two decades there has been an amazing and uplifting focus on such perspectives as business ethics, corporate social responsibility, and sustainability. Major companies throughout the world have developed executive positions and reporting systems that are intended to demonstrate that the corporate world, in spite of—or perhaps because of—its classical focus on wealth creation, is becoming increasingly sensitive to the needs of the public and the environment.

However, without in any way attempting to play down the important role played by such perspectives, something crucial is still missing. When one analyses the positive discourse and the fine 'triple-bottom-line reports', it becomes clear that underlying the implementation of these perspectives into the vocabulary and policies of our corporate bodies is a very traditional economic rationale. When leaders are questioned as to why they and their organizations should promote this new and expanded sensitivity to ethics, responsibility and the environment, their 'default' answer typically is: 'It pays to do so! It protects our reputation and enables us to maintain our licence to operate and to continue to increase our wealth.' Ethics and values and responsibility and sustainability are not important in their own right. They are simply efficacious means to promote classical business ends of increasing earnings and share prices.

What is missing is a paradigm of leadership that looks upon social responsibility, ethical behaviour, and concern for the environment *not* simply as instruments, but as fundamental principles and values in their own right. In the moral language of the mind, what is missing is responsibility. In the emotional language of the heart, what is missing is love. In the spiritual language of the soul, what is missing is compassion and unity.

A new concept of success

But how and why should such an expanded concept of leadership develop? What should provide the motivation for our leaders to find their way in an increasingly complex business world by using a compass that points not only to a pot of gold, but also to a path to deeper meaning and purpose in business?

This book does not provide answers in the form of proposals as to new rules or laws or moral injunctions. Rather it provides a collage of perspectives in the form of stories of highly respected and successful executives who have integrated their spiritual search into their leadership so as to be 'whole' people—leaders whose thoughts, words and deeds are in harmony with their most fundamental truths and longings, both at work and in their private lives. These stories tell of an emerging culture where business becomes a primary domain for both individual and organizational spiritual growth. As some of the leaders in our research told us:

- I think a business exists to provide an innovative answer to a compelling societal need. A spiritual sense of the inner journey and touching the transcendent will shape this purpose in many ways. The problems you start listening to, and the needs you start becoming attentive to, shift.

- There is such a need for a complete rebirth of trust in our business leaders. Somewhere along the line, leaders have lost their humility and in doing so they have lost their compassion and empathy, and their inner connection to God. I think this is something we need to come back to.

- Business must benefit society; there is no question about it. You cannot be a spike of prosperity in a sea of poverty. If we become cost-competitive we will make a profit and out of that profit we will serve the community.

- Our responsibility is to ensure that the company will survive and thrive for the next 120 years. We cannot just attend to the short term. When you begin to think this way, you are really entering into the spirit of family, into the spirit of a multicultural environment, and into the spirit of humanity as a whole.

Spirituality as the basis for leadership is not always an easy journey. You will see in the chapters to follow that not one of the leaders was spared from the ethical dilemmas and challenges of leading a business in an increasingly complex, demanding, and globalized business environment.

However, no matter what challenges these executives faced, all of us in the research team found that their guiding principles were fundamentally different from most of what we had come to know during our own years of corporate and academic experience, and their perspectives and actions were often quite out of the ordinary. For example, they have all grappled with the pressures of financial performance and success—but each according to his or her own unique guiding principles, founded in their spiritual views of life:

- We need to make money, but the reason why we exist, our *raison d'être*, is much more than that; there are things that are more important than making money. We are a team with a common purpose, a moral purpose, and we do everything we can to live up to that purpose.

- My concept of business is the harmony of ethics, energy, excellence, economy, ecology—with effectiveness and efficiency that leads to enlightenment. All this occurs through wisdom, coming from purity and beauty. This is my vision of the future of business.

- If you have a sound policy based on caring for people, not harming anyone or anything, and a profitable business strategy, then financial success will come automatically.

- Yes, we must make a profit; but, most importantly, we must ask: how did we make this profit?

- You should not measure success or failure at all. What is most important is to determine: Have I followed my inner conscience? Have I given my best effort? Have I done what was right? Have I learned from my effort? Have I used all of my senses and values that I am conscious and aware of? This is what is most important.

The individual stories are personal and reflect experiences in specific contexts. In their entirety, however, they provide powerful and uplifting evidence that the paradigm of economic rationality that dominates our concepts of 'success' can be expanded to include fundamental concerns regarding one's own well-being as well as the well-being of all those affected by one's leadership. They illustrate overarching questions such as: 'Is there a place for spirituality in the workplace?' 'Can spirituality drive success?' 'Should it?' 'Can leaders integrate their spiritual longings and values with the down-to-earth demands of a highly competitive global economy?'

Such questions may not be new; presumably leaders in all cultures and all times have more or less unconsciously dealt with similar considerations. What is new is that these questions are being explicitly raised in a rapidly increasing number of forums where business leaders and/or academics interact.

These very questions were addressed at a conference exploring issues of leadership, values and spirituality in business at Harvard Business School in the spring of 2002. Here, executives from all over the world, representing a wide range of industries, discussed how they twine their business leadership with their values, and how their spirituality helps them to be powerful leaders. In the spring of 2006, another highly respected American university, Yale, hosted a conference with a similar focus: 'Faith and Ethics in the Workplace'. Those attending were not established business leaders, but MBA students from prominent universities and business schools in the USA, including Chicago, Duke, Harvard, MIT, Pennsylvania, Yale and Virginia, representing an impressive degree of diversity along racial, ethnic and gender lines.

In India, as early as 1995, the prestigious Indian Institute of Management in Calcutta inaugurated its 'Management Centre for Human Values' to bring a grounded spiritual reality to business. On the walls of its inspiring conference centre, where business executives regularly meet to update their knowledge of leadership, as well as to improve their ability to still their minds, hang paintings of modern India's most highly revered spiritual leaders—not business leaders, not political leaders.

An article titled 'God and Business' in the 9 July 2001 issue of *Fortune* magazine related how a former IBM executive and investment banker, David Miller, now leads a faith-in-the-workplace group of business leaders and senior executives called the Avodah Institute. Avodah is a Hebrew word meaning both 'work' and 'worship'. According to Miller, 'People often talk about the sacred–secular divide, but my faith tells me that God is found in the earth and rocks and buildings and institutions, and yes, in the business world.'

During the last decade, dozens of major conferences focusing on spirituality and business have taken place in countries as diverse as Mexico, Guatemala, UK, Holland, Canada, USA, Hungary, Slovenia, Australia, India,

Switzerland and Brazil. There has also been a surge of international non-profit organizations devoted to spurring this awakening, including 'Spirit in Business', the 'European SPES Forum' (Spirituality in Economic and Social life), 'The Bahá'í Business Forums', and the 'Association for Spirit at Work'. And in 2001 a special-interest group was formed on 'Management, Spirituality, and Religion' at the Academy of Management[2] in the USA. This prompted André Delbecq, former dean of the Graduate School of Business, Santa Clara University, USA, to proclaim during our interview with him: *There are two things I never thought I would see in my lifetime: one was the fall of the Russian empire; and the other was hearing the word 'God' spoken of in the Academy of Management.*

The 'missing link'

Thus, there is an increasing belief amongst both academicians and business leaders that faith and fortune can mix, and that spirituality in business is here to stay. However, in spite of all the many new business theories, methodologies and training programmes that have emerged in response to this spiritual awakening in business—even IQ and EQ have now evolved to SQ, spiritual quotient—one thing is still glaringly missing: practical, real-life stories of business executives who are leading from a spiritual basis. Stories that reveal their ups and downs, their struggles and successes. Stories that demonstrate to the sceptics that you can be both deeply spiritual and highly successful in business. Stories from credible sources that put to rest concerns that spirituality will undermine the 'business of business'. Stories that give us a realistic glimpse of what might be possible if business and leadership were defined and conducted from a spiritual basis. Stories that reveal the 'spiritual thread' that connects all human beings, regardless of race, beliefs, religion, culture and location.

In the profiles that follow, business executives from around the world—and from industries as varied as IT, health care, retailing, manufacturing, food, agricultural supplies, investment management and telecommunications—bring such stories to life. They are part of a global culture that is slowly but surely emerging in business leadership: executives who are able to express, from their first-hand experience, what it is like to lead a business from a spiritual basis.

---

2 The Academy of Management is a leading professional association for scholars in the field of leadership, management and organizations. It is the oldest and largest scholarly management association in the world and has over 16,000 members in 97 countries.

Having interviewed these executives, we have grown in our knowledge of, and confidence in, the far-reaching impact spiritual-based leadership can make in our world today. That it can, and will, provide the long-term wisdom and guidance to bring us into a new era where wealth creation, business ethics, values, corporate social responsibility, and sustainability are all deeply rooted in a spiritual view of life, a view that integrates heart, mind and soul.

We believe that this book will provide you with knowledge and inspiration that will enable you to better lead your lives and organizations from a spiritual basis—to lead with integrity, and with the confidence and faith that leadership and spirituality can be mutually supportive. You *can* be a successful and joyful leader whose life and leadership unfold from your consciously held spiritual view of life.

Section 1

Love

In this section

In this first section, entitled *Love*, we have gathered the inspiring stories of four executives from four continents. Their personal styles, industries, working environments, and cultural and religious heritages are as different as their geographical locations. Nevertheless, when one distils their statements as to their spiritual views of life and how these impact on their leadership, all four of them demonstrate a strong focus on *love* . . . even if this focus finds expression in very different ways. You will meet:

Janiece Webb, Senior Vice President, Motorola, USA

In *Expressing love and compassion*, Janiece Webb talks about the 'tough love' that she may give to employees to 'create giants out of ordinary people' and of the love that lifts her above her ego and enables her 'to appreciate people at all levels and express my compassion and love to others in an open way.' Ultimately, this led her to see how business can be both competitive and compassionate—business with a soul.

Lars Kolind, former CEO, Oticon, Denmark

In *Making a difference through love*, Lars Kolind tells the story of a dramatic turnaround and rejuvenation of an ageing company, taking it from near bankruptcy to global eminence. He concludes that, 'if you serve a purpose based on care and love, then you can be successful in almost anything.'

N.S. Raghavan, Joint-founder and former Joint Managing Director, Infosys, India

In *Love and trust*, N.S. Raghavan speaks about trust being a by-product of love, where 'love is unconditional' and trust is obtained simply by trusting others. 'I am a person who implicitly trusts people. It is important to me to see the good in people and to care for people.' From this basis, he helped create at

Infosys a corporate culture, characterized by sharing both information and the power of making decisions.

Francisco Roberto Cañada, Director/Partner, Errepar S.A., Argentina

In *Loving God and aiming at excellence,* Francisco Roberto Cañada sums up his spiritual principles and values 'in one word: Love'. He says, 'I pray that all people can do their duty with love and care. Therefore, as a leader, I make an effort that all our companies do good business, do good work, and make good products in the way of God, without breaking His laws.'

1

Janiece Webb

Senior Vice President, Motorola, USA

When she was interviewed, Janiece Webb was 47 years old and a Senior Vice President with Motorola Corporation where she had the responsibility to 'take the technology assets of the company and either incubate them, sell them off, get them into a business, or license the technology.' Those technology assets included over 8,000 US patents and almost 13,000 foreign patents. Motorola is a *Fortune* 100 globalized technology company, known for its innovation in wireless, broadband and Internet communication technologies. In 2005, the company had roughly 70,000 employees at more than 300 facilities in over 70 countries worldwide, generating revenues of roughly US$37 billion.

Janiece Webb has had a rather amazing career, having started out as a production worker on the night shift and rising to the top echelons of Motorola Corporation's leadership. As she told us, 'I've been in marketing. I've run engineering, manufacturing, software, equipment businesses, and service businesses around the world. I've run businesses from $2 million to $3.5 billion. I've had from zero people to eight people to 8,000 people working for me.'

This has provided her with extensive experience in contracts, business development, engineering management, research technology, manufacturing and international businesses in Motorola's communications businesses. For example, when she was with Motorola's International Networks Division, she installed network-operating companies in 18 countries and managed 21 major businesses. Janiece Webb has since retired from Motorola.

Our research colleague William Miller knew Janiece Webb for almost a decade before her interview, and spoke of her reputation for being tough in her business decisions and heartful in her support for each employee. It is clear from the long interview that forms the basis of the following profile that her spirituality thoroughly permeates her leadership and her ethical standards. She has long held a spiritual view of life that starts with 'getting in touch with the essence of God inside of me—finding God inside myself,' and that she lovingly extends to seeing 'God in everyone . . . we're all connected.' This expression of her love as the interconnectedness of all human beings impacts on her view of her role and responsibility as a leader: 'I believe that you can create giants out of ordinary people when you act in balance and harmony with people. Sometimes this requires tough love and that can be done within proper bounds. And yes it can be hard to see God in everyone. I have worked with so many incredible teams of people, and I have seen parts of life that I never thought I would see. To me this is what success is all about.'

Expressing love and compassion

I think that God intends us to find a way to not be judgemental, to not be envious and greedy, all those cravings that keep us separate. I think that my spiritual path is to leave all of these cravings behind me and to replace them with compassion and love.

Janiece Webb's career with Motorola Corporation started in 1972 as a night shift employee on the production line. 'People ask me all the time how I became a Senior Vice President of technology at a major corporation like this. Truthfully, I don't know. It wasn't something I had planned. I came here because I needed a pay cheque in order to eat. I moved out of my parents' home when I was 16 years old and I wanted to go to school, so I worked the night shift in order to go to school during the day.'

When the production lines were down, Janiece Webb started listening and watching what the engineer was doing, wrote it down, and fixed the problem herself the next time it happened. When she began writing training programmes, an inspiring enthusiasm developed among her co-workers and productivity increased considerably. It was only a matter of time before management realized she should be in the office and not on the production line. She went on to receive a graduate degree in Business Administration and post-graduate training in electronics engineering and management (the Leadership Institute at Northwestern University's Kellogg Graduate School of Management).

'How I progressed, which is the same pattern over and over in my career, is that there was always a problem that needed to be solved and I had the courage to tackle it. I've always known that I could push a barrier. I have always been a visionary and have always found the problems that nobody else wanted to solve but needed to be solved.

'I feel that I'm in a very good place right now in my career because I do not feel lost in my ego and I like that. What that means is that I can appreciate people at all levels and I can express my compassion and love to others in an open way.'

A spiritual purpose

'I have known that I have a spiritual purpose ever since I was ten years old. I grew up in a very poor dysfunctional family yet somehow I knew that life would be okay. I remember running home from school one day in the desert and feeling somewhat afraid. I thought to myself that I will find my way and I will be all right. I knew this even at ten years old.

'I know that I am to inspire and coach people. I know that, when people are feeling downtrodden, I am supposed to pick them up and give them some wind to their backs so they can move forward. I know that I love to mentor people who feel wounded. I know that I practise courage and I love to break through barriers.

'I know that my spiritual purpose includes a deep practice of spirituality, but I do not completely know the details. It's exciting and it's troubling because I don't have my finger on it. I also think that my years of work have given me wisdom and comprehension of life and the issues that people walk around with every day, and that plays a part in my soul's work.

'For me, spirituality is getting in touch with the essence of God inside of me . . . if I really get quiet, let my brain quit talking to me and get a feel for the essence, I can find God within me. Someone asked me the other day what my goal in life was and I said, "To take all of the chatter out of my head". I will know that I've made it spiritually when I can sit and not jabber, when both my mind and mouth can be quiet.

'I read a lot of different things on spirituality because I did not get a lot of formal spiritual education growing up. I took classes on Islam when I was in college. I've gone through Christianity. I've read a lot of the Buddhist teachings. And I listen to a lot of tapes dealing with religious and spiritual matters.

'I think spirituality is taking the principles that are taught in most religions and living them as a natural way of life. I very much relate to and appreciate the Buddhist practices, even though for me God is the higher power, the creator of our earth and creator of all this magic. I think that all religions are connected. I see people manifesting their God in a way that works for them. I am searching for my own personal relationship and I know it doesn't have to be like anyone else's.

'I pray every day, several times a day. I ask for guidance and am humbly grateful, and I let that be known. I do not try to control things, whether it's my work environment, my husband, or my family. I come to work to live; I do not live to work. I can feel my spiritual growth as I realize that I do not need material things in order to live. I could go back to living in a shack and I would be fine.'

Building trust through integrity

'I believe that God put us on earth to find joy and happiness and to become enlightened. I believe He will test us with a thousand episodes and it's our job to learn how to walk through them. Numerous times people outside of the company have asked me to cheat in the name of business. I have run into this all over the world. Within myself, I have always known that I didn't have to go behind the law.

'I have stood firm many times to not paying bribes and as a result people realize that they can trust me. I have had people that worked for me in the past come and tell me that I have the highest ethics of anyone they have worked for. This is always a surprise to me when people say these things because to me this way of operating in business is so natural.

'A wealthy man in an Asian country once attempted to get me to hire a person so that he could buy some property for his personal use through Motorola. I stood firm that I would not do that. He reminded me that he was one of our largest customers in that country and I told him I didn't care. To this day my contacts in that country tell me that they want to deal with me because they know they can trust me.'

Spiritual fitness in the ups and downs of a career

'In my career I have been through some extremely difficult downsizing situations and personal attacks. I have been put into some impossible situations when I felt that I was under intense pressure by those in power above me to solve an unsolvable problem, or when the organization just wouldn't work together to get things done. Every once in a while I have lost my way and those were really dark periods. And yet I knew I would be okay. I've been demoted and I've been celebrated and through it all I have learned not to get attached because none of this is what's real.

'If your goal is to be successful, there will be a day when you will come down—someone else will come to replace you. If your goal is to live your principles and make sure that you leave life better than you found it, then you will be able to ride through the ups and downs and accomplish many things.

'In my 30-year career, I have experienced all kinds of bosses. I have seen numerous executives rise all the way to the top and then at some point they came back down. When an executive rose to the top by taking advantage of people, then on their way down people ganged up against them. But, when an executive rose to the top in a spiritual, respectful way, then on their way down the people caught them and cushioned their fall.

'Most often people do not know why they succeed or why they fail. They are afraid to look closely at themselves because they don't want to see their own frailties, or the things they may have done wrong. It is important to know why you are succeeding and why you are failing. It's also important to know what you contributed and what you didn't contribute; both are just as valuable. I think it is just as important to accept the perfection in each of us, as it is to accept the imperfections, the parts that are so fallible.

'I used to affirm that I wanted to be intellectually fit, physically fit, emotionally fit and spiritually fit. But now I realize that if I get in touch with my spirituality, then the rest takes care of itself. I don't even have to worry about all of those others things—they happen naturally when I am spiritually fit.

'For me, the single most important issue we have to conquer in life is fear. And the way I conquer fear is by getting in touch with my spiritual Self. I believe that faith is an important part of life; it's what gets me through the bumps. Faith is a heart- and soulful knowing. I don't have faith in man-made systems or man-made judgements, but I have faith that I will survive them. I know that my relationship is with God and that's where I place my faith.

'I have had several companies come to me and offer me a CEO position in the last few years and I have turned them down. Why? If I took a new job like that it would take my husband and me completely off the spiritual path we are walking in our lives, and I am not willing to do that.'

Seeing others as equals

'I've never looked at people in high power positions and been in awe. I've always been able to talk to the janitor, to the street person, or to the CEO, or to the president of our country, because to me they are all the same. Yes, some have different circumstances or environments or experiences, but inside they are all the same. I also think that we don't need to be embarrassed with our feelings of love for each other. At work, I embarrass people with my warmth, and I don't care.

'What I have done is make sure that I communicate in every meeting that anyone can speak up and say whatever they need to say to me. I tell them that I am just as fallible as they are and that I don't have any more grand ideas than they do. I encourage them to enlighten me if I say dumb things. I remind them that we are all trying to solve this problem together.

'In truth, I believe that a position of power is a position of serving the people around you. I feel it is my job to serve people. No one gets anywhere by themselves. I am only as good as the people around me. I can only achieve our organizational goals by nurturing the people. I encourage people to believe in themselves and not let the system dictate who they are. I also encourage them to forget about the corporate hierarchy structure. I don't identify myself with my title; that's a label someone decided to put on me, and I ask them to not let that get in the way.

'I do believe in the pure potentiality of every single being. It really is unlimited and we are the ones who put limits on it. I believe that you can create giants out of ordinary people when you act in balance and harmony with people. Sometimes this requires tough love and that can be done within proper bounds. And, yes, it can be hard to see God in everyone, especially in a large corporation like this one where there are people who can be quite cruel with blind ambition. God gives us such potential and we can take it in any direction we want.'

Being competitive with compassion

'I believe that a corporation has a soul and what that means to me is that, yes, you do perform in a capitalistic model, but you do it with integrity, with absolute deep respect for people—not hollow words, but really treating them with dignity. A company that has soul has compassion. It doesn't mean they can't be tough and it doesn't mean they can't strive for big goals. You can be competitive with compassion, but if you are competitive without compassion you will lose your soul. Leaders who are sincerely compassionate hurt if they have to downsize. People know the truth and they know when you are sincere.

'When you stay true to your spiritual principles you can walk lightly. I have found that people who are phenomenal spiritual leaders are not entangled with the world; they have empathy and compassion and can even look at the world through your eyes. However, they do not attempt to control you. If you feel joy, they will also feel your joy; if you feel hurt, they will feel your hurt, but not to the point of losing their own spiritual centre. They have a compassionate observance of others and of themselves.

'Bob Galvin, the former Chairman and CEO of Motorola, was once asked what kept him awake at night and he said, "The fear of arrogance and if we become arrogant, we will no longer be watchful". I believe this is very critical. I give career talks a lot and tell people to watch out for arrogance, believing you are invincible, letting power seduce you, getting into the wrong crowd and selling out on your personal principles. If your organization is succeeding, you should be lying awake at night thinking about how you will handle it when it comes back down.'

The role of business in society

'The role that business could play in benefiting the world could be huge. It could help education by investing in kids and showing them, by example, how to lead in a spiritual way. It could channel the money it makes into giving back to society. I honestly believe that if a CEO came forward and was willing to genuinely show his or her spiritual side in making and selling good products as well as using the profits to help society, the results could be unbelievable.

'I truly believe that people want to follow goodness and are looking for these kinds of examples. I believe if people could see that corporations are investing the profits they are making back into the society without a self-serving interest, it could be a new recipe for attracting and keeping shareholders.

'Whether in our personal life or corporate life I think that it is a principle of life to give back. I have found time and again that every time I give in this pure way that it comes back to me many times over, sometimes in even embarrassing ways. You give and it comes back, that's just the way it works.'

Being open about spirituality at work

'I have found that it's okay to admit that you are spiritual and have certain beliefs at work; it *is* possible to speak openly about spirituality at work. However, it's important not to try to get someone else to believe the way you do. When I know that someone can handle the subject of spirituality, I talk and discuss it openly. When I know someone cannot handle it, then I just "be" my spirituality and I don't talk about it openly. I can be it, I can show it, and I can exhibit it in my behaviour and attitudes, and I don't have to label it.

'I give career talks a lot, and one of the things I always tell my audiences is to look way into the future and think about how you want people to remember you. What do you want to be known for? What would you like to have written on your epitaph? It's important for you to get in touch with your principles early and let them guide you. For myself, when I die I want people to say that I cared, that I worked hard and tried my best to make a positive difference every day, and that I was spiritual and treated people fairly.

'I know that, unless God has different plans for me, I'll be a little ole' lady on roller skates. I realize how precious life is and I don't take anything for granted. One attachment I do feel is to my husband. I feel as if I have found my soulmate and I would not want to lose him and yet I know that at any instance he could be taken away. I know that will be one of my biggest tests.'

2

Lars Kolind
Former CEO, Oticon, Denmark

Lars Kolind is former CEO of Oticon in Denmark, the world's oldest manufacturer of hearing aids (founded in 1904) and a world leader in products for the hearing-impaired. Lars Kolind acknowledges that spirituality is so woven in the fabric of his life that he rarely notices that it is his fundamental operating principle. As he told us: 'Spirituality has simply permeated my life. It is just there and I realized it was there early on. My values come from my spiritual views. When I see what I have done and the decisions I have made in different situations it is clear that spirituality has always been there; I've just become more conscious about it.'

Having known Lars Kolind for many years, it is very clear to us that he is a staunchly ethical executive with a strong Christian upbringing, striving for noble goals that 'make a positive difference', a phrase he emphasizes. But, if you look more deeply at his profile, you will also see that the unique perspectives he exemplifies, and the decisions he has made, have come from the love that he speaks of when he says, 'Love God and love your neighbour'. This is especially evident in his memorable story of downsizing a business that was experiencing severe financial difficulties and a loss of market share.

The profile presented here focuses primarily on Lars Kolind's time as CEO of Oticon (1988–98), but also on his period after leaving Oticon to serve as Chairman of Grundfos, a Danish-based billion-dollar multinational corporation that is the world's second largest manufacturer of pumps. Over and above these activities, Lars Kolind has been chairman or member of the board of several other major corporations and has been instrumental in starting new businesses within such fields as electronics, telecommunications, home security, and design, often in collaboration with the investment firm PreVenture which he founded and chairs. He has masters' degrees in both mathematics and business.

He has also made significant contributions to public-service activities, including the founding of the Danish Business Network for Social Cohesion—a partnership with the Danish government to reduce social exclusion, and chairing the National Council of Children and Culture, an advisory body to the Danish Minister of Culture. Lars Kolind has been actively engaged in scouting (the Boy Scouts) throughout most of his life and is currently a member of the Governing Board of the World Scout Foundation.

Amidst all these activities, this father of four, together with his wife Vibeke, has found time to revitalize a magnificent manor house in Denmark, as well as to write a visionary book on leadership.[1] To keep his strong contacts with Danish academia alive, he has accepted to be Adjunct Professor of Management at the Aarhus Business School, Denmark.

Making a difference through love

I have a vision, which I dare generalize, that organizations will survive, develop and prosper if they build a very strong culture that ties the staff together—a culture that creates a strong sense of 'we-ness'. It should not be done only for financial reasons, but primarily for a common purpose of doing something important. This is a key to being successful. If you are serving a purpose and you are doing it based on some fundamental values, and those values have to do with care and love, then you have great potential and you can be successful in almost anything.

Lars Kolind, 54 years old at the time of the interview, was for 11 years the visionary Danish CEO of Oticon, the major international producer of hearing aids. Here he created what became internationally known as the

---

1 *The Second Cycle: Winning the War Against Bureaucracy,* published in 2006 by Wharton School Publishing, USA.

'Spaghetti Organization' which transformed Oticon from a traditional manufacturing company into an amazingly creative knowledge-based organization without paper, offices and titles.

When Lars Kolind was asked to take over as CEO of Oticon, it was in great trouble and was very close to bankruptcy; a dramatic downsizing was in the offing. When he left 11 years later, in 1998, Oticon was a uniquely creative, innovative, fast-growing organization with an unbelievable financial performance. Since then, Oticon has continued to produce incredible growth and financial results.

Having grown up in a family with strong Protestant Christian ties, Lars Kolind is still heavily influenced by his religion. 'I probably see spirituality in a relatively narrow sense because I was brought up in a home that had a quite strong Lutheran touch. This early interest in Christianity led me on to be active in that part of the Danish Boy Scouts that was associated with the Danish national church—roughly 85 per cent of the Danes are members of this church. I might add that later on I became a leader of the scouting organization in Denmark and then of the World Scout Foundation.'

It was the combination of his Christian upbringing and active participation in scouting that opened his eyes to spirituality. 'I first became aware of my spirituality when I was 18 or 19 years old. I was very, very active in scouting. Through that work with scouting I met a lot of interesting people from all walks of life. What really struck me was that these people that I admired from a professional point of view were so influenced by spirituality. I realized that this was a turning point for me.'

'Spirituality began to influence my decisions even at this early time; however, I have become more conscious about it as I have matured. For me spirituality is the acceptance of the existence of a God, whatever that is, and to adhere to my religion. It is not really very distinct from religion.

'When I look back on the major decisions I've actually made, they are very intuitively based and values-oriented. My values come from my spiritual views. There are many situations where, afterwards, I wondered why I made a particular decision and realized it was clearly related to my spirituality. But I must admit that only on rare occasions did I ever think about my spiritual basis while making the decision. I was tuned into the situation at hand, thinking about the issue and how to solve it. But afterwards it was obvious that I was strongly influenced by my spirituality.

'I try to live and act and lead according to the principles of Christianity, the way I understand them. I have become conscious of the fact that I am much more Lutheran than I thought I was. I am in particular very strongly influenced by the Lutheran tenet that it is your duty to work hard. I am so strongly influenced by that principle, that I hope that in ten years times I can have a little more relaxed attitude towards this feeling of obligation.

'I am trying the best I can to live a Christian life, which to me means to do something for the poor, to do something for the underprivileged, to try to do to other people what I hope that they would do to me, and all of that. This all came from my parents, basically, and I never really questioned it, which is strange because I tend to be both curious and critical, and have questioned lots of other important things. My spirituality is just there and I don't currently see a reason to question it. It works. Prayer is a part of everyday life. I may pray at certain times during the day, such as at a meal or when I feel thankful for the day, and I also pray in difficult situations. There are difficult situations where I think it is a great strength to be able to express yourself via prayer and to feel that you are in dialogue with a higher being. I must admit, though, there have been periods when I have had my doubts—and I still have a few existential doubts.

'In rare cases people ask me why I am so obsessed with the idea of *making a difference*. I reply that this is fundamentally why we exist and that has something to do with our relation to a higher being.'

In summing up his spiritual view of life, Lars Kolind simply states: 'Love God and love your neighbour'.

The Oticon story

When Lars Kolind took over at Oticon in 1988, after having had leadership positions at the major national nuclear research centre, Risoe, and an international manufacturer of medical electronics, Radiometer, he was given the power to do whatever he thought was relevant. Looking back at the Oticon story, he sees two phases. One was the dramatic downsizing in order to survive in 1989. The other was the building of the new company. This included not only developing a completely new and revolutionary organizational concept in early 1990 (for which the company became world-famous) and implementing it more or less overnight in August 1991, it also included discovering and living the new purpose of the company.

'In the downsizing phase, we were under extreme pressure because the whole company was falling apart. We were forced to reduce staff very dramatically. On one occasion we cut away ten per cent of the staff overnight. I took the decision, which *no one* understood, that we would not fire anyone over 50. Neither would we fire people who were so essential that we didn't think we could survive without them. But, other than that, we would let those people go who we thought would have the best chance of getting another job quickly—even though these were obviously the ones I would have preferred retaining. I just couldn't look into the eyes of all of the people that we would kick into prolonged unemployment in order for the rest of us to make money and prosper. I just couldn't do that.

'Normally someone in my position would let the department heads talk to the people. But I didn't do it that way. I talked to every single person that was to be laid off and told each of them that they were going to be fired and that we would work with them to get a new job the best we could. I was experiencing all their bad feelings as I was confronting myself with the doubts and fears of all of these people. To me it would have been an act of cowardice to let others do this for me.

'The interesting point was that we got through this amazingly well. There was total acceptance, even though no one really understood it. But once it was done, people said '"wow" and really respected my decision. Obviously this had a price for me and for the company as well, and the price was that there were lots of people that I would have rather laid off that we retained.

'Later I realized that this was really an expression of my spiritual principles. But I must admit that while doing it I didn't think much about it. Yes, I did follow my conscience and that is certainly the voice of spirituality.'

Company with a purpose

'After the downsizing of Oticon, it took us two years to find out what the essence of the company actually was. We came out of a tradition where our tag line was "Leaders in hearing technology", but we were far more than a technology company. I worked day and night to find out who we really were and what our fundamental purpose should be.

'What inspired me was the fact that we were dealing with people who had enormous personal problems due to lack of hearing. Our job was to add to the quality of life of those we served and to help them to live a decent life. So this is what led us to phrase the essence, the vision of the company to be: *Help people with impaired hearing to live as they wish with the hearing they have.*

'I later realized that this came out of my desire to involve myself in doing something for these people, to improve their situation. It turned out to be a fabulous expression of what we stood for. It was so powerful, even though it was not developed by marketing people; there were no consultants or advertising agencies involved. It was from working on the questions: "What can we do?" "What should we do?" I am sure this was highly inspired by my fundamental beliefs about what's truly important in life.

'This all had a tremendous effect on our employees, customers and dealers. We were not only saying all of this; we were living it. We went through the process where we examined every corner of the company. I asked the question a hundred times, "Does this help people with impaired hearing to live better with the hearing they have or does it not?" We were closing departments and initiating projects in order to actually live this.

'What struck me was that if you phrase your purpose that way, and if you demonstrate that you mean it, then you earn a tremendous respect from everybody, not just the employees. This included researchers and knowledge partners at universities and clinics . . . To practise what you preach is the key to personal and organizational success.'

Looking back, Lars Kolind recalls that it took considerable time for him and the organization as a whole to become consciously aware of the values underlying this purpose and the revolutionary organizational changes that took place at Oticon. 'Phrasing the values, discussing the values, achieving consensus first occurred about five years after I started. I felt that the organization would be much more sustainable if all the employees were conscious of the values on which it was built.'

He summarizes the broad values that emerged as follows:

'First of all, it was to "focus on your neighbour", where your neighbour in this respect is primarily your customer. These were people whose hearing was impaired and were in very difficult situations. So we focused on what we could do for these people.

'Second, we created a culture in which people were responsible not only for what they did, but also for what we all did together.

'The third thing emerged clearly from the first two and how they were implemented, and that was a clear element of caring for your neighbour—your colleague.

'The last thing was creativity; the culture urged everyone to continuously question what they were doing and to find a better way and new ways to do things.'

Shared ownership and purpose

'After half a year of a lot of turbulence, the company really took off. The financial performance was unbelievable. We took the company public in 1995; together with practically all of the employees, I bought shares.

'We need to make money, but the reason we exist, our *raison d'être*, is much more than that; there are things that are more important than making money. We are a team with a common purpose, a moral purpose, and we do everything we can to live up to that purpose. In that context it is totally natural to introduce shared ownership. I have always argued that shared ownership means that you share responsibility; you make an investment. So I have worked against stock options, but I have worked strongly for shares that people pay for. To me there is a tremendous difference between the two. We give them a discount in the price, that's okay; but we are now taking joint responsibility to run the company by sharing ownership.

'When I bought my shares in December 1990 the value of the company was 150 million Danish crowns. When I left in May of 1998, the value of the company was 6 billion crowns, and now [March 2002] the value is 20 billion, roughly 2½ billion US dollars.[2] I think it has been a surprise to a lot of people, but not to me, that Oticon has also continued to produce incredible growth and financial results *after* I left.

'What we did was a role model for others and Oticon is still perceived as one of the most attractive places to work for engineers and other groups of staff. People were desperate to work with us, we were making a major difference with our customers, and we were recognized by our peers. And it all ended up creating financial value like crazy.

'In connection with the new organizational concept, the management changed dramatically. There were two of us who ran this whole process and we were completely, 180 degrees, each other's opposite. Although I had doubts about having two people manage the company, I nevertheless went ahead and chose my opposite, Mr Niels Jacobsen, to be my deputy manager. We ran the business together and Niels took over as CEO when I left. He has done amazingly well and the company is still providing excellent products and record profits.'

Making a difference

'The key thought I have is that the motivation for what we do is beyond the bottom line, and I think Grundfos, where I am now the chairman, exemplifies this very, very well. Everyone knows we are in business to make money, which goes without saying, but that is only part of the story. Everything we do is so clearly focused on environmental, social and ethical issues.

'I was asked to chair Grundfos because they wanted someone who would express values that were based on a concern for both social and environmental issues. Grundfos is an expression of these values. The founder was a strong Christian and the company is led 100 per cent from those values. I believe that almost all employees honestly feel that this company is not only in busi-

---

2   The market value continued to increase. In 2005 it was 24.9 billion crowns, roughly US$4.23 billion. Note that the value of the US dollar *vis-à-vis* the Danish crown decreased considerably from 2002 to 2005.

ness to make money; we are in business to make a difference. If you look at Grundfos, that is an essential part of their success. This was also true with Oticon. The staff felt that we were doing something that was more important than making money.

'With both Oticon and Grundfos I faced a lot of social and environmental challenges, as well as major issues about our product focus. When I look back upon the decisions that I've lobbied for, they've been on behalf of the environment and social issues—even though if I had been asked at the time what was most important, I probably would have said to make money. As it turns out my focus was and is a very good basis for strategy—and we're making money . . . I can see that I have a much stronger interest in non-financial issues and I am happy that they turned out to make financial sense.

'I know what I want to do but I cannot always express why. That can be a problem when you deal with the board and all of the financial guys, because it is hard for them to accept things just based on "knowing it is the right decision." They are so used to focusing on rational arguments based on short-term economic results.

'In business, if you dare speak about values, then most people perceive you as a guy who makes decisions that make no sense from a financial point of view and who is really not a good businessman; you are considered a preacher and not a businessman. I just hate this. I have asked people to cut this out. I show them what I have been doing and all of the money I have made.

'Yes, it can be dangerous and you may be open to attacks, especially in a small homogeneous country like ours. I have been unable to avoid publicity about my manor house in Jutland, and I've been asked many times. "With your Christian background, how can you accept owning so much?" I say: Wouldn't it be better that I own it? Look at what I am doing with it. My wife and I really take care of it, we have restored it to a high level of quality, maintain it and the grounds, and we share it with others, opening it to the public for concerts, meetings and the like.

'I personally have no doubt that being in contact with a higher power increases the quality of one's life in the broadest sense. This applies to everyone. I am only happy because I started by making a difference, whether it was for the family, or the environment, or the hearing-impaired or whatever it was, that is what gives me satisfaction.

'Personal success to me is the feeling that I am doing the right things and we are doing it right. I would not say that money is not important, but for me success is to be able to do right and to have a good feeling of what you are doing, and to run a wonderful team of people who are dedicated.

'If you are serving a purpose and you are doing it based on some fundamental values, and those values have to do with care and love, then you have great potential and you can be successful in almost anything.'

3

N.S. Raghavan

Joint-founder and former
Joint Managing Director, Infosys, India

N.S. Raghavan, one of the joint-founders of Infosys in Bangalore, India, helped to build this radically successful information technology firm, putting India on the 'silicon map' and producing numerous millionaires in the process. N.S. Raghavan expresses his spiritual theme as 'love and trust', which accurately describes how he demonstrates love in his leadership—through trust.

When asked to explain more of what he means by love, N.S. Raghavan said, 'To me "love" is unconditional. It is a natural phenomenon and is spontaneous. It cannot be based on logic and reasoning. When you expect something in return, then it is not pure love.'

Some of his 'experiments' at Infosys clearly demonstrate his sincere trust in his values, trust in those who work for him, trust in the goodness of people, and trust in life itself. Elaborating on the concept of 'trust', he told us the following story from the Second World War that he had read: 'The War Secretary at that time was asked, "Sir, how do you make people trustworthy?" His answer was cryptic and profound: "Simply by trusting them." To me, this is such a strong way of building a trusting environment.'

Infosys, the company that Raghavan served as Joint Managing Director for so many years, has in fiscal year 2006 surpassed $2 billion in sales and has more than 66,000 employees in India and 22 countries worldwide. It was the first

India-registered company to be listed on the NASDAQ (largest electronic equity securities market in the USA). Its market capitalization in 2005–06 grew by 35 per cent to Rs 821.54 billion (roughly US$18 billion). Infosys currently trains thousands of new recruits every year at its US$120 million Global Education Centre. According to an article in *Fortune* (March 2006), 'Securing a position at Infosys is more competitive than gaining admission to Harvard. Last year the company had more than 1.3 million applicants for full-time positions and hired only 1 per cent of them; Harvard College, by comparison, accepted 9 per cent of its applicants.'

Infosys has won a huge number of awards, including 'India's Best Managed Company' and 'India's Most Respected Company'; it has been ranked number one amongst companies as 'The best company to work for in India', number three amongst 'The World's Top 100 IT Companies', amongst 'The 100 Best Places to Work in IT', and amongst the '100 Most Respected Companies in the World', where it is ranked ahead of IBM, Intel, Microsoft, Dell and Nokia. *Fortune, Forbes, Business Week, TIME* and many more have written articles praising the company and its leadership.

We have followed the incredible development of Infosys from a distance. In 1999 we interviewed the newly appointed Managing Director/President and COO, Nandan Nilekani for a major Danish newspaper. Like N.S. Raghavan, he was one of the seven 'computer freaks' who founded Infosys as India's first software house in 1981. We think of that original founding group as 'The Beatles of the Indian IT industry'. Somehow they found each other, inspired each other, and had major positive effects on the lives of hundreds of thousands of people first and foremost in India, but also in many other parts of the world.

Love and trust

The most important values to me are fairness, love, caring and trust. For me, 'love' is unconditional: when you expect something in return, then it is not pure love. When you are operating from a strong sense of values, you don't change your behaviour and treat people differently just because circumstances change. I am talking about fundamental ethical and moral values here.

N.S. Raghavan retired from Infosys in Bangalore in 2000 as Joint Managing Director when he was 57 years old. Since then, he has been Director of his own new investment company, Nadathur Holdings & Investments Pvt. Ltd, and an independent non-executive director for a large conglomerate, the Murugappa group of companies. In addition, he established in 2001 a social trust, Foundation for Action, Motivation and Empowerment (FAME India); to contribute to the well-being of physically and mentally challenged children.

For N.S. Raghavan, the source of his love comes from his spiritual views. 'I believe very strongly in the part of religion that says you should show love, kindness and compassion towards people and try to make a difference in the lives of those you touch. To me, if you are doing things that are not meant to further your personal interests, but which are meant to help others, then it is spiritual.

'I also think of spirituality as something that is beyond body and mind. It is something that gives a certain purpose and meaning to our existence. It is something that gives you joy, happiness and contentment, which cannot be gotten through material pursuits and knowledge. It is also something that gives you the motivation to do something for others and makes you feel happy when you do it.'

In alignment with this view, N.S. Raghavan believes that the purpose of business and wealth creation is to enable both a company and its employees to share with others, rather than acting out of self-interest. 'Every business is really a social organization, which has to ensure that it does create wealth so that it can be shared with others. I also subscribe to what is called "high sociable" organizations, where employees tend to do a lot of things to help their colleagues; they are not just looking out for themselves. They interact closely with their colleagues as if they belong to the same family, which creates an environment of trustful relationships and community spirit.

'I believe that it is the responsibility of the company to make sure that employees continuously develop their skills, that they are happy and feel recognized and rewarded, and that they are doing something that is worthwhile and useful. I think that the employees actually put in a lot more than even the capital that the shareholders put in. Therefore, it is important to help the employees create their own wealth so that they can help others who are not in a position to help themselves. As a result, the community as a whole benefits.'

N.S. Raghavan's sense of 'giving to the community' is in tune with the establishment by Infosys of a foundation in 1996 operating in the areas of health care, social rehabilitation and rural upliftment, education, arts and culture, so that they could intentionally contribute to society. 'I think that a business should contribute to the upliftment of the people that it employs and strive to improve the community that it is operating in, including the state and country as a whole. I think that businesses need to realize that by giving attention to all of these, including due importance to environmental issues, they will be making a significant contribution to society and the country.'

The birth of Infosys

N.S. Raghavan's early career shows his aptitude for human resources and technology, both of which were vital to his role at Infosys. 'My first job was with Andhra Pradesh State Electricity Board as a junior engineer. Soon I realized that there wasn't really much of a challenge, and I landed a job in Madras (now Chennai) as head of the electrical department in Kothari Sugars & Chemicals Ltd. My tenure of nearly two years was an enriching experience, especially in dealing with workers. As a senior manager, I was fully exposed to the two strongest trade unions at that time in the country and was a witness to all kinds of management–union problems including strikes and lockouts.

'I wanted to get first-hand experience of working in other parts of India, so I decided to take up a job with the Ministry of Defence, Government of India. As I was leaving the Kothari factory, I met the General Manager to say goodbye, and he told me, "I want to congratulate you because you are the only officer in all of this organization who has been able to manage good relations with both the unions and the workers."

'My first work in computer programming and systems development happened between 1973 and 1978 while I was working for the government in Delhi. In the late 1970s, I went through the first Data General computer training programme offered by Patni Computer Systems (PCS), where Mr Narayana Murthy, one of the eventual co-founders of Infosys, was a teacher. Later, I became an employee of PCS. Then, in September 1981, seven of us, all employees of PCS at the time, began Infosys. Our first job was when I and another colleague, Nandan Nilekani, went to Tampa, Florida in the USA, to customize an apparel manufacturers' software package.

'In 1983, the government regulations would not permit import of a computer into India even if you had the requisite finances, unless you were a software exporter willing to accept a large software export obligation. We were well positioned to use this opportunity and could import computers for use by a large group or multinational companies. The bureaucratic procedures for importing computers were, of course, still quite stressful. One time, I stayed in Delhi for three weeks just to get a letter of approval modifying a small clause.

'We all wore many different hats at Infosys in these early days. We went through many stages of development and experienced tremendous growth after economic liberalization in 1991. Since Human Resources Development was my forte, I was responsible for HR since day one, except for a short one-year period when I was made responsible for total delivery.'

Acting in accord with a common value system

'I always encourage people to work together as a team and to build trust and respect among everyone. I believe that one of the reasons Infosys was so successful is that we knew our individual strengths and we respected the strengths and contributions of others. We were very fortunate that everyone believed in a common value system. We could be very open and frank with each other as our relationships were based on a foundation of trust and respect.

'When I was offered the Managing Director position at Infosys, I told them honestly that I felt I was ready to retire. I did not feel that I had the energy to run the company at that stage of its scorching pace of growth; I felt that a younger person with lots of energy would be better suited, and I told them this with full honesty and sincerity. It took them some time to convince themselves that I was serious about what I said before they accepted my decision. A CEO position with a company like Infosys is, after all, a coveted post; however, integrity and openness are something that I value a lot.

'When it comes to building an organization culture, I do not think you have to formally speak about it. I think people automatically observe and follow the way you behave and act. Even if you have a rulebook that says differently, people will still follow what the leader does. They will follow the behaviour that they observe, not the behaviour that they read about in the rulebook. It is not the rules; it is the spirit in which the work is undertaken.

'Leaders must be very clear about what they expect and the right way of doing things. For example, financial goals are important as long as there's no compromise on the means to achieve them. We did set financial goals and encouraged our employees to strive to reach those goals, but we were not willing to do anything unethical or unfair in order to accomplish them.

'Whenever we set up a new centre at Infosys, people would ask us, "How do you ensure that your organization culture is going to be followed?" I found that if we sent a few of our veterans to set up that centre, the new people would follow their example and reflect their attitudes and behaviour. So the only way I have found for a culture to be created is for senior leaders to demonstrate the behaviour. At Infosys, we proved that it is possible to run a business successfully without compromising on values and beliefs. That makes me feel very happy and proud.'

Taking things lightly

While N.S. Raghavan cannot point to a specific time or incident to explain how he gained his values of fairness, love, caring and trust, he does draw from the rich heritage of Indian philosophy to guide him. 'In Indian philosophy, there are three paths to enlightenment. They are: "bhakti yoga",[1] which is devotion; "jnana yoga", which is discrimination and knowledge; and "karma yoga", which is good deeds and actions. The bhakti yoga requires you to do certain rituals to build strong devotion, but this ritualistic form of religion has never appealed to me. I am also not such a great intellectual to understand clearly the jnana yoga; unless I experience something and go through it myself, I am not able to really appreciate it that much. So I follow more the karma yoga path where you should put forth your best actions and not worry about the results. I can take very calmly almost everything that happens and not really worry about it. I find it quite natural to take things lightly; this is what I have internalized.'

However, N.S. Raghavan's inner calm and 'taking things lightly' did not prevent him from addressing behaviour he thought was not in accord with caring and respect for others. 'In my long career, one of the areas where I had disagreements with some of my colleagues is the mistaken notion that if you are powerful or intellectually brilliant, you can be arrogant and step outside the purview of rules and norms. In the public-sector bureaucracy, the powerful get away with arrogant behaviour. Interestingly, I also found that, in the private sector, the so called "outstanding performers" who produced results by trampling over everybody got away with serious infringements on the dignity and self-respect of other employees. I have fought my own mini-battles against these people with various degrees of success.'

Trust as a by-product of love

One expression of 'unconditional love' in N.S. Raghavan's life is how he sees the inherent goodness in people, and thereby strives to treat them with trust and respect. 'I am a person who implicitly trusts people, and unfortunately

---

1 In this context, 'yoga' means 'union with God' by any of three means (devotion, knowledge, good deeds).

this has brought difficulties to me in the past. But I still argue that people are born as good people. They are not born to cheat; I believe it is the circumstances that affect them and their behaviour. So I prefer to treat a person from the viewpoint that I trust them. I start with full trust and, if I find out that they are cheating, then I will move away from them. People who work for me have a lot of freedom.

'I like to distinguish between the individual and their attributes and actions. I do not feel that any person is bad; instead I say that their actions are bad or good, or that they have good and bad characteristics. If we want to have a good relationship with anyone, we need to give more emphasis to their more endearing qualities and downplay their less desirable traits. After all, all of us have our own set of not-so-good aspects.'

According to N.S. Raghavan, as an executive building a trail-blazing international company in a fast-paced industry, he continually demonstrated his belief in the inherent goodness of people by trusting them with information and decision-making power. 'There are probably very few organizations like Infosys where even the project managers were aware of the full financial profitability of their projects; they were very clear about their costs and whether they were contributing or not to the profit of the company. We were very open and shared all this information throughout the company. I always felt that we should share financial information with the employees and trust them with this information.

'I tried some interesting experiments in human resources at Infosys. When we were recruiting the new head of HR, I asked him if it was okay for the current HR team to speak with him. He said he didn't mind, so I called the team who would be working for him. I told them to spend an hour with him, ask him any questions, and then come back to me and tell me how they felt about him. So they went and interviewed a person who could become their new boss. It worked out very well.

'Similarly, we had a team of four people to whom I gave the job of deciding their own salary increments. I gave them the total amount that was available for pay hikes, had them sit down in a room and decide how to share this amount, and then come back to me and let me know. I also gave them a few rules. Rule number one was that it could not be distributed equally among the four. And rule number two was that they all had to agree as to the distribution among the members. Initially, each had the attitude that his/her contribution was better, but once they got over that then it became a very open discussion. So I really was fortunate to have a free hand to try all kinds of experiments at Infosys.'

Life after retirement

After his retirement from Infosys, N.S. Raghavan continues to seek ways to exercise his spiritual values of fairness, love, caring and trust. 'Given the tremendous success of Infosys, I became convinced that India has tremendous entrepreneurial talent which, if nurtured well, could put India in the forefront of the world economy, so I also wanted to help budding entrepreneurs. While a lot of teams came to me for guidance, the entrepreneurs who approached me were also in need of funding and financial support. So I started an investment company, Nadathur Holdings & Investments Pvt. Ltd. Suddenly I realized that we had invested in 14 companies, and I had to recruit specialists into the company to support these enterprises.

'Then, there was an opportunity at the Indian Institute of Management in Bangalore (IIM-B—one of Asia's top business schools) to set up a centre. I chose to set up the "N.S. Raghavan Centre for Entrepreneurial Learning" at IIM-B, where I am the Chairman of the Advisory Council for the centre. I funded from my personal resources the setting-up of the centre and the "Chair on Entrepreneurship". In the last couple of years, we added an incubation centre for supporting up to ten start-up teams.

'Soon after my retirement from Infosys, I was approached by the Chairman of the Murugappa group of companies to join their corporate board. This family business is a diversified group of companies spanning fertilizers, engineering goods, financial services, sugar, abrasives, etc., with a turnover of US$1 billion, with 22,000 employees. Mr Subbiah narrated how his grandfather started the company in Burma and about the strong values that formed the basis of their growth. Even in the 1970s, they refused to pay bribes to get any licences and, as a result, for ten years they could not expand. Then they decided on a strategy which did not require licensing. They decided to acquire other companies by aggressive bidding and did a lot of acquisitions in the 1980s.

'I wanted to meet the other members of the board and found in each of them a great humility and a strong sense of values. After this, I joined the Murugappa Corporate Board as an independent non-executive director. I am now the non-executive Chairman of the group and we are close to hiring a full-time chairman.

'I believe that if you can make a difference in the lives of people that you touch, if you can make their lives happier and bring them some joy, you should do this. This brings my wife and me a lot of satisfaction. It is important to me to see the good in people and to care for people. I have compassion for people who are underprivileged and I want to do something for them. That is why, at this stage in my life, I wish to be involved in social work.

Towards this, I started in 2001 a social trust called Foundation for Action, Motivation and Empowerment (FAME India) to help physically and mentally challenged children to lead a life of dignity and self-reliance.'

4

Francisco Roberto Cañada

Director/Partner, Errepar S.A., Argentina

Francisco Roberto Cañada, whose university degree was in accounting, is from Buenos Aires, Argentina. During most of his professional career he has been a leader of and partner in Errepar S.A., the major Argentinean firm for the publication of books and other materials for accountants. In addition, he has in more recent years also been a director and partner in the publishing and manufacturing companies Longseller S.A., Eco. Errepar S.A. and Deva's S.A., all of which are co-owned with his two partners in Errepar S.A. He was 47 years old at the time of the interview and had been in an executive leadership position for 20 years.

His entire career seems to have been an expression of his love and his search for true happiness, which he equates with spirituality. As he told us, 'My spiritual principles and values can be summed up in one word: "Love".' He has continually attempted to unite the spiritual and the material dimensions of life. As an expression of that love, and in spite of his having to deal with periods of severe illness, he has considered it to be his leadership responsibility to help others find their own true fulfilment. He told us, 'The concept for business we work with, our goal, is to make people aware of their inner potential, to help bring out this potential, and to always strive for excellence. Excellence is the way God made the world. I also think this should be the purpose of business in general.'

Since his childhood, Francisco Roberto Cañada has been strongly influenced by the prevailing Catholicism in South America. While still practising his Catholic faith, he now also finds spiritual upliftment, both in his private life and in his work life, in the teachings about religious tolerance and the underlying unity of all religions of the spiritual teacher, Sathya Sai Baba, whom he visits in India. He cited his teacher: 'There is only one religion, the religion of Love. If you are a Christian, go home and be a better Christian; if you are a Hindu, go home and be a better Hindu; if you are a Muslim, go home and be a better Muslim; if you are a Buddhist, go home and be a better Buddhist; if you are a Jew, go home and be a better Jew; and if you are an atheist, go home and be a better person.'

The interview was conducted in English with the help of a Spanish–English interpreter.

Loving God and aiming at excellence

For me being a businessman has not always been easy, as I am a man of silence. All of my life, I have rejected the material world, and still I have become a big businessman. It is not easy for me to be the head of four companies as a member of their boards. It's difficult, it's a problem; it's not my nature. But I have been guided to do my work, so that I am able to live in the material world and combine work and doing business with spiritual growth . . . Excellence is the way that God made the world. I also think this should be the purpose of business in general.

Three themes kept reappearing in our interview with Francisco Roberto Cañada: 'hard work', 'doing your duty with love and care' and 'loving God'. For example, he said, 'I pray that all people can do their duty with love and care. Therefore, as a leader, I make an effort that all our companies do good business, do good work and make good products in the way of God, without breaking His law.'

'In the beginning, work was a burden for my spirituality. But in the last ten years I have come to realize that happiness in life is to do all the work for God, to take part in God's creation, and to leave the fruits of my actions, my products, to God. In doing this, I hope that my products in some way or another send people to Him.'

Francisco R. Cañada graduated as an accountant from the University of Buenos Aires in 1977. 'I had worked in an accountancy company for five years when the owner of the company decided to publish books for other accountants. That was the start of the publishing company 25 years ago.' Francisco R. Cañada, who is one of three partners of that company, told us: 'We became strong because we worked very, very hard; we had two years without one single holiday. We worked on publishing and marketing, and in ten years we became a very successful company. Today Errepar is the leading company publishing books for accountants in Argentina.

'We made some acquisitions in this field and started another company for the publication of books on cultural subjects (psychology, philosophy, spirituality, etc.) and educational books for the different school levels. We also have a company dealing with products from India, including fragrant oils and organic products for health care. The fourth and last company is a firm that produces and sells agricultural products such as wheat.

'For many years and up until roughly three years ago, I was managing the editorial staff in the company that publishes books and other materials for accountants. Now, however, we have general managers in each of the four companies, and a single board of directors for all these companies. The board consists of the three partners who own these companies, and as one of the three partners I have been on the board from its inception. Together, the companies employ about 300 people.'

Human values as the guidelines for business

'Like all difficult things, leading a business becomes easier as time goes by. Seven years ago we developed some principles of action in our company. We began to hold weekly meetings where we discussed leadership according to the principles of my and my partners' spiritual teacher, as we read about them in a book on management, *Sai Baba's Mahavakya on Leadership*, by retired Lieutenant General in the Indian army, Dr M.L. Chibber. In these meetings, we discussed how to grow the company using spiritual principles.

'When the company went through hard times for a period of roughly three years, the weekly meetings stopped. The difficult times arose when the company was being split from just one firm into four companies, each with its own newly hired general manager and with the three partners as the board for each of these companies. Recently we have taken up the weekly meetings again, but have changed them. Now the meetings are being run by trainers in each company and on different levels—with the managers, with the middle management and with the employees. These trainers have been trained in working with human values, and the first results of the meetings are beautiful.

'We talk about how to apply the teachings and principles of spiritual leadership, both at work and in our daily life. In these weekly meetings, we focus on principles based on the human values of *truth, right action, love, peace and non-violence*—not on religion. We use examples from all religions, but each person has his own spiritual way. The employees accept this in a wonderful way.

'But not everyone finds working with us to be so beautiful. Sometimes it happens that an employee doesn't get on well with the company. They find that, with the family spirit and the spiritual orientation that permeate our way of doing business, it has a different vibration than they are used to, and so they leave.

'When we, the three owners, worked directly with everybody, there was a certain family spirit in the company. When we began growing as a business and then changed the organizational structure by installing general managers for each of the companies, the spirit of the overall organization suffered. People who have stayed with us through all the 25 years tell us that they feel that with these weekly meetings, which we began again three months ago, the whole organization, all four companies, are going to revive the old family spirit.

'The book on management by Lieutenant General Chibber has helped me to clarify my thoughts on the purpose of business as seen from my spiritual point of view. The book begins with a message where our spiritual teacher tells the students at his schools and university to always act with high dignity with the people they work with. That is the concept for business we work with; our goal is to make people aware of their inner potentials, to help bring out these potentials, and to always strive for excellence. Excellence is the way that God made the world. I also think this should be the purpose of business in general.'

Responsible leadership

'A concept from Buddhism and Hinduism, *dharma*, has had an enormous impact on my life. Ordinarily, this term is translated into "right action" or "acting righteously", but to me this term is much more than these definitions imply. For me it really is all about *responsibility*. Given my nature, my wish to be silent, it is difficult for me to be a business leader, but my concept of *dharma* as *responsibility* has helped me a lot to understand my position as a leader. It has also helped me to make the difficult decisions I have had to make, such as those dealing with firing people. Whenever we have to make a decision, and we don't do it in a *dharmic* way, in the long run it becomes obvious that it was not the right way to decide and not the right decision to make.

'In the weekly meetings, we replace the word *dharma* with responsibility: responsibility for the whole company, responsibility for the areas the people work in, responsibility in the relationship between the manager and his employees, responsibility in the relationships among the employees, responsibility in the relationship between the manager and his family as well as the employees' families, and the responsibility of all of us for ourselves.

'The conceptual framework for these meetings has not been written down; it is transmitted orally. Sometimes the managers have to make decisions that are so subtle, that they say: "Well, there is a thin red line between what is a good decision and what is not a good decision, between what is right to do and what is wrong to do." We try to make people aware of what has to be done in those situations. For example, some people discover in these meetings their own difficulties in making decisions, and we help them find out how to overcome that. But it's also important to point out that everyone brings not only his or her personal values but also their personal problems—from inside or outside the company—to the weekly meetings. We not only deal with problems of leadership and decision-making, we also go beyond the company and deal with the individual employee's personal affairs that have a direct connection with the work. Of course, privacy is always respected.'

Quality not quantity

'We are working to include the principles of the human values that are so central on our spiritual paths, in the books we are publishing for primary and secondary schools. Our evaluation committee is working on this, contacting our authors and trying to integrate the human values into our books—not only into books about societal affairs, but also into books about mathematics, biology or history. And in all our publications we want to produce products recognized for their high quality. We aim at excellence in everything we do. This also applies to the charitable donations we make, e.g. in supporting schools economically.

'On some occasions we have had to refuse to publish a book if it did not align with our principles, even if the book would clearly have sold many copies and made financial gains for the company. The managers are very focused on earning money, and in many cases they have proposed publications that were not *dharmic*—meaning in these cases that they would not inspire people to act in a proper way. Such books we have turned down.

'In the beginning, this attitude sometimes created confusion, but little by little the employees understood that their work was to lead them, and those affected by their work, in the direction of spiritual growth. When we select a book for publication, we focus on quality, in the broad, spiritual sense of the word. One of our activities is publishing spiritual, cultural and educational books. These kinds of books are a reflection of the view of life, shared by all three of us partners. We look upon this activity as an opportunity to help to create a better world.'

Do good business, do good work

'I have had major health problems all of my life. I was born with a serious heart problem. I went through major heart operations at the age of 18 months and again when I was ten years old and, in spite of these problems, I always felt God's close presence in my life in the form of Christ or Mary. At the age of 20, I forgot a little about my religious practice, but in my heart I always kept my love for God. I always desired to live a God-loving life.

'I am a Christian and I have loved my religion all of my life. Especially I love the Christian mystical writers, Santa Theresa de Jesus, St John of the Cross and others. They transcend the religion and go beyond it, as true spirituality transcends religion. Spirituality and religion are not the same. Religion is the necessary structure to bring forth awareness of a God-presence in you. This is the first step towards God, which is the first step on the spiritual path.

'The spiritual purpose of my life is to realize God in my heart, to have God working through my own self. God gave me this work for me to be able to unite the spiritual and the material world. He teaches me to go through the material world to the spiritual world. My spiritual principles and values can be summed up in one word: "Love".

'When I was in high school, which was a Catholic religious school, there was a new student who hadn't received the first communion. The director asked me to help the student to be prepared for it, and I explained to that student the basis for communion. We went to church on the day that I finished teaching him. We knelt and I told the new student: "Everything I told you is important, but there is one thing that is more important than anything else—that you love God." This is my advice for aspiring spiritual-based leaders: "Love God".'

Section 2

Looking and listening within

In this section

Here you will meet six top leaders; one from Colombia, two from the USA, two from India, and one from the Netherlands (also known as Holland). Once again they appear to be a very heterogeneous group—including a North American leader of a large, multinational consulting company who has written books that have sold almost 20 million copies; a South American Governor who owns and leads a construction company; the CEO for Europe, Africa, the Middle East and Russia of a huge Japanese hi-tech corporation; the leader of a traditional Indian manufacturing company; the chairman of an innovative biotechnology company in the USA; and an Indian in-house expert on leadership and HR. But, just as in Section 1, we were able to decipher a 'code' that links them all, a common theme or 'red thread' that interweaves their spiritual views of life and leadership. We have called this synthesizing theme *Looking and listening within*. Here you will meet:

Stephen R. Covey, Co-founder and Vice Chairman, FranklinCovey Co., USA

In *Peace of conscience*, Dr Stephen Covey says that 'To be a spiritual-based leader is to have universal principles integrated in your inner life and to be true to them in your actions. When you have that integrity, then you have peace of conscience. It means that you are truly true to that which you have internalized as being right and that gives you tremendous courage. Integrity is the highest form of loyalty—and over time it produces loyalty.' He shares how he has witnessed the tangible impact of living by such principles in country after country around the world.

Ramon Ollé, President, Epson Europe B.V., the Netherlands

In *Know thyself,* Ramon Ollé tells us: 'Whenever I am passing through a critical period in my own life, if I try to first put my priorities on things outside, on the external world, I never succeed. Everything works out after I put myself in order inside. When I am capable of reflecting within myself on what my internal problems are, what my internal dreams are, and what the internal consequences of the acts I am considering are, automatically I can also work with others to help them to look within and to put themselves in order.'

Ricardo B. Levy, Co-founder and Chairman, Catalytica, Inc., USA

In *Deep inside we need a humility compass*, Dr Ricardo B. Levy relates an internal conflict he faced: 'When we sold the pharmaceutical company it involved the dismemberment of the business that we had built over 27 years . . . It helped me throughout this period to be able to live in the unknown: to let the problem be with me and just rest there, to quiet my mind and get into my deeper inner self and allow my inner spirit connected to God to give me the signals of my path.'

Anand Pillai, Head of Centre for Leadership and Management Excellence, HCL, India

In *Connecting with the source of being*, Anand Pillai shares how he called upon his 'spiritual quotient' to handle challenges from angry vendors and employee errors: 'When I started doing research on spiritual quotient, I went from intelligence quotient (IQ) to emotional quotient (EQ) to spiritual quotient (SQ). Spiritual quotient measures the extent that you do what you do because of who you are. SQ brings together my thoughts, intentions and activities and correlates them with my inner being, my inner voice, my inner self-worth.'

Alvaro Cruz, CEO, I.C.M. Ingenieros Ltda, and Governor of Cundinamarca, Colombia

In *Listening to your intuition*, Alvaro Cruz recalls several experiences he had where listening to his intuition actually saved his life. 'Being spiritual means being able to listen to one's intuition,' he told us.

'Spirituality is a permanent attention to the inner self: to be able to perfect one's behaviour and attitudes, both inwardly and externally with others, basing one's conduct on fundamental human values such as love, truth, peace, right conduct and non-violence.'

A.K. Chattopadhyay, Senior Vice President, ACC Ltd, Refractories Division, India

In *Manifesting the perfection within*, Dr A.K. Chattopadhyay tells of how 'looking within' enabled him to maintain peace of mind and serve those in need in the aftermath of a dramatic accident. 'Spirituality,' he says, 'is the manifestation of the perfection that is already there within you. Spirituality is when I look at myself, I look within and not outside, and respond from my inner feelings where we are all perfect beings.'

5

Stephen R. Covey

Co-founder and Vice Chairman, FranklinCovey Co., USA

Dr Stephen R. Covey is a highly effective man who has written hugely successful books about being effective, including *The 7 Habits of Highly Effective People*,[1] which has sold more than 15 million copies in 38 languages throughout the world. In addition he is Co-founder and Vice Chairman of the FranklinCovey Co., which provides global professional services. He has held this position for nine years. He lives in the Rocky Mountains of Utah, USA, and was 73 years of age at the time of the interview.

He attributes his success as a business leader and leadership authority to his dedication to principle-centred living and spiritual-based leadership. His leadership and teachings are founded on a fundamental assumption. 'I think that our work was born with us, and that it is a sacred stewardship to find and fulfil our work, our duties,' he told us. 'My basic approach to helping people to develop awareness as to spiritual principles is to get them to think in terms of their mission and vision and the values that they want to put into their life, and then how

---

1 *The 7 Habits of Highly Effective People* has been called the #1 Most Influential Business Book of the Twentieth Century and one of the top ten most influential management books ever. Other bestsellers he has authored include *First Things First*, *Principle-Centred Leadership*, *The 7 Habits of Highly Effective Families* and, most recently, *The 8th Habit: From Effectiveness to Greatness*.

to set up an information and accountability system to get them institutionalized. This applies to both individuals and to organizations.'

Stephen Covey has an MBA from Harvard University, a doctorate from Brigham Young University and seven honorary doctorate degrees. He has also received numerous awards dealing with contributions to peace in the world, entrepreneurial leadership and service to humanity. However, he has no doubt that the most meaningful award he has received is the 2003 Fatherhood Award from the National Fatherhood Initiative—as a father of nine and grandfather of forty-three. Dr Covey has been recognized as one of *TIME* magazine's 25 Most Influential Americans.

Peace of conscience

Spiritual-based leaders respect others and are guided by the fundamental ethic: service to others comes before serving oneself. From an existential perspective, the raison d'être of organizations is to serve human needs. Really, there is no other reason for their existence. Individuals and organizations grow when they give themselves to others. Relationships improve when there is a focus on serving the other, be it at the level of the individual, the family, the organization, the community, the society or all of humanity. The phrase so eloquently developed by Greenleaf sums this up: servant leadership.[2]

Dr Covey moved from academia to the world of business, but never subdued his dedication to learning, writing, teaching and serving. He told us about his business, 'Earlier I was professor of organizational behaviour and business management at Brigham Young University[3] in Salt Lake City, Utah, USA. At present I am Vice Chairman of the global services company, FranklinCovey which focuses on leadership, effectiveness, empowerment, organizational

---

2   Robert Greenleaf (1904–90), former Director of Management Research at the American telecommunications company AT&T, developed the concept of servant leadership. See for example the book *Servant Leadership: A Journey into the Nature of Legitimate Power and Greatness*.

3   Brigham Young University, although open to the public at large, is heavily steeped in the religious beliefs of the Church of Jesus Christ of Latter-day Saints, which is unofficially but generally referred to as the Mormon Church.

change, time management, work–life balance, communication and sales performance.

'The company was consolidated in 1997 as a merger of Franklin Quest and the Covey Leadership Centre. Our clients include 90 per cent of the *Fortune* 100, more than 75 per cent of the *Fortune* 500, as well as thousands of small and medium-sized businesses, governmental bodies and educational institutions. We have global operations in 129 countries, run more than 140 retail stores, and have more than 2,000 associates worldwide who provide professional services, products and materials in 38 languages. We train several hundred thousand people each year in effectiveness, leadership and productivity programmes. We also sell more than 1.5 million books a year and our FranklinCovey Planning System is used by more than 15 million people worldwide. Sales in 2005 were roughly $300 million.'

Stephen Covey is now 73 and still going strong, to put it mildly. When asked about his future work, instead of speaking about retirement he shared with us one of his mottoes, which serves as a powerful spiritual theme for him: 'Live life in crescendo'. He clarified: 'In other words, the most important work you'll ever do is still ahead of you.' And he adds: 'Another such spiritual theme for me would be: "Educate and obey your conscience". Educating as I speak of it here involves getting into the sacred literature of all the great traditions that have had enduring value and then consciously living true to what you have learned.'

Referring to his own obligations to the company he leads, FranklinCovey Co., Stephen Covey told us: 'I provide strategic direction to the board and to the company itself, and I attempt to get us to practise what we preach. But my main interest is in writing and teaching. I find that the administrative work is like the pounding surf; it beats you up and casts you in all directions. So I pretty much have empowered other people to do all of the business activities, and I just focus mostly on trying to write meaningful books. I am working on six of them right now. They are all co-authored, and the *leitmotif* underlying all of them is the role of principles as the timeless and universal basis for lasting effectiveness at the individual and the collective level.

'Such principles are fundamental to my thinking and leading, and to the way we organize our company and our work. It is my experience that to know something and not to do it is really not to know it.'

Universal spiritual principles

Stephen Covey often uses the metaphor of 'leaving a legacy': 'To be able to leave a legacy that is sustainable over time requires institutionalization of principles,' he told us. 'If you actually get a person to think in terms of their legacy, what they are trying to really do in the long run to bless people's lives, it gets them immediately into a spiritual frame of mind. I use this approach all the time in my leadership.'

'To me spirituality is three things: First of all, you are dealing with the whole person. That includes the person's spirit or soul. You cannot separate their body or their mind or their heart from their spirit, because they are all so interrelated, and there is a synergistic relationship between all these four dimensions of our nature.

'Another dimension would be that you are dealing with those principles that are universal and timeless.

'Third, spirituality deals with peace of conscience. Obeying or following your conscience means that you are true to that which you have internalized as being right and this gives you tremendous tranquillity and courage.

'I just finished going through four countries in Africa, three countries in the Middle East, India and Sri Lanka, with the effort to bring together principles that are universal and timeless. I taught from Hinduism, I taught from Islam, I taught from Christianity. I just did a satellite interview to China explaining what this material can do for a Confucian[4] nation. I teach the exact same principles no matter where I am and show that there is a universal character to these principles.

'I make a real conscientious effort in my leadership, writing and speaking not to refer to any one particular religion, but only to deal with that which is universal. Although I am an active member of the Mormon Church I don't get any Mormon theology snuck into it in some secret way.

'Certainly principles have a moral and spiritual foundation, but no religion has a patent on them. So if people have certain cultural definitions of what these universal principles are, and of what their values are, I say to them, "I'll just go with yours." The key is to live the values and to be true to the principles that underlie them—to be integrated around principles—not around people or organizations. Personally I believe that the source of all the principles that give your life its integrity, and its power and its meaning, all of them link up to the Divine.

'If controversies arise or if people start feeling that I am being too religious, I say, "Let's just stick with those principles that we all agree on. Let's see if we can follow the principles of fairness, kindness, respect, the development and

---

4 Confucius (551-479 BCE) was a leading thinker, political figure and educator. His philosophical, ethical and religious ideas provide the basis of a universal moral system that has survived even Chairman Mao's Cultural Revolution (1966-76) and to this day plays a fundamental, though often implicit, role in the mind-set of the Chinese people.

use of people's talents, having meaningful work, and living with integrity. Let's see if we can agree upon these, let's go to our hearts and our souls and live with integrity."

'To be a spiritual-based leader is to have these universal principles integrated in your inner life and to be true to them in your actions, even when it's dark—when you have power over people and can do things and not be found out. When you have that integrity, then you have peace of conscience. Peace of conscience is much greater than peace of mind. It means that you are truly true to that which you have internalized as being right and that gives you tremendous courage. Because then you can be strong with a loving spirit. Integrity is the highest form of loyalty—and over time it produces loyalty. It's far better to be trusted than to be liked.'

Competence in designing win–win systems

'Following your conscience is a long-term approach to win–win; even though all your decisions may not be popular, you don't ever violate the relationship of win–win towards people. One time in the USA, I was working with a man whose insurance company was suffering under internal competition. I had attended their annual celebration where about 20 to 30 people received big awards. I asked, "Did you hire the other people as losers?" He said, "Oh, no, they will have their chance next year." I said, "Nevertheless you have got about 800 losers out there and only 30 winners. Everyone can be a winner; you have just got to change your mind-set from scarcity to abundance." He had a fine character and said, "I would like that, but how do we do it?" He didn't know how. It was not a character issue, it was a competence issue.

'I said, "Turfism in your company is a result of the way you have designed your reward system; it nurtures cut-throat internal competition." He asked, "What can one do?" I said, "Set up win–win agreements. These are agreements where the people you want to inspire participate in designing the agreement where, if some achieve their goals, all the rest benefit; this is a win–win system where everyone can win. Get off this internal competition." He had an abundance mentality and immediately responded to the need. Now that he was aware of the challenge, he had to develop the competence for designing and institutionalizing participative win–win agreements. He became so inspired that he and his employees designed the new reward system—and within one year 80 per cent of his organization was producing per person what 3 per cent, 30 people, had produced the year before. The pie got so large.'

Partnering and setting goals

'Recently I was with the sheriff of greater Los Angeles County. I asked him, "What is your goal?" and he said, "For Los Angeles to be the best and the safest large city in the world." I said, "It's way too small of a goal, you have to think in terms of a mega-goal, an extraordinary goal, one that allows your city to be a model for other large cities throughout the world, and to send ambassadors out to mentor these cities, so that they can better deal with their crime issues." Such goals require the creation of the kind of partnerships that I am promoting in my leadership activities. Such partnering definitely is a spiritual approach; it integrates the temporal and the spiritual, based on a whole different approach to preventing crime. And crime is going down. Where this approach has been used, the rate of crime is falling and is now reduced between two-thirds and 90 per cent.'

The same basic ideas of partnering based on principles are not only being successfully applied in businesses, they work in educational institutions as well. Dr Covey told us: 'In the schools I have worked with to introduce principle-based character into the curriculum, the results are measurable and very dramatic. There is a clear connection between learning and principles, between academic performance and character.'

In this connection he said, 'I find that spiritual intention drives perception, which drives behaviour, which then drives results. Let me give you an example. I was working with a large college in Ontario, Canada. They really had a terrible culture; it was characterized by turfism and fighting and interdepartmental resistances, with everyone looking out for themselves, protecting their own situation, silo thinking, and all that kind of stuff. I worked with them over a period of a year to develop a mission statement that would be supra-ordinate. By this I mean larger than oneself, larger than one's own institution. It took them about two years before there was broad agreement, and eventually what happened was that they developed a mission statement to become the yardstick educational institution for all of the state of Ontario—the institution others could measure themselves against. When they really bought into that intention to leave a legacy, the littleness of their souls completely submerged, and the magnanimity of soul exploded inside them.'

Seeking first to understand

'I had an interesting experience recently in India. I had just read the book *The Argumentative Indian*. Essentially it's a very well-written cultural history of

India and how the argumentative tendency is part of their cultural DNA. When I got into that, I could see how underdeveloped their country was with respect to teamwork and how overdeveloped their democracy was. They have so many parties and so much fighting and contention. I spoke to an audience of a thousand people about the spiritual principle of seeking first to understand before seeking to be understood. I then opened things up to the audience and said, "Let us see if we right now can listen to each other and re-make the other person's point before we make our own." They were unable to do it. So I said, "Let me see if you could ask a question on what we have covered to this point without making an oratorical statement." They were unable to do it. So I had one half of the audience just observe if the other half could practise this principle. They could not do it. And they could see that they could not do it.

'Then I said, "Look at what has happened to your infrastructure here in India, look at the bureaucracy, the extent of rules and regulations that have taken the place of human creativity—which is really interesting when you consider that you have more knowledge workers in this country than any other country in the world." I said, "You are capable of transcending your cultural DNA, because deeper than that is your spiritual DNA, it is deep in your natures, you really are capable of doing it." They were aware of their cultural DNA. Rather than looking at life through it, they now chose to look at it. They could then see that true leaders don't work through systems, rather that they work on the systems, and they do this through a principle-centred approach that rests on universal spiritual principles. This was a fascinating learning experience for all of us.'

The soft stuff is the hard stuff

'Business has a definite spiritual role as regards its responsibility for the whole because its influence is so enormous. And business leaders are increasingly aware of this relationship between the spiritual and the responsible. They are aware that the human dimension, particularly at the level of trust, is the root source of so many of the problems that follow in the slipstream of globalization. They know that the soft stuff is the hard stuff—and that leadership is increasingly becoming an art, an enabling art.

'We must continually renew ourselves physically, socially, emotionally, mentally and spiritually. In an organizational context, the top people have to be out in the field, and they have to get to know the people they affect and know their families and their situations. This is not a waste of time, it is renewal; if you don't feel the pulse of people, you can't serve them and you can't feel the pulse of God. You can only serve God as you serve other people, and you don't feel the pulse of people unless you also feel the pulse of God.

'The problem is, when you are in a huge, growing organization, how do you do it? It's so abstract; you are so insulated and isolated from what is in fact going on.

'In my country the HR [human resource] person has kind of been driven out of the front room and replaced with the CFO and the auditors because of the fear of not complying. But compliance has to come from the heart. There is such a fear of being challenged legally that in many organizations it takes the place of spirituality, and formal authority replaces moral authority. I think that to get people to be *independent* and to then choose to be *interdependent* based on principles is the real challenge to those leaders today who realize that moral authority underlies formal authority, and that the purpose of the organization is to serve.

'To become a spiritual-based leader, you have to teach the principle of service, to apply it, to live it, and then to be accountable to those you serve. Service can start at the very local level, but real stewardship requires expanding one's vision to include all of the world. But good character is not enough. A talented person with a fine character and good schooling also needs organizational competence in order to develop organizational trustworthiness. Trust is a function of both character and competence.'

Write your mission statement

'My advice to aspiring spiritual-based leaders would be: "Write your personal mission statement or creed." This is the most effective way I know to begin to focus on what you really are searching for in life. Developing your personal mission statement gets you to focus on what you want to be—your character—and what you want to do—your contributions and achievements—as well as on the principles and values upon which your character and contributions are to be based. Developing a mission statement is not a simple task; it requires considerable introspection, analysis and thoughtful expression. When developed, it becomes your constitution, it expresses your values and vision, it provides you with the criteria for measuring everything that you do in your life.

'Having developed your own mission statement, I would advise a spiritual-based leader, together with his or her associates, to write a mission statement for the organization. In this process all the associates should be treated as partners, as co-creators. So I would tell the leaders to start the process of developing such a mission statement which embodies vision, mission, values and strategic goals for the organization.'

6

Ramon Ollé

President, Epson Europe B.V.,
the Netherlands

When we interviewed Ramon Ollé, he was President of Epson Europe. He joined Epson in 1985 as Managing Director of Epson Ibérica, S.A. in Spain, following a joint venture between the Japan-based multinational Seiko Epson Corporation and his own electronic and computer products company. In 2000 he was appointed Executive Vice President of Epson Europe, the regional headquarters of the Epson Group for Europe, Middle East and Africa, and he became the company's President in 2001.

Seiko Epson Corporation, the parent company of Epson Europe, develops, markets, sells and services information-related equipment (computers and peripherals, including PCs, printers, scanners and projectors), electronic devices (semiconductors, displays and quartz devices), precision products (watches, corrective lenses, factory automation equipment) and other products.

Ramon Ollé's spiritual view of life centres around the concepts of 'wholeness' and 'inner force'. He told us, 'I do not understand man in terms of duality—that he is matter and mind, or matter and spirit. I see man as both, fully integrated. For me spirituality is the inner part of this total, integrated concept of humanness. In my background as an engineer, I also studied some theology and philosophy. At a later point in my life, I tried to find explanations to things that exceeded my logical capacity and my mathematical reasoning. I decided on my own to go back to explain my faith, and to explain why certain things affected my life in the way that they did. These new insights supported my managerial work. When you study these things, it helps you to discover the inner part of man.'

His spirituality has for many years found external expression in his leadership of Epson Europe, his teaching as guest professor at several universities in Spain, and his interest in organizational ethics and cross-cultural relationships. Due to his long working relationship with a Japanese company, Ramon Ollé also has a particular interest in Japanese culture and business management.

Ramon Ollé was born in 1950 in Barcelona, Spain, and received his degree as an engineer in telecommunications from the Ramon Llull University of Barcelona. He also has a Theology Licence degree from Catalonian University in Barcelona, as well as a master's degree in Industrial Management from EADA in Barcelona. In addition, he has followed postgraduate programmes at Stanford, Harvard, Columbia and Michigan universities in the USA, and at the Institute for Management Development in Lausanne, Switzerland. When we interviewed him, he was also pursuing his doctoral degree in Ethics and Engineering at the University of Barcelona.

Shortly after our interview with him, Ramon Ollé was appointed CEO and Chairman of Epson Europe; he now has responsibility for Epson's activities not only in Europe, the Middle East and Africa, but also in Russia.

Know thyself

I consider that life is like a pendulum. Do you see any middle managers today that are happy with their stock options? Do you see any organizations that have senseless and unreasonable priorities with happy and satisfied employees? Once again, the pendulum is moving back and compelling us to reconsider certain basic concepts. It has been proven that when executives make short-term big money, it just creates more desire for the future. As a Japanese organization, we do not have these big benefits; we are always looking ahead, even to future generations. As a result, we are much more committed to our sustainability when we face difficulties, because our commitment is long-term.

After 17 years in the Japanese-based organization Epson, for the last year Ramon Ollé has been the President of Epson Europe B.V., dealing with electronic equipment and services. He was born and educated in Spain. At the time of the interview he was 52, working in the headquarters of Epson Europe in Amsterdam, the Netherlands.

'I was an engineer in telecommunications for a limited period of time, acting as a technician,' he tells. 'Following that, I worked in design and manufacturing and had the opportunity to have a lot of communication with colleagues around the world, especially with the Japanese and Americans. When I returned to Spain after a trip to the United States, the company I was working for went bankrupt. During that period, I felt very uncomfortable because I was newly married, with a small child. Here I was, 27 years old and starting all over again.

'But then I decided to build my own company, and that was probably the best experience I have had. From 1978 to 1985 I ran my own business with electronic and computer products. This was a very good experience because I started from zero and grew the company to a good size. During that period of time, I had a lot of connections with Japan because I dealt with imported electronic products. Epson gave me exclusive distributorship of their products; and then in 1985 they proposed to enter into a joint venture with my company.

'We were in this joint venture until 1989 when they took over all of the capital of the company and I was appointed the President and Managing Director in Spain. In the next ten years, I developed the company from a very small level of US$10 million to almost US$100 million. I was then appointed President of the company in Portugal as well.

'In October 2000, the President of Epson appointed me as Executive Vice President for Europe. We had to merge two large organizations in Europe at that time and I was put in charge of this entire reorganization. This includes Europe, Africa and the Middle East, which totals 103 countries, with a large number of dealerships, 16 branch offices, six subsidiaries and three factories. I call that time period my "black year" because of the things I had to do in connection with the reorganization.

'In May 2001, I was officially appointed President of the organization in Europe. Epson worldwide [in 2002] has 84,000 employees with ¥1.4 trillion yen turnover [roughly US$12 billion] and in Europe we have 2,600 employees, with a turnover of €2.2 billion.

Spirituality as the inner part of the integrated human being

While Ramon Ollé was working, he started once again to study philosophy in order to 'understand why people are reasoning in certain ways, and what influences our thinking,' he told us. 'In my background as an engineer, I also studied some theology and philosophy. At a later point in my life, I tried to find explanations to things that exceeded my logical capacity and my mathematical reasoning. I decided on my own to go back to explain my faith, and to explain why certain things affected my life in the way that they did. These new insights supported my managerial work. When you study these things, it helps you to discover the inner part of man.

'What I have always wanted to be, and the inspiration of my entire life, is the integrated man, the whole human being. I do not understand man in terms of duality. I gladly accept that as a man I am both material and spiritual. I see man as fully integrated . . . fully complete. For me spirituality is the inner part of this total, integrated concept of humanness.

'In our Christian culture we were educated to believe in the duality of matter and spirit. Today the big mistake is to equate man's spirituality with religion. And that's why the new generation doesn't have much to do with either spirituality or religion. People tend to think today that everything about man is rational, whereas I believe that not everything about man's life is rational; otherwise, we have to deny a very big part of ourselves.

'It seems that today we have a lot of resistance to expressing our spirituality because it seems that the spiritual life belongs to the past; it is easy for people to misunderstand what you mean. In today's language we seem to avoid strong words, and spirituality is a strong word. This avoidance of strong words is why we don't say that people are dead; we say that they have passed away.

'If you understand yourself as a full human being, you will understand that your inner force is spirituality. Nobody can deny its existence. It is the most inner part of us. And it is a force as the main driver of our human nature. When we are experiencing, say, the emotion of love or resistance to others, these are very strong feelings that are not simply related to our chemistry. Spirituality is really the inner force—not only in the exceptional moments, the super tasks, but also in our daily life.'

Changing mind-sets in a multicultural organization

Referring to his 'black year' reorganizing the company, Ramon Ollé says, 'The most difficult part of changing an organization is to change the mind-sets of the people. Designing change is a logical matter with a certain risk. But, in the end, what makes it really happen is when everyone aligns their mind-sets in one direction.

'The company I lead is very multicultural with 31 different nationalities represented in the headquarters, so it is much more difficult to bring forth transformation in this kind of environment. One reason is because everyone has been educated and raised in a different manner and we are not sharing the same values. Our ways of listening, interpreting and understanding are embedded in our cultures. Then, when people have to adapt to an organization's way of doing things, it can be difficult.

'I try to help them clarify their inner understanding of the problem we are facing so that we can move from the inner understanding to the outside action. I have 100 per cent trust in the Chinese proverb: First know and help yourself, then your family, then your village, then your country.

'I discovered that when it is not possible for a person to change his mindset, even when he has had training and coaching, then he must be let go and replaced. We are talking about the human spirit and we must do all we can to bring out this spirit, but sometimes there are limits.

'We implicitly think that our global world is a common world. However, you become aware of the richness when you discover and respect all the differences. It requires a lot of skill to navigate in these different waters. Just like the physical world has a lot of hills and mountains, which is more interesting than a flat landscape with only desert, an organizational world that has many different cultures is richer than an organization without such complexity, when we are able to integrate all of this, while respecting the differences.

'Whenever I am passing through a critical period in my own life, if I try to first put my priorities on things outside, on the external world, I never succeed. Everything works out after I put myself in order inside. When I am capable of reflecting within myself on what my internal problems are, what my internal dreams are, and what the internal consequences of the acts I am considering are, automatically I can also work with others to help them to look within and to put themselves in order. All of the people in the world have basically the same desires, the same emotions, the same loves, the same fears. So, if I am capable of understanding this, then I can understand the different cultures we work with and in. If I do not do this, then I cannot really understand anything.'

The value of family

'It is vital for leaders to have a lot of contact with their employees. It requires them to walk around the organization and to learn employees' names. Before reaching my current position, I knew most of the employees in my organization by name.

'Today, what makes me most happy is when people are friendly towards me, when we say hello to each other, and I ask them about their family and their lives. If you ask people what the most important thing is for them, they will immediately say it is their family. People think that this is more so in their particular culture, but it is not really the case. It is the same in all cultures. This becomes the first value in order for man to live in society.

'A company has to create profit because the main part of that profit is going to our employees and their families; it is not going to the shareholders. Thus as part of our social obligation, if we really want to contribute to putting order within the family, we must make sure that our employees' families have the means to get proper food every day, to sleep in a comfortable place, and to be trained and educated.

'In my house in Spain we are a family that spans three generations: my father, my wife's mother, my wife and my four children. I don't have a lot of time with my family; however, my family life is still very rich. All of my free time is devoted to my family and not to anything else. And I give time alone to every member because every person needs me in a different manner.

'I have a son who is 28 years old and I have a son who is two years old. I am now enjoying, like I have never enjoyed before, the learning capacity of a small child. When I was younger, I was incapable of realizing this. As a result my way of training and educating my employees is very different. When our life's experiences like this begin to happen on a global scale, things will begin to change.'

Surviving and thriving for the next 120 years

'All organizations are working to survive and to thrive in society. A company can only be excellent as long as its people are happy to work there and to develop themselves as human beings. When this happens, our organizations will fit more into the network of society and will create more value for society. When everyone is happy in the organization, it will be totally integrated in the society. This is much more than providing economical value.

'All of the top leaders throughout this international organization imbibe the spirit of contributing to the long-term well-being of everyone, even of future generations. There is a great respect for human beings in our organization. There are certain measures in a corporation that cannot be evaluated in a month, in a half year, or even in a year. Our responsibility as leaders is not about ensuring that the company survives for even the next few years. Our responsibility is to ensure that the company will survive and thrive for the next 120 years. We cannot just pay attention to the short term. When you begin to think this way, you are really entering into the spirit of family, into the spirit of a multicultural environment, and into the spirit of humanity as a whole.'

Consistency between thought and deed

'I have always asked myself one critical question throughout my life" "Is there consistency between what I am thinking and what I am doing?" My thoughts and my practices must be the same. This is perhaps the most difficult part of being a public figure, which I am as a leader in a large international company. I have tried all of my life to be consistent and to be a whole person. This has created problems many times in my day-to-day business because, if others do not share these same views, then it has sometimes been difficult for me to explain my decisions to them.

'Many of the stands I have taken in my life were based on the conviction that everyone is as equal in their total integrity as I am. I must always be aware of how the decisions I make will affect their lives. When we look at re-engineering, we have to take care of others; it is our duty as leaders to consider their personal lives.

'When your leadership is founded on a value and belief system that considers the person as a total unity of the spiritual and the material, you cannot segregate which part of your daily activity is which and just consider one side of your total integrity.

'I believe in God. I pray. I think my life is more than my job, my title, my career and my salary. And, when you speak about this publicly, there is a lot of respect for you. When people lose the capacity to speak about these things openly in public, things change for the worse.

'Today, especially in my country, so many people seem to be very proud to say that they are, for example, atheist; it seems to be a sign of liberation. I am not upset that these people talk freely in public or in the media. But, unfortunately, it seems easier to talk about wealth or sex or not believing than to talk about your values, about faith, and even about God. I am a spiritual person and I speak openly about these things—about my values, my faith, God. But there does seem to be a resistance in others to speak out like this. I do not believe you can be true to yourself, stay consistent with yourself, by just ignoring these things.'

7

Ricardo B. Levy

Co-founder and Chairman, Catalytica, Inc., USA

Dr Ricardo B. Levy is another example of a multicultural spiritual-based leader. He is the son of a Jewish businessman who fled from Nazi Germany to Ecuador, one of South America's smallest nations. Here he learned to communicate freely in three languages: German at home, Spanish at school and with friends, and then English such that he could attend three of the most prestigious universities in the USA. Dr Levy has an MS from Princeton University, a PhD in chemical engineering from Stanford University, and is an alumnus of Harvard University's Executive Management Programme.

But it is not only at the level of language that he straddles cultures. Born into a Jewish family, and although considering himself Jewish, he does not follow Jewish religious practices. And, although he follows practices from Christianity, the major religion in Ecuador, he does not consider himself a Christian. He derives inspiration from both of these major religions, but is first and foremost spiritual, not religious. As he says: 'A particular religion is just one *approach* to the spiritual journey. Spirituality has a much broader context that encompasses religious practice. For me spirituality is a deep connection with a force greater than myself. It is an individual journey that includes longing and belonging, and the fruits of this journey are love and compassion.'

After a short spell with Exxon's research laboratory, where he was a founding member of the company's chemical physics research team, Ricardo Levy teamed with a colleague from Exxon in 1974 to start Catalytica in the basement of his house. They developed promising technologies in the fields of combustion systems and pharmaceuticals, raised venture capital, took the company public, acquired other firms, and grew Catalytica from a consulting firm into a Silicon Valley-based pharmaceutical and energy company with 1,600 employees, three factories and a market capitalization of US$750 million in the late 1990s.

His world became extremely complicated and he turned to spiritual practices to obtain the sense of peace and fulfilment that no amount of business success could provide. Over the years, these practices included meditation, reading spiritual literature, t'ai chi, practising humility, quieting the mind, and living in the unknown. As he told us: 'I think the problem with leaders in our Western business is that we are not aware of the need to go inside. We have to connect with a much more human universe and be willing to take the time that is needed to make our decisions from this deeply felt inner guidance. Deep inside we have to have a humility compass and we must have a way to tune in to that compass repeatedly, especially as we grow and begin to have successes in business.'

When he sold the pharmaceutical part of the business to a huge Dutch company, DSM N.V., in 2001, what remained was the combustion division, Catalytica Energy Systems, Inc., where Ricardo Levy is chairman of the board. He is currently also on the board of Accerlys, Inc. and StemCells, Inc.

Deep inside we need a humility compass

Spiritual resonance is in my view a very important aspect of good leadership and good teamwork. It permits the meshing of different personalities without jealousy or resentment. It permits one partner to cherish the limelight of the other partner. It permits listening even in the most difficult situations. It overcomes the dark shadow of the ego. The story of Catalytica is very much a story of spiritual resonance. With my co-founder I had that relationship. It permitted us to build a successful enterprise that transformed multiple times over the 30 years that we were together. Without it I doubt that this would have been a success story.

At the time of the interview, Dr Levy is the acting CEO and Co-founder of Catalytica Energy Systems, Inc., based in Mountain View, California. He is 57 years old, born in Ecuador, where he lived until he came to study at Princeton and Stanford Universities in the USA.

When his father passed away suddenly, Ricardo Levy returned to Ecuador to run the family business that made paintbrushes and different forms of bristle-based products. 'My parents were German immigrants who fled from the Nazi persecution of the Jews and went to Ecuador, and so they were true entrepreneurs. They lived in the house in the front, and had the business in the back. We had about 100 employees, and I had grown up in the midst of many of those employees. But, suddenly, at the age of 22, I became their boss. They still called me Niño, which means little boy.

'After that I came back to Stanford University and finished my PhD in 1972. I joined Exxon so I could work in a large corporate research laboratory. There I had the good fortune of meeting my business partner for a lifetime, with whom I started Catalytica in 1974. He is a remarkable visionary technologist.

'We started with the idea of developing proprietary technology that we would then commercialize. We had developed enough of our own ideas to get financing and by the late 1980s we began developing some inventions that were important. In the early 1990s we decided to focus our attention on two markets in which our catalytic inventions looked most promising: pharmaceuticals and energy. We ended up doing this by forming two subsidiaries, which developed much on their own path.

'By the late 1990s, our pharmaceutical company had become a major outsourcing supplier to the pharmaceutical industry. We had three manufacturing plants and 1,600 employees throughout the USA. We did about US$500 million a year in gross sales, when a company decided they wanted to acquire us. So we sold the pharmaceutical business and kept the energy business as its own separate entity. The basis of our energy company was a catalyst we had invented in the late 1980s that allowed fuel to be burned without pollution. I retired from active duty and became the Chairman. I am currently also filling the CEO role because our CEO left just a few weeks ago; however, this is temporary until I find a replacement. Today the energy company has about 150 employees. We only have research and development revenues at this point.

'For me the purpose of Catalytica is to create value for society. Unless we have a clear sense that what we are doing has a positive societal purpose and our actions will make the world a better place, it is very difficult to achieve wholeness. I do not hesitate to talk about my own spiritual struggle, when the opportunity is appropriate. The people in my company know that this holds an important place in my life. Being able at any moment to say that the struggle and effort is worth it when judged against the whole spectrum of one's life is perhaps the greatest measure of success.

'How does this translate to my company? By how I treat my employees, whether I display empathy, compassion, fairness, or consistency.'

The deep inner search

'A few months ago I was asked to give a talk at Harvard University where they had a one-and-a-half-day forum on "Leadership, Values and Spirituality". For that talk, I brought with me this definition of spirituality: *The deep inner search for a fuller personal integration with a transcendent greater than our narrow self*. I find that for me spirituality is a deep connection with a force greater than myself. It is a very individual, lived experience that includes both longing and belonging, expressed often and perhaps best through love and compassion. One of my favourite quotes from Abraham Joshua Heschel[1] is: *Needs are spiritual opportunities*. I find this so true, just as longings are also opportunities for us to learn about our spirituality.

'I am by heritage Jewish and a lot of my social and personal history is Jewish. But I am not deep enough in my knowledge of Judaism to claim that I am really following that path as my path. Nor am I a Christian, yet I respect both of them and connect with both of them. I even have a strong commitment to a group that meets each week with other business leaders that is based in the contemplative traditions of the Jesuits.[2] The important thing for me is that, while I am Jewish by heritage, I have overcome any barriers to Christianity and can share some of the holiness of that tradition.

'I have always had a yearning, a drive to seek, and reflect upon, spiritual matters. In 1997 I was sailing in Turkey with André L. Delbecq, a professor at Santa Clara University who teaches a course on Spirituality and Business Leadership. We began to exchange books and engage in dialogues about this subject. Then he asked me to be a part of his first course at Santa Clara on this subject. The group consisted of nine executives like myself, and nine MBA students. This course offered me a wonderful opportunity for deep immersion into spirituality. It had an enormous syllabus; I read for about a year and am still reading today. My spiritual studies are the best moment of my day.'

---

1 Abraham Joshua Heschel (1907–72) served as Professor of Jewish Ethics and Mysticism at the Jewish Theological Seminary of America from 1945 to 1972.
2 A Roman Catholic Christian order of priests.

Downsizing with empathy and compassion

Looking back, in 1991 Ricardo Levy was having one of the most difficult times he had ever had in his career—one that called upon his sense of deep connection and compassion. 'By then we had about 80 scientists working for us and we were in a transition, forming focused subsidiaries and moving into the commercial world. We had 17 years of history behind us, so we weren't just a start-up. In our dream to become commercial, we thought it would be best to partner with some larger companies in order to supplement the skills and capabilities that we didn't have, such as sales infrastructure and market capability. There was one company that we thought would be a good partner, and we focused our innovations in the areas of interest to them. The partner was a very large private company that was run by two brothers. Then one day one of the brothers decided he wanted to get out of technology. I got a call and was told that they were pulling out. I was so upset I went home and cried.

'It was so difficult because I had no choice but to cut the company. I had personally recruited each individual in this company and we had to let about 25 per cent of them go. I admit that I was not equipped to really do this. But what I was able to do is that I was able to downsize the company in such a way that I have remained a friend or colleague to everyone who was dismissed. No one was left with bad feelings toward me or toward the company. Even in the face of the extremely difficult complexities of the moment, I was able to do this with respect for the dignity of each individual.

'What enabled me to do this was that I felt the same pain that they were feeling. I was thinking deeply about what would happen to them and their families. And thinking about how I could help them get through the trauma of the layoff. I have never managed my company as just a job to do. When I deal with people it must be with compassion and empathy. Empathy is deep connectivity. Compassion is *with passion*. I think if one displays passion for another person, you can do what needs to be done and you can do it with dignity. I think this is one of the most important spiritual behaviours of a leader. You are living the experience, there is no artificiality or ulterior motive about it, and people feel it. You are honest and sincere.'

Hiring a spiritual-based CEO

'In 1997, we decided we wanted to grow our pharmaceutical side and become a more significant player with our customers, who were multi-billion-dollar companies. We knew this would be a major change for us. We looked for a new facility and found a huge one that was being sold. We were able to do what seemed impossible: a small, research-based company with sales of less than US$12 million and a market value of less than US$80 million purchased this magnificent US$300 million facility. Needless to say, it put us on the map. All of a sudden, in one step, we found ourselves with 1.8 million square feet of building space, 60 acres of industrial site and 600 total acres of land. In making this move we became a company with sales of over US$300 million. And then we continued to grow even larger than that over the next four years.

'In that growth, it became evident that the people I had hired as CEOs for our subsidiaries in the early years were just not the right people for the new stages of the company. In retrospect, as I faced this dilemma, I could have used one of the more important spiritual lessons that I have learned over the last few years: the ability to quiet the mind and let the unresolved issue sit while discerning the right path. The whole concept of living in the unknown has become more and more important for me. I was never trained in how to do this. In fact, as an engineer I was trained to do just the opposite. I am still so hard-wired to jump in and solve problems, and my comfort zone is to take action. If I had been more seasoned in my ability to live in the unknown and accept it, I could have handled this much better. Interestingly enough, I believe that I would probably have made a replacement decision of those CEOs much sooner. As it turned out, I did eventually make the change and it was the right step.

'When I hired a replacement CEO for the energy business I was much more aware of the spiritual connection to my business leadership activities and one of my important requirements in identifying this new CEO was my sense of that person's spiritual centre. I acted accordingly and chose a man that I felt was quite genuine. In our initial interviews, I did not have to ask him specific questions. Because this is now such a natural part of who I am as a leader, it comes across when I speak, and the dialogue flows easily with the resonating partner.'

Letting the problem be with you

'When we sold the pharmaceutical company it involved the dismemberment of the business that we had built over 27 years. There were many areas to think through. Perhaps the most difficult one was the future of the employees. People that we had attracted because they wanted to be a part of our dream of an entrepreneurial company were now going to have to face being sold to a large European conglomerate.

'It helped me throughout this period to be able to live in the unknown: to let the problem *be with me* and just rest there. I also followed the Jesuit practice of discernment, which is learning to quiet my mind and get into my deeper inner self. And from that place to listen to the voice of God and allow my inner spirit connected to God to give me the signals of my path.

'I am still an amateur at this. It takes an enormous amount of practice to be able to sense these signals and make sure that I am not using my ego to rationalize my actions. During the intense negotiations that followed, lasting over nine months and involving numerous bankers, lawyers, accountants, board members and executives, I was required to convince many sceptics and make many complicated and far-reaching decisions. It made such a difference to come from this centre point, which I had found through this deep spiritual process.'

If you have compassion and love, you will have humility

'There is such a need for a complete rebirth of trust in our business leaders. Leaders in business have an important role and responsibility to help society. Somewhere along the line, business leaders have lost their humility and in doing so they have lost their compassion and empathy, and their inner connection to God. I think this is something we need to come back to. And all of these concepts are connected. If you have compassion and love, you will have humility.

'I think the problem with leaders in our Western business is that we are not aware of the need to go inside. We have to connect with a much more human universe and be willing to take the time that is needed to make our decisions from this deeply felt inner guidance. Deep inside we have to have a humility compass and we must have a way to tune in to that compass repeatedly, especially as we grow and begin to have successes in business. If we were to train leaders in such a way that the biggest fear they have is of becoming arrogant, we will be on the right path.'

8

Anand Pillai

Head of Centre for Leadership and Management Excellence, HCL, India

At the time of the interview, Anand Pillai was 43 years old, and head of the Centre for Leadership and Management at HCL, Hindustan Computer Ltd, New Delhi, India. HCL has two major arms: HCL Technologies (the major part of HCL dealing with IT and BPO services aimed at global markets) and HCL Infosystems (IT hardware and system integration aimed at the Indian market). HCL has 34,000 employees in 15 countries, most of whom are employed in HCL Technologies.

The Centre for Leadership and Management was started in 2002 by Anand Pillai, who at that time was Vice President of Sales and Marketing for HCL COMNET, a subsidiary of HCL Technologies Inc., which had about 600 employees.

For him, spirituality is intimately related to the concept of 'being'. It is this concept that is also fundamental to his leadership. 'Spirituality is that state of "being what you were meant to be",' he told us. 'Our self-worth comes in being who we are, not in doing what we do, not in achieving what we achieve, not in having what we have. For me, what is important is the *internal* motivation, not the external motivation. I bring lots of people together and make it a collective process, so that everyone is responsible and participates in the success. I don't come to the office to enjoy myself alone. I come to the office to enjoy others. I come here to enjoy the system and to contribute to the system. As a result of my contribution of being, I am inspiring others to contribute their being and, as a result, the organization's being is enhanced. This is true service. When I focus on my being and the others focus on their being, then all the rest becomes incidental.'

After completing his BSc from Bangalore University, India, and postgraduate studies in management, he worked for highly respected Indian companies in Bangalore and Delhi, then for multinational companies in the USA and Canada, before returning to India in the late 1990s.

When our research team once again was in contact with Anand Pillai in 2006, he was Vice President—Talent Transformation at HCL Technologies Limited and a member of the Senate (operating board) reporting directly to the President. He was also strategically involved with major Indian business educational institutions (such as the Indian Institute of Management, Bangalore; Institute of Management Technology, Ghaziabad; and S.P. Jain Institute of Management and Research, Mumbai) where HCL Technologies has academic partnerships. This keeps him on the move, primarily between Delhi, Bangalore and Chennai, where the company has its major development centres, and the USA, Europe and South East Asia, where it has its major business operations.

Connecting with the source of being

I bring lots of people together and make it a collective process, so that everyone is responsible and participates in the success. For me, what is important is the internal motivation, not the external motivation. My desire and dream is to take this same kind of vision forward to the one hundred managers in our organization. Today these managers come to me for training modules; what I want them to discover is the spirituality that is within them and have them manifest it in the way that they know best. Then, this movement can be passed along.

Anand Pillai has for many years been strongly motivated to help others to live and lead from a spiritual basis. 'Several years ago I decided that I did not want to get so caught up in the corporate world that I wouldn't have the energy later in life to share with others the importance of living and working from spiritual values, and how to manage by those values. After teaching a course for the Indian Institute of Management and Research in Bombay, the Director of the school wrote a letter to our executive vice president about the course and how well it had been received. The executive vice president forwarded this letter to the president of HCL and told him: 'Training is Anand's passion, preaching is his passion, and coaching is his way of life.' That in turn started a dialogue about what I most wanted to do for HCL in relation to sharing my spiritual values and how to manage by those values.

'As a result, I ended up as head of the Centre for Leadership, Intrapreneurship and Management Excellence (CLIME) at HCL. I was very happy with this decision and felt that my prayers had been answered. I realized something very important. My core competence was living a life of spirituality and then translating my life's experiences into something I could teach to others and train them to implement in their own work.'

Being—not doing, achieving or having

'For me, spirituality is the state of "being what you were meant to be". In 1979 my spirituality shifted from the religion I was born into, which was Hinduism, to my faith, which is in Christ. I have not changed my religion. What has changed is inside me.

'I recognize that spirituality is different for every person. Spirituality for a religious person is to be lost in a personal God, or to be lost in a formless God, or meditation. Spirituality for a materialistic person is to be lost in possessions. Spirituality for a workaholic or achievement-oriented person is to be lost in success. But spirituality for a "being" is to be lost in "being".

'In each category I just mentioned, there is a careful and conscious detachment. In the case of the religious person he is definitely detached from the world. In the case of the materialistic person, he is definitely attached to the material, and therefore is detached from anything else. In the case of the workaholic, he is definitely attached to his work, so much so that he is detached from the natural relationships of a husband, or wife, or a child, or other people; because he is so task-oriented, he does not have the opportunity or time to be people-oriented. Whereas if I am a "being", a spiritual being, and I do everything out of that, then the coordination factor is within me, it is not outside. I become attached to my inner being and detached from the outer world.

'Have you ever noticed that we are the only creatures who are called "beings"? We do not refer to any other thing or animal as a being. Our self-worth comes *in being* who we are, *not in doing* what we do, *not in achieving* what we achieve, *not in having* what we have.

'When I started doing research on spiritual quotient (SQ), I went from intelligence quotient (IQ) to emotional quotient (EQ) to spiritual quotient (SQ). Spiritual quotient measures the extent that you do what you do because of who you are, not because of your nationality, or title, or position in life. Who you are is your spiritual essence. The closer we relate every activity to our inner being, the higher our spiritual quotient is. SQ brings together my thoughts, intentions and activities and correlates them with my inner being, my inner voice, my inner self-worth. This motivation that comes from within will last. I really understand this, and I feel that my purpose is to share it.'

Summing up his thoughts here on 'being', Anand Pillai says that his spiritual theme is: 'Connecting with God, the source of "being". When I connect with God, I have everything necessary for a life of productivity. All this is my conviction to live and to share my spiritual values with others.'

From pain to peace

'Through a series of tragic incidences that happened in my family I came to a deeper understanding of spirituality when I was a university student, 20 years old.

'At the age of ten, I lost my father. Due to some family disputes over a piece of property, his brothers cast an evil spirit on him. He then became so tormented that he committed suicide. Four years after my father passed away, my elder sister got married and some money was given for her dowry. After the marriage, more money was demanded and her in-laws subjected her to mental persecution. She could not bear this and so she consumed poison and died. Two years after that, my auntie, who had been childless for ten years, could not bear the curse of not having a child, and so she killed herself.

'This brought me to question and to seek answers about how there could be an end to this misery, this suffering, and how to find salvation, which in Hindu terms is called *moksha* (liberation). I felt I needed to get answers to these questions. I was looking for assurance in a definite sense because I wanted to know where I would go when I die. I myself was contemplating suicide because I did not feel that life was worth living.

'Then in July of 1978 my younger sister was diagnosed with cancer. She was told that she had four months to live. When I heard that I felt ashamed that I was living and everyone else was dying. About three months after my sister passed away, I was still in confusion. I got a rope and decided that it was time for me to end my own life. I had a New Testament Bible in my room that had been given to me by my Christian college, but since I felt it was for Christians I had never read it. For some reason on that day, I decided to read it. I found an index for where to find passages to help you when you have a specific need, such as when you need peace, or when you are feeling sad, and so on.

'My name is Anand, which means ultimate bliss. In fact, it is the culmination of peace, bliss and joy. I knew that my need of the hour was peace so I looked up the passage that it referred to. The verse was John 14:27, "Peace I leave with you. My peace I give to you. I do not give as the world gives. Do not let your heart be troubled, neither let it be afraid." I said to myself, this is a very strong, very assertive and confirmative statement. I continued the reading and got really excited, and decided to postpone my decision to take my own life. My death could wait; I needed to explore this.'

Today Anand Pillai is so filled with the spiritual peace he has found, that he says, 'I come to the office to enjoy others. I come here to contribute to the system. As a result of my contribution of being, I am inspiring others to contribute their being and as a result, the organization's being is enhanced. This is true service. When I focus on my being and the others focus on their being, then all the rest becomes incidental.'

Responding to a large mistake

'At HCL, we had a situation in Calcutta where we were submitting a bid that was due the next morning at ten. This was a World Bank tender for US$4.5 million. We worked all through the night to prepare the documents. We had to prepare three sets of the commercial bid and three sets of the technical bid. Everything was done, and we split up to check that all of the documents were correct. We gave the bid at 10 am, just at the time it was due. That day the bid was opened at 4 pm and it was discovered that our supporting document for the annual maintenance contract was not there. As a result we were disqualified.

'The first reaction everyone had was to find the guy who made the mistake and sack him. However, I said, "No, there is no point in doing that. It was a mistake. If he did it intentionally, then yes, but if he did it unintentionally, that is a different matter." So, instead of getting angry and upset and sending nasty emails, I said, "Let's take control of this situation and let's see what we can do to salvage this situation. Let us focus our creative energy on supporting him, so that he has the initiative to stay on through the night when we have the next bid."

'This is what motivates people to go beyond the call of duty, to do what they are supposed to do. I told them to go to the evaluation committee and explain what happened and give the document to them in writing. I also asked them to request them to consider our secondary bid as our primary bid.

The committee said they would not honour our second bid. They said that they instead would follow another law, which says that if you have not submitted a bid for a component, it will be assumed that your quote is the highest quoted figure from among the other competitors. As a result, our quotation became costlier and we became outpriced and were out of the race.

'Again we kept our focus on trying to find a solution. After some further research, we found out that the other competitor had also violated one of the specifications. They had quoted their bid in Indian rupees, whereas this was a World Bank tender that needed to be quoted in US dollars. We pointed this out to the committee and as a result they applied the rule that said a bidder must then use the highest exchange rate, plus a deemed export rate. So this premium was added and ultimately this vendor was disqualified. We won the bid and for that year it was the largest contract we received.

'The spiritual basis that I came from in this situation is that I knew that this person had not made this mistake intentionally. I focused on the process and showed him respect. The moral of this story is simply this: We focused our creative energy not on the person who made the mistake, but on the process. The question that we asked ourselves was "what" went wrong, not "who" made this mistake. The customer also had a lot of respect for us because they watched us go through this process.'

Responding to an angry supplier

'There was a time when I had just moved into a new assignment and a vendor had not been paid because he had not supplied what he was supposed to have supplied. This vendor was upset because he had not received his money. This conflict had been going on for quite some time when I took this position.

'My secretary received a call from this vendor, and she came to ask me if she should tell him that I was not there. While she had the receiver covered she told me what a nasty fellow he was, and how he was going to shout at me. While she kept the receiver down for a minute, I told her that I did not want to hurt her, but I wanted to take the call. I asked the man what I could do for him. He said that his payment had not come. I told him the truth; I said, "Sir, I have just moved into this position one week ago. Give me your details, phone number and invoice. I cannot promise you a payment; however, I can promise you that within the next half-hour I will tell you why your payment has not been made. Then we can see what we need to do so you can receive your payment."

'He shouted that everyone promised to call back, but no one ever called back. I said with a calm voice, "Sir, you have spoken to me for the first time;

please give me that respect. If I don't call you back then you can yell at me also." In that half-hour I talked with my secretary, first about how she was avoiding rather than solving the problem. I said, "By your saying that I am not here, you are only solving the symptoms. We want him to be a satisfied vendor."

'I then went to the accounts department and found out that he had short-supplied an item. In less than 15 minutes, I called him back and told him exactly what the facts were. I told him that if he supplied the item that was not supplied, then we would pay him. He said, "Sir, I don't even want the payment now that I am talking to you. I want to thank you for giving me the full details. Yes, there was initially a short supply, but the reason I did not supply the full amount was because I talked with a person in your company and he told me I would not be paid even if I supplied the rest of the order." He supplied the item and got his payment. From this experience, my secretary gained a clear conviction to solve the problems and not the symptoms.'

Inner control during an extremely difficult situation

'I must give you a personal example of how I responded in an extremely difficult situation by connecting with my spirituality—an example that can also be applied to work situations. A little more than two years ago, my son met with an accident: a fully loaded car drove over his right foot. It caused a lot of damage to his foot. My wife rushed home from work in order to take him to the hospital. I was travelling in Bangalore and received a call that this had happened, so I had to catch a flight back to Delhi.

'Everyone who knew what had happened wanted to stone the driver; they wanted to beat him. My wife took control of the situation and said, "Listen, this is our child. Please let us take care of it." This driver was pleading with my wife not to make a police case because then he would lose his job and would not be employable again.

'When I arrived in Delhi I went to the operation theatre and there was my wife, along with the head of HR and vice president of operations from our company. One person had paid the bill and one person had arranged the doctor. My entire company was involved, even though it happened after office hours and outside of the company business. The vice president of customer support and his wife had also come to be of support to my wife, and his elder daughter went to be with our daughter at home.

'When I came, everyone was there and their immediate reaction was one of anger and wanting to know what had happened. For me, I simply asked the doctor two questions: "Will there be any irreparable damage? How long will he take to recover?"

'In all of this, my wife was not crying or throwing a tantrum. She had the presence of mind to keep her focus on and take care of our son, even though it was a very emotionally draining situation. Instead she took control of the situation as a practical person. When I came we were both in complete control. We kept focusing on our son, to support him. Everyone else wanted to focus on what happened, on the driver, on everything else, except our son.

'Delhi is a very vindictive society; if you do something, people want to make sure that you pay for it. Afterwards, my neighbours all got together and said, "Forget the driver, you must go after the owner." We told them that we would take care of it. The owner of the car came and apologized and offered to pay for the damages. I told him, "Take your money and go back; we don't need your money. Whatever you do will not be able to pay back the flesh that my son lost or the two inches of tendon that my son lost. Recognize that this situation was not in your control or in my control. It was in someone else's control. However, I want you to recognize that you have a role in maintaining order and discipline. I want you to incur a cost, and the cost I want you to incur is to first go to the community association and apologize to them, that you have been irresponsible in this community and you have let your car driver run over a small boy's foot. I want you to put that apology in writing and to feel the pain. Then I want you to put boards all over the streets in the community that say 'Children at Play. Drive Carefully'. You write these boards yourself and put them up." Our neighbours had never heard of anything like this being imposed. They were used to using this as an opportunity to receive large amounts of money for damages.

'This has become an example in our office. That situation was an uncontrollable situation, but we were in control. By being in control I mean: there is a sphere in which you have control and there is a sphere in which you do not have control. I am in control of my emotions, I am in control of my actions, I am in control of my intentions, and so on. I am not in control of others' emotions, others' actions, or others' intentions. If I try to control that which I cannot control, then I lose control. So if I operate in this zone of control and expand this, it is what I call the sphere of influence. If I stay in this zone that I can control, then I can increase my sphere of influence. In my office, this has become an operating principle for responding to situations.'

Doing things out of conviction

'Sometimes you must focus more on the value-based leadership, instead of going deeply into the spiritual-based leadership. Most people can more easily recognize what is of value and can make sense of what they need to do.

'You can do things out of conviction, or you can do things because you are convinced. If I first do something because I am convinced, then afterwards I will do it out of conviction because, while I am doing it, I will recognize the value and realize how it will make my ability to manage or lead much more effective.

'Appreciation is a result of being convinced, but being able to reproduce in others what you believe will come as a result of conviction. Conviction can also be positive or negative. I am talking about positive conviction from within. This is beyond age or status; I can pass on my convictions to my children, to my wife, or to my team members . . . Conviction comes from an inner deeper realization and not just an external convincing. It is not an easy step. You must move from coaxing, to cajoling, to convincing, to having conviction.'

9

Alvaro Cruz

CEO, I.C.M. Ingenieros Ltda, and Governor of Cundinamarca, Colombia

Alvaro Cruz straddles two worlds: business and politics. He has been the CEO of a large construction company in Colombia with several hundred employees and the Governor of the major state in Colombia, shifting his time and energy between these two activities.

In both of these leadership positions, as well as in his private life, his spirituality is continually guiding him, he told us. 'Spirituality is a permanent attention to the inner self: to be able to perfect one's behaviour and attitudes, both inwardly and externally with others, basing one's conduct on fundamental human values such as love, truth, peace, right conduct and non-violence. Being spiritual also means being able to listen to one's intuition. Spirituality is something you must persist in every day, every hour. Together with my wife, I have worked on being able to apply and reflect on this every day.'

Speaking about his governorship, he told us how his spirituality has resulted in his being respected as a leader who could get people to agree and work together in his otherwise strife-torn state: 'As the Governor of Cundinamarca, which is in the centre of the country with Bogotá as the capital, I was elected the President of the Governors' Federation in Colombia. Among the 32 Governor members I was considered to be a conciliatory figure who brings people together. The 19 representatives and senators in my state whom I worked with during my three-year period as Governor [until 2004] approved 100 per cent of my plans and proposals. And at the level of the republic, at the senate and in the national government, I am acknowledged as the man who keeps his word.'

Alvaro Cruz told us that he is not certain as to whether he will focus his future energies on politics or on business, but that, whatever he does, it will be in accord with his spirituality—'Spirituality is a way of life.'

As background for his activities in Colombia, he told us: 'Colombia has drastically changed from the 1930s, when it was primarily a rural country to now, when it is an industrialized country. Since the 1950s, there has been guerrilla warfare going on in Colombia, which has been related to drug activities, which are a source of great income generation. This has been terribly harmful to the country. It has created a loss of values, which has caused havoc throughout our society.'

The interview was conducted in English with the help of a Spanish–English interpreter.

~

Listening to your intuition

Spirituality is a permanent way of life where you are working towards attaining two main principles or goals; these goals are love and happiness. At work, if you have a spiritual outlook, you will have a wider outlook, you will be more patient and you will have greater respect for and a better understanding of the people you work with. Spirituality is very applicable to my work as a business leader in a construction company, as I have seen how much love, happiness and smooth working spirituality brings to the recipients.

Alvaro Cruz is owner and CEO of the engineering/building company, I.C.M. Ingenieros Ltda, in Bogotá, Colombia. He is also a former Secretary (minister) of Finance in his state and Secretary (minister) of Public Works with the Government of Colombia and has just ended his term as Governor of Cundinamarca, the major state of Colombia. The state, which surrounds the capital, Bogotá, but does not include it, has a population of 2.5 million. He is 54 years old at the time of the interview and has held leadership positions for 23 years as partner and manager of several different companies in the building construction industry.

For some years, Alvaro Cruz has been able to shift his emphasis from leading a successful business to serving his country as a politician. He feels that the secret that has made this possible is being able to feel love and respect for others as well as the ability to focus on non-attachment. 'Non-attachment to your work attracts more income and better results. The less attached you are to the fruits of your work, the more you are likely to get higher profits. Simultaneously this has a positive effect on co-workers, because they will be feeling more love and more happiness in working together', he says. For him as well as for his wife Zoraida, a lawyer and former vice mayor of the capital of Bogotá, 'spirituality is a way of life'.

'Long before I started practising spirituality, my experiences in life were that, when you treat others with respect, there is a sense of commitment, and therefore the people work better and the results get better. Because of this respect, I have experienced that, when I meet workers again who worked for me even 20 years back, we feel a mutual affection between us.'

Applying the principles of spirituality at work

As a civil engineer, Alvaro Cruz was only 34 years old when he was elected to the House of Representatives. He has combined being a politician with being a businessman: 'Since 1993 when the engineering building company was founded, I have had an associate partner and, when I serve in a public office, he runs the company, I.C.M. Ingenieros Ltda. Now I am very much trying to set my main partner in the company on the spiritual path, because he is materialistic. He is a person who suffers if he needs to give increases in wages to the workers. It's a big task facing me now, to try to influence my partner to change. Not only could he himself be happier, he could also make others happier.

'Sometimes I have given up major contracts or possibilities of business in order to be happy and peaceful. There have been a number of occasions where the government invited bids for different contracts. I studied the situations and found that there would be a lot of potential difficulties. It might be difficulties in getting the right supplies or doing the work in the right way in a certain area of the city or state, or there might be problems arising from employees, and so I wouldn't go for it. Even though there might have been a lot of money involved, I would avoid giving bids in such situations. It would only have given me a lot of trouble; it wouldn't have made me happy.'

Murals with spiritual values

'I will tell about an event that happened when I was about to enter the competition for governorship, when I was running against very traditional and very strong political forces: I was visiting Whitefield, near Bangalore, in South India. One day the people there were singing a devotional song speaking of righteousness, truth, harmony, family, order and peace. At that moment, when I received the essence of this, I adopted it to be my slogan for my election campaign. I applied it and talked about it in all my programmes and presentations thereafter. In no political campaign before had any politician ever come up with a spiritual slogan describing a moral situation. Adopting this poem really made me win. I always began my campaigns with these words, and I swept the voters:

> *If there is righteousness in the heart, there will be beauty in the character.*
> *If there is beauty in the character, there will be harmony in the family.*
> *If there is harmony in the family, there will be order in the nation.*
> *If there is order in the nation, there will be peace in the world.*

'I took this message to 69 municipalities out of the 116 there are in the state. In many of these municipalities one of the main ideas in my campaign was a mural painted by children where these words would be inscribed.'

Intuition saves lives

'Spirituality is a permanent attention to the inner self. Being spiritual also means being able to listen to one's intuition. In my country terrorists want to destabilize the order, and on many occasions I represented law and order. On one of several occasions of attempts on my life, terrorists had mined my armoured car. Ten minutes before I was supposed to use it, my intuition told me to move to another vehicle. Shortly after, the first vehicle blew up, and I was saved.

'Already by 1983 I was listening to my intuition. At that time the company that I was working for as a consultant was building a major hydroelectric dam. One evening I was talking to the engineering chief of the night shift; this man was an old college friend. I had asked him to come with me for ten minutes. Because of this, he arrived ten minutes late for work. Just as he was getting there, the engineer heard and saw an explosion at the entrance of a tunnel. More than 130 people were trapped and died. This friend felt that my calling him had saved his life.'

Happiness and service

'After serving as Governor I returned to my company. It has between 100 and 500 workers, depending upon the construction work we are doing. It is one of the first few companies in Colombia certified both nationally and internationally for excellence in delivering. As far as my business goes, the purpose of business is personal fulfilment, then happiness and, third, entering into activities enabling me to contribute to the well-being of my country. I find financial goals secondary to the goals of happiness and service. If in order to obtain good profits, I have to go beyond my principles or the rights of my workers, I don't do it.

'I feel that through achieving my goals, which are happiness and service, I will be able to know and understand myself better. I would define success as being happy, attaining happiness through what I do, and contributing to the happiness of others. Unquestionably, however, when I pursue business activities, it is certainly also with the object of making a profit.

'At my desk at work I keep a little statue reminding me of my spiritual self, and whenever I have a chance, I look at it and remember God.

'I feel there is a difference between spirituality and religion because, although religion might be one way of living a life, spirituality can lead into expansion, into greater consciousness. Most religions coincide on the basic principles of spirituality: love, respect, human solidarity and non-attachment are taught in these religions. I grew up in a religious environment as more than 90 per cent of the Colombians are members of the Catholic Church, and for a number of years I was an active participant in all of the Catholic practices. I believe that if you practice certain principles for a long time, you can evolve yourself spiritually, whether it is within a religion or outside a religion.'

It is important to know how to listen

'I try to select individuals who are ethical, righteous, honest and loyal to work for me. I tell them this when I hire people. The world is the sum total of every part. Just as at work, if you make a good team, it is a very positive beginning. If you have individuals who are not working as a team, you cannot achieve anything. We can achieve meaningful betterment, in Colombia, in my state, and in my company, if we daily perform positive actions, framed in spiritual principles. This applies as well to your family and your colleagues at work, to anyone you are associated with, or any person you interact with during the day.

'Women have a pre-eminent key role to play in participation in society. As the Governor, I had a high percentage of women working at all levels. The main posts were given to women: they were Heads of Education, Planning, Finance, Press and Communication. In my private company the main general administrator is a woman.

'It is important to know how to listen. I need to realize that not everyone must think the way I do or agree with me, and I must also be able to interpret what people are trying to put forth to me. I see very clearly that if I can do that I can obtain even better results at work. If I can really see and understand that this person doesn't have certain skills or needs to learn a little something, then I can work on that. But if I pre-judge my workers or my staff, then a person might be hurt, and there is no cooperation.

'I would advise aspiring spiritual-based leaders not to offend others, not to judge them, and to try to understand that, if another person takes a decision, he is acting in good faith, even though he might have been mistaken. I would also advise them to be ethical and righteous in their actions and to be able to forgive and forget. Above everything, I would stress non-attachment to the material results and rewards of one's deeds and the practice of love: love for oneself and love for others.'

10

A.K. Chattopadhyay

Senior Vice President, ACC Ltd, Refractories Division, India

A.K. Chattopadhyay was 50 years old at the time of the interview. For six years he was the Senior Vice President of ACC (Associated Cement Company) Limited, Refractories Division in Nagpur, India, dealing with the manufacture and installation of refractories. These are products that are resistant to corrosive, erosive and abrasive action of hot gases, liquids and solids, and are employed in high-temperature production processes.

Like many spiritual seekers from the 'East', Dr Chattopadhyay's spirituality is oriented towards inner peace and inner guidance. He told us that 'When I have peace in what I have, rather than looking to what I don't have, this is spirituality. My spiritual view of life calls for me to align myself with a superpower; go within myself to find out the reason for things within myself, not looking to the external environment; have faith in others, even when I am cheated; have a caring nature, which to me is caring for everyone in society.' This spiritual perspective, which has grown slowly and surely over time, permeates both his private life and his work life.

Dr Chattopadhyay has a master's degree in chemistry from the Danrupa Ramakrishna Mission, and master's and PhD degrees in chemical engineering and technology from Calcutta University, India.

Soon after the interview he joined Tata Refractories Ltd., as Executive Director, a position he still holds today. In 2005 he was elected Deputy Chairman of

IRMA, the Indian Refractory Makers' Association, with a membership of more than 60 refractory manufacturers throughout India.

Manifesting the perfection within

Spirituality is the manifestation of the perfection that is already there within you. Spirituality is when I look at myself, look within and not outside, and respond from my inner feelings, where we are all perfect beings.

Dr A.K. Chattopadhyay's life has been centred around the north-eastern and central parts of India, and his career has been centred around refractory materials (materials used to line vessels that undergo high-temperature operations). 'I grew up,' he says, 'in a small village. From there my father took us to a town in the eastern part of India where I studied at a school for the children of employees of the railroad. I was always number one in the class, and my father tried to put me in a good college. Danrupu Ramakrishna Mission was a good college. It is situated near Calcutta. This mission has a heritage all together different from other universities. Everything is there inside the campus so, once students are inside, they do not have to go outside. In this mission, the monks are the teachers.'

Their behaviour left an indelible mark on the young student. 'I got inspired by the monks who had left everything to spend a life there at the college to help the society. There was a flood one time and I saw the monks work almost 14 or 15 hours a day—relentlessly working for the villages that had been washed away. They are highly educated people; they could have found good jobs, but still they chose to sacrifice a lot of things to live this simple life, trying to do good to others.'

A.K. Chattopadhyay graduated with honours in chemistry and then studied chemical engineering and technology at Calcutta University. After working for about eight years for a few companies, he joined Associated Cement Companies (ACC). 'At that time ACC was looking for a business revival. They had a plant in Katni (known as "the City of Lime", in the state of Madhya Pradesh) that was on the verge of closing down; there was a lot of unrest and a lot of strikes. They were trying to find a different business model and hired me as a part of the new business leadership they wanted. So in 1991 I was brought to the ACC, Katni. In those days I was head of operations. Today I am heading up the whole refractory business as the Senior Vice President. We are focused just on the manufacture and installation of refractory lining material. I have two plants that report to me. Along with the plant managers, the managers of marketing, R&D, technology and such all report to me. We have about 700 employees.'

Spirituality as the manifestation of perfection

'My spirituality has grown slowly, especially as a leader. I can remember thinking that if I react in a certain manner it may do harm, and if I react in a different way it will not harm. This is how it began to grow in me and I still think that way today.

'All of us go for short-term pleasures and we end up with serious problems. Even those who have plenty of wealth are doing these very same things. For me, spirituality is when we do not think in terms of these short-term gains,' he says, and elaborates: 'If you have a sound policy based on caring for people, not harming anyone or anything, and a sound business strategy, then financial success will come automatically. When leaders start working from the mind-set that "Yes, I love society, I care for society, I love my colleagues and people", then this will be transmitted to all the levels of the organization and society. Then our actions will definitely bring prosperity to all of us.

'I do feel that my very existence has a spiritual purpose. 'If I am here,' he says, 'I have a purpose to serve; God has created me not just to hover around and do nothing. There is some superpower that creates things in a systematic and organized manner, and I can align my thoughts with this.'

Workers having faith in management that cares

'When I initially came in to head operations at ACC in 1991, I saw right away that there was a big distance between the management and the workers. There was also not enough information being shared between them, so the workers felt totally disillusioned about what was going on. They had completely lost faith in management. To me, the workers are a part of the whole game and you cannot win the game without taking them into proper consideration.

'So I started by working with the people. As a management team, we started working closely together with the factory workers and started sharing information with them. Slowly the workers responded to this very nicely. I regained the faith of those people. After two years or so, they began to listen more to us than to their union leaders. So naturally the senior management people became their leaders and this was a big transformation.

'My spiritual philosophy behind all of this was that I was trying to do good for our employees. They were not aware of the things that they were doing that were actually harmful to them. So I wanted to do good and show them how to do good.

'I believe that when a worker comes out of his house dressed in his uniform and carrying his tiffin [lunchbox], he has a mind-set that he wants to work that day. How can he be thinking anything other than this? I used to tell my managers this in response to their complaints that the people did not want to work. I believe we are the ones who have created an environment that has given him the feeling that he does not want to work. Either he does not like this place or the equipment is not working right. For me, happy people produce happy results. So productivity is a matter related to people and working toward the happiness of the people.

'When a man says his prayers and puts on a full uniform and leaves his house at seven in the morning, he has come to work. Let us create a good environment for him to work. When we create an environment for the people where they want to work, then they will automatically change. I cannot tell them to change; I can only create the environment in which they feel that they want to change.

'We revived the business, and today I can tell you very proudly that a ten-times growth has occurred just by using a proper strategy to run the business and giving value to the people. In 1991 we were almost a non-entity, and today we are a force to be reckoned with in the country. Our products are good, our services are good, and our quality is good. During this same period the refractory industry overall was in very bad shape. However, we still managed to grow and grow.'

Feeling strength while being abused

'Once an employee in our factory got caught in the conveyer belt and his hand was chopped off. This happened during the night and he was taken to the hospital. You can imagine that his family was in total distress. The newspaper came to write stories against me since I was head of the plant, saying that not enough safety measures were being applied.

'Personally, I reacted in a totally different manner altogether. I stayed in the operating theatre the whole night that he was being operated on, in order to give moral courage to his family members.

'There were some local union leaders who wanted to influence the head of the local police to arrest me. All these things happened while I was sitting inside the hospital. I felt strength inside me that enabled me to stand up to all of these people who wanted to abuse me, due to no fault of my own. I continued to feel this strength inside me because I knew that I was doing what was good for this man and for his family.

'The proper safety measures were there, but unfortunately this fellow had not followed them. I did not tell this to the press or to his family members. I called his family all together and I explained that I would take full responsibility to take care of this man and them. I explained that, "No, we cannot get back his hand; this is most unfortunate. However, we can give the monetary compensation that needs to be given and we can give him a job where he can still work peacefully without his hand."

'I called groups in our company together and explained what had happened and how we handled it. Later, after all of this was over, I reflected back on this strength that I felt and realized it came from my connection with this superpower.'

Listening to one's inner self when facing moral obligations

'One incident happened sometime back when a man who had previously worked for ACC supplied and installed some refractory material to one of our customers. He represented himself to his customer as an ACC employee and claimed that the material had come from ACC, which was not true. So the client agreed to let him do the work because he used the ACC name. It so happens that the work that he did failed after two months.

'The customer came to me and talked with me about what had happened. I went through all the purchase orders, but could not find one for that specific job. Then he mentioned the name of the man who did the work. I told him that that man had not worked for us for over six months. The customer assured me that this man told him that he worked for ACC and that he was using ACC materials.

'In this situation, we had no legal obligation. The work was not done by our people or with our materials. But I felt it was our moral responsibility to stand behind this job because this customer gave the job to this man based on the ACC name. I replaced the material and sent my engineer out to install it. We lost heavily as there was no income whatsoever on this job. Even though I faced a lot of audit queries about this, I had the support of ACC management behind me.

'People who want to be spiritual-based leaders sometimes face conflict when they try to listen to their inner self. They are sometimes afraid to follow their conscience because they do not want to lose money. When I gave the approval to have our people install new material for this job, that we had not originally done, losing a lot of money on it, I clearly told our people, "I am willing to take this loss, because I know there is a much bigger gain." This is the dilemma that we must face sometimes, when we listen to our inner voice. We will face opposition and difficulties. However, the more the aspiring spiritual-based leaders do this, the more they will be successful. As a leader I must also help them to achieve these successes. As there are successes, then they will grow in their courage to continue on this path to being a spiritual-based leader.'

Composing oneself

'My own spiritual view of life calls for me to try to find out the reason for things within myself, not looking to the external environment, to align myself with a superpower, to have faith in others, even when I am cheated, and to have a caring nature.

'Of course I pray to God Almighty, but I don't do rituals and ceremonies like a lot of Hindus do. I do have a temple in my house where God is. I go there and pray for two or three minutes. I ask to think in a positive way, to think in a way that is good for others . . . I also ask for courage to face any type of adversity.

'There is so much suffering because of competition among people to see who can have the better shirt, the better house, which I feel is unhealthy. This is the source of many of the problems arising in our society today. I try to stay focused on what I have, rather than what others have. I see harmony in nature; I try to find peace in everything.

'One thing I also do is to compose myself each evening. I think about all the things I have done that day, where I went wrong, and how I can rectify that. Tomorrow I can start again as a composed man. A lot of things will happen during the day that I cannot avoid, but again in the evening I will compose myself for ten minutes. By doing this I go to bed in peace and start the next morning as a very fresh man.'

In this section

In this section you will meet five spiritual-based leaders from five continents, including an American who runs mining operations in Africa from his office in the USA; the Chief Operating Officer of the major development bank in the Philippines; an expatriate from the USA who for over 20 years has led a food supply business in El Salvador; the Executive Chairman of a major manufacturing company in India; and the CEO of a business training and consulting company in Australia who has also had leadership positions in China and the USA. These spiritual-based leaders from so very different cultures and industries share a vitality in their spirituality—they are really 'doers', people who appear to be fearless and unattached to the fruits of their deeds. Yet they are also characterized by their deep concern for contributing to society in general and, in particular, to serving those who are affected by their leadership. Therefore, we have labelled the overarching theme that connects these five leaders: *Live it and serve!* Here you will meet:

James Sinclair, Chairman and CEO, Tan Range Exploration, Ltd, USA/Tanzania

In *The key to success is the 'power to be'*, this internationally recognized specialist and trader in precious metals says, 'Making money is not the driving rationale for my being in business. That is the popular misunderstanding. Success or failure is not our focus. Our focus is to serve. I face total financial disaster without fear of lack. I cannot lack since abundance is everywhere. The only place a recession exists is in the closed mind of ignorance.'

Flordelis F. Aguenza, President and COO, Plantersbank, the Philippines

In *What would the Lord do?*, Floy Aguenza tells us how she and the development bank she leads are committed to being role models in nation and character building and helping small and medium-sized businesses grow: 'I believe that there is a purpose for our life and we need to discover what we are here for. The truth is we are here to do good—to make the world a better place, to be a better person, and to help others to have a better life. This is what I keep trying to do every day.'

John R. Behner, former Country Manager, Nabisco, El Salvador

In *Realizing God by serving others*, John Behner tells of how his practice of instilling in the employees 'the idea of serving, and that the reason for them to be there was to serve our clients and to do the best possible job' led to extraordinary service to the public during a period of civil war and following a major earthquake.

G. Narayana, Executive Chairman, Excel Industries Pvt. Ltd, India

In *Work is worship*, G. Narayana—Guruji as he is reverently called by those who value his wisdom—tells about how 'I was able to assist people to bring out the latent energies within them. I became a hero builder. The people and the companies brought out their inner potentials and excellencies; people became leaders and heroes.'

Niran Jiang, CEO, Institute of Human Excellence, Australia

In *Co-creating a world that works for everyone*, Niran Jiang speaks of her new company, Institute of Human Excellence: 'We are building it on a whole new business model based on collaboration and transparency.' Drawing upon her Chinese heritage, she says, 'The most important thing for me is the interconnectedness of everything. I believe in true equality because of this. In my spiritual practice it is important that the relationship is equal. Prayer for me is a co-creation. I pray for all that is. I pray to the work-god and the spirit of the soul.'

11

James Sinclair

Chairman and CEO,
Tan Range Exploration, Ltd, USA/Tanzania

James Sinclair is a highly respected precious metals specialist and commodities trader[1] who has also headed numerous firms dealing with securities and commodities as well as metals and currency arbitrage. He has been a gold market-maker[2] on New York's Wall Street, owner of a research company working for banks in Luxembourg, as well as a 'warrior in a battle of ethics' in Tanzania. At the time of the interview he was 62 years old and CEO and Chairman of Tan Range Exploration, Ltd, Tanzania and USA.[3] 'I am not a gambler; I am an intelligent speculator,' he states.

---

1 A trader is a person who buys and sells things (stocks, commodities, currencies, financial derivatives) as distinguished from a broker, who is a person who executes buy-and-sell transactions on a market as an agent for clients.
2 A market-maker is a person or a firm that quotes a buy and sell price for a financial instrument or commodity.
3 Prior to his founding Tan Range Exploration, Sinclair was founder of the brokerage firm Sinclair Group of Companies (1977–83), with branches in the USA, Canada and Europe. From 1981 to 1984 he served as Precious Metal Advisor to Hunt Oil. He was also a general partner and member of the executive committee of two New York Stock Exchange firms and President of Sinclair Global Clearing Corporation and Global Arbitrage (derivative dealer in metals and currencies). He was President of James Sinclair Financial Research SARL in Luxembourg, Chairman of Sutton Resources from 1989 to 1995, and Chairman and CEO of Tanzanian American International Development Corporation, Ltd, until it was acquired in 2002 by Tan Range Exploration.

James Sinclair is not only an 'intelligent speculator'—as will be clear—he is also a 'highly intelligent spiritual-based leader'. 'Spirituality,' he says, 'is not a code of morals. Spirituality is unity with Divinity. It is a constant event within the human experience. It is included in our thoughts and activities that take place in our day-to-day lives. There are means of allowing these wonderful spiritual moments to happen; and the means to allow this is to simply get out of its way. We need to cease our busyness, physically and in our minds, and then something wonderful can happen. In order to do this, there are activities that can be undertaken that can lay the groundwork—but we must recognize that spirituality is ripeness. The apple doesn't say it's going to fall from the tree, it just knows it and it happens.'

His beautiful home, which also serves as the offices of Tan Range Exploration, is located on a 40-acre estate north of New York City. It is beautified by many religious pictures and statues with figures from the world's major religions. Every day his employees start their day with meditation—a policy that was also applied when he was running a larger organization with hundreds of employees. Although he travels widely, having his offices at his home has permitted him to balance work and family life—something that he told us is more precious than gold.

Dealing with gold is something that Sinclair has done with flair, and with an apparently amazing foresight. In 1980 he called the top of the gold market, proclaiming that its price would rise from US$150 per troy ounce to $900. It never reached that high, but almost—it peaked at $887.50 on 21 January 1980; the next day he sold his entire gold position. Later, when analysts predicted that the price of gold would go as high as $2,000, he declared that the bull market was dead (within months this came to pass) and that it would languish for the next 15 years—and it did. Since 1996 he has invested millions of US dollars in developing 5,600 square kilometres (2,163 square miles) of barren land in Tanzania, where he believes there are rich deposits of gold.

The key to success is the 'power to be'

The business of business and the business of life are one. The reason for living and working is to act and the reason to act is to seek excellence in everything that you do. If you are going to run a business, then run it well. The most successful person is the person with the least desires. The successful individual is the contented individual. So success could be as much about planning a garden as it is about running a major corporation.

James Sinclair is an extraordinarily active, intuitive and eloquent leader, who is known internationally for calling the top of the gold market in 1980. Being a trader came naturally to him, he told us. 'I am the son of an upper–middle-class family in the USA. My father was a man of extraordinary discipline and extraordinary human capacity, and was one of the greatest traders ever on Wall Street. As a result, I already knew what I wanted to be when I was six or seven years old.

'In 1959, I was attending the University of Pennsylvania when my father became ill, and so I postponed going back to the university and started working in his business as a professional market-maker; I was 19 years old at the time. I ran my father's business successfully and became the boss of other senior traders, making all of the decisions about their over-the-counter⁴ dealings with the New York Stock Exchange. This is where I found out that I had a talent: I had to make the decisions; I had to make the bids and offers; I had to buy and sell.

'When my dad got well and came back into the business, I went back to the university and found myself bored out of my mind. I came home and said to my parents that I wanted to leave school and work in my father's office, which put them into total shock. I wanted to learn from my father, and I learned from a master. I became a partner of the firm when I was in my mid-twenties. Overall, I was a professional market-maker from 1959 to 1975.'

The power of silence

'Even as a kid I always wanted to know God, and I prayed, "I don't know where you are or who you are, I just know you are. So you've got to find me 'cause I don't know how to find you." My mother was a strong Catholic, but I wasn't too much into church. However, I did know that there was something out there making it all happen.

'My spiritual practice has matured since I've known Sathya Sai Baba, my spiritual teacher. For me spirituality is a constant event within the human experience. It is included in our thoughts and activities that take place in our

---

4   *Over-the-counter trading* is the trading of financial instruments (stocks, bonds, commodities or derivatives) between two parties. This differs from *exchange trading*, which takes place on stock exchanges or futures exchanges.

day-to-day lives. Watch your words, actions, thoughts, character and heart—then you'll be happy. Be brave, don't lie, do your job, quiet your mind and at the end of the day fold the cards. Wake up the next morning, see what's dealt and play it the best you can, don't worry about it. See the job, do the job and stay out of the misery. If there's anything that attracts God, it's having courage and having courage is doing what falls in your lap and doing it right, no matter what it is.

'At one time, when looking deeper into the subject, I found one thing in common among the more successful people: introspection. What is introspection? It is quietude, a period of time for reflection. So in my organization, every day we start here with meditation, right in this office. Previously, I had an office with hundreds of people and even then we started exactly the same way. I tell them, "Take your time and be quiet; begin all activity in silence. Before or after lunch, however you do it, be silent. And before you leave the office at the end of the day, be silent." '

Live it!

'Making money is not the driving rationale for my being in business. That is the popular misunderstanding. Success or failure is not our focus. Our focus is to serve. Therefore the business of business and the business of life are one. An attention to the results is not my business, but attention to each day will bring me the results, and I am living proof that this is true. We certainly plan—we've got statistics and plans to the point of nausea—but that's not why we are where we are today.

'So is there a spiritual purpose to my life? No. Am I on a mission? No. I want to live my life with courage; I want to live my life with honour; I want to live my life with dignity, and I want to be harmless—not necessarily in that order. As a businessman, I live by the code, which some people call spirituality, which is to never hurt, steal or lie. I take risks that few on earth would even consider. I face total financial disaster without fear of lack. I cannot lack since abundance is everywhere. The only place a recession exists is in the closed mind of ignorance. My theme for spirituality would be "Live it!" '

Listening to the inner voice

'I got into investing in minerals because I always had the basic education from my father that, if you intend to keep anything for significant lengths of time, value lies in products of the earth, more so than paper assets. When I decided to open up my own trading firm, in six years we became the largest gold traders in the world. I had the good fortune of actually having called the end of the gold market. My decision to liquidate our position in the gold market when the price was at a high of US$887.50 per ounce was made in an environment with a huge room of traders running some of the largest positions in the history of the marketplace.

'In the midst of all of this, I heard inside, *"it's over; this market is over"*. I sat in shock. Then I went to all our technical expertise and saw that everything was yelling and screaming that the market was over. *"How could I have not seen this?"* is what came to me. Then I said, "We have to get out, this is over." In one night, we kept every trader busy, and spent the whole night selling all of our gold positions all over the world. We sold a huge amount, 900,000 ounces at over US$800 per ounce, close to US$1 billion. When the market opened the next morning, the price of gold had dropped US$150 an ounce and never stopped falling until it hit a low of US$400.

'Even in doing what we did, we faced the possibility that the market might have continued to rise as it was predicted to do. But my intuition perceived that the rise was not substantiated by underlying demand and could not continue. Maybe I listened and acted fast because in my office we take the time to meditate and to listen to our intuition.'

Hearing the message, "It's over" inside and listening to his intuition is natural for a leader who tells of his spirituality in the following way: 'Spirituality is a perspective that comes in glimpses, but has the capacity of being a constancy. Spirituality lies in the musings of the musician, or the reverie of the professor teaching just that one point that's been built over a long period of preparation, that gives him or her a moment of success. And the perspective in which it is looked at is the perspective of the observer.

'Spirituality is that point when the mind is quieted, and the circumstances, situation, problem or event is looked at in a different perspective. You know those moments in your life when time didn't exist? Those moments of joy when you had no body consciousness? Spirituality is not an active individual; spirituality is not a code of morals. Spirituality is unity with Divinity and it's the closest you'll get to unity with Divinity because God exists in the quietude between these words and is the source of these words.'

As an aftermath to this experience of foreseeing the collapse of the gold market Sinclair told us: 'I was feeling burned out due to the tremendous intensity of the business, so I decided to sell all of my businesses. I did this selling off in bits and pieces starting in 1980.'

Being a warrior in a fight for ethics

'When I was the Chairman of the Board of a public company in the late 1980s/early 1990s, their stock price grew from US 19 cents to US$56 and was then bought by a major corporation. How did we do this? We raised our corporate profile by our personal behaviour. I went to Tanzania, Africa and lived with the people and we acted as responsible citizens, undertaking the needs of an area of a developing country that was within the scope of our economic impact and environment. We saw to the needs of the people and their health; we built a hospital. My influence with this company was from 1989 to 1995. The last book that I wrote dealt with this subject—how you do business in a developing world.[5]

'But then after this level of success, the management began to act in extremely unethical ways. They were doing some very bad things like stealing money from the stockholders for themselves and hurting people. I first went to my management and said, "Can I convince you not to act in this way?" "No." "Can I plead with you not to act in this way?" "No." "Can I pay you not to act in this way?" "No." So I fired the management. The problem with this was, the management was also on the board, so they turned around and fired me. Then I called a special meeting of the shareholders to determine what to do with all of this, and that is called a proxy.

'In all of this, I became a warrior and fought against them. I asked them to cease and desist and change their policies and asked them to liquidate their major asset, which was a piece of land that they were going to build a mine on to extract gold. When they refused, I executed the public proxy against them, which cost me personally US$5 million. Even though this was a modest company, the legal battle reached the level as if it were between two of the largest corporations in America.

'The management immediately began to throw dirt at me, but through all of it, I never deviated from the high road. The way I handled this publicly was to say that they weren't capable of building a mine and therefore the asset should be sold. I knew if you put US$300 million in these guys' hands, it would have been a disaster. So that's why I executed a proxy to force the sale of the company.

'Do you know what hell is like? Hell is having 21 lawyers working for you. I put every cent I had in the world into it. No one paid me anything to do this.

---

5   James Sinclair has authored many magazine articles and three books dealing with investment matters such as precious metals, trading strategies and geopolitical events and their relationship to world economics and the markets. The books are: (1) *How the Experts Buy and Sell Gold Bullion, Gold Stocks and Gold Coins*; (2) *Gold and International Finance: An Emphasis on Timing*; and (3) *Investing Internationally: Stocks, Commodities, Options*.

I did this because following God through my spiritual teacher and my sense of ethics had made me a warrior.

'I was drinking 16 double espressos every day just to stay awake with all the tension and fatigue, and eventually I went blind in one eye. They attempted to ruin my reputation. They sued my wife, they had detectives trailing my children, they said I was part of the mafia. They took my money on three different occasions using legal manoeuvres, but even after all of that I ended up beating them.

'Initially I lost the proxy because they paid one of the stockholders to get his votes, but even then I got 47.3 per cent of the total vote. But that didn't stop me. They had so many lawsuits that they couldn't get financing to build the mine. What won in the end was nature. Nature was on my side. This property was so valuable that a company came in and bought it.

'Even during this extreme tension, I took the time to be quiet. I wouldn't miss that time for anything in the world. When I couldn't sleep at night, I went to my meditation room. Even if you can't meditate, you can pray. Prayer for me is not "God help me". Prayer for me is "Give me courage, give me strength".'

Doing the right thing

'I will be the first to admit I never wanted to go back to Africa to do business after the horrendous experience I had in the mid-1990s. But my spiritual teacher told me to go back. Right now it's taking all of the money I have and the strangest things in the world are happening. I am the first guy in this type of business (gold mining) to do this without any investors.

'But even then I am standing strong to only do what feels right. For example, an African local lost his concession (piece of land) because he didn't pay the money required and so the licence went back to the state. Here is this very desirable piece of land with a mine already on it. I wanted that piece of land and the government was ready to give it to me. But I said, "No, give it back to the man who owned it. I'm going to make a deal with him because he wasn't sophisticated enough to keep it." I got him back into the loop and now he owns 30 per cent of the option and we're paying him US$50,000 for the privilege and we'll buy the rest of it as his participation in the joint venture.

'I did this because it seemed like the right thing to do. As a result, the word has gotten around that I'm a straight shooter who is going to treat these African locals like human beings with respect. I paid them the same amount of money that I would pay someone in the USA. As a result, my company ended up with 52 pieces of land for mining, about half the size of the state of

Connecticut. We gave all of the landowners the respect of being real partners; we paid them and didn't even take the land out of their name. I have made a lot of Tanzanians wealthy. Am I helping them or hurting them? I don't know. But I do know that to hurt someone requires an intention. If your intention as a human is to hurt, you are looking for disaster. I don't care if you've got the oracle of Delphi giving you insight.

'If you really want to save the world, then save yourself. If you really want to be successful in business, then be quiet. If you want to be able to handle that success with dignity and grace, then also be quiet. If you've got a problem, sit back and shut up. The greatest thing you can do in that moment is nothing. Our inner being is supportive of true evolution and to the movement towards something. Let's say that the key to success is the "power to be". What you are offering people as a spiritual-based leader is the easiest, simplest, most accessible thing on earth in the human experience.'

12

Flordelis F. Aguenza

President and COO, Plantersbank, the Philippines

Maria Flordelis F. Aguenza, generally known as Floy Aguenza, is President and Chief Operating Officer of Planters Development Bank, the largest privately owned development bank in the Philippines. In her description of the bank, prior to its receiving the *International Spirit at Work Award*[1] in Geneva, Switzerland in 2004, Floy Aguenza noted that the bank 'is dedicated to serving the financial needs of small and medium-sized enterprises (SMEs)'. In the Philippines, the SMEs account for 90 per cent of the registered business enterprises, contribute 25 per cent of the GNP and provide employment to roughly half of the labour force. Nevertheless, they remain largely unserved by financial institutions, which tend to be risk-averse; SMEs are considered to be more costly, risky and difficult to lend money to. Planters Development Bank, commonly referred to as Plantersbank, has chosen to focus on this sector that needs help the most. According to Floy Aguenza, 'Throughout our support to the SMEs, there was always this overarching objective of supporting an often neglected

---

1 The International Spirit at Work Award was created in 2001. It honours organizations that are deeply committed to nurturing the human spirit. According to its website, the award 'is dedicated to honouring companies that have implemented explicit spiritual practices, policies or programmes inside their organizations'. It is co-organized by: the Association for Spirit at Work; the Spirit in Business Institute; the World Business Academy; and the European Bahá'í Business Forum.

sector and contributing in a vital way to national progress; not only doing business and making a profit.'

The bank has grown from a single office and a tiny asset base of less than US$10,000 in 1961 to over US$650 million in 2004 and more than 65 branches nationwide. Among its shareholders are the International Finance Corporation (IFC) of the World Bank Group, the Asian Development Bank, and the Netherlands Development Finance Company. At the time of the interview in 2004 it had over 800 employees, and has grown considerably since then. In recognition of its success in SME financing, the bank has been called upon to help financial institutions in other developing countries (Pakistan, Yemen, Vietnam, Laos and Cambodia) through training and consultancy, and it has received numerous awards from multilateral and government sectors for its excellence in SME financing.

Commenting on the 'International Spirit at Work Award', Floy Aguenza said: 'Spirituality in the workplace and business success go hand in hand. There is certainly no conflict here at Plantersbank. Spirituality is a way of life for us because it is deeply embedded in our culture and structure, and emanates from our personal convictions. We have incorporated corporate social responsibility and integrated a culture that nurtures spirituality into the way we do business and, indeed, there is tremendous and unparalleled gratification and fulfilment in that.'

Concurrently with her position as President and COO, Floy Aguenza is also the Vice Chair of Planters Development Bank affiliates and a member of the Board of Directors of a number of development centres and financial institutions in the Philippines, as well as member of the Board of Trustees of the University of the Philippines Foundation. Mrs Aguenza completed her postgraduate studies in Economics from the Ateneo de Manila University.

What would the Lord do?

I didn't start my work with Plantersbank with a grand vision to lead this bank spiritually. It just came. I believe we are here to do good—to make the world a better place, to become a better person, and to help others have a better life. Financial success is not the 'end all' here in our bank. I believe success lies in the values we live as an organization, in living by a certain code where we treat each other and our cus-

tomers with fairness and caring. Our strength is our people . . . Profitability and social impact are fundamentally intertwined.

For the last 12 years Floy Aguenza has been the President and COO of Planters Development Bank (commonly referred to as Plantersbank) in Manila, the Philippines. She was 62 years old at the time of the interview and has held leadership positions for 30 years, 23 of which have been with Plantersbank. Earlier in her life, she had absolutely no idea that she would be recognized as a spiritual-based leader of a major financial institution in her country. 'I had no brilliant, eloquent answer to the question, *"How do you see yourself five years from now?"* when I was being interviewed for my first job with a bank after graduating from college,' she recalls. 'Though I knew I would become a good career person, I had no grand ambition of heading a company, spiritually or otherwise, much less play a role in the development of the small and medium enterprise (SME) industry in the Philippines. It just goes to prove, however, that God has His ways of accomplishing His plans through us, no matter how unwilling or unwitting we may be at the start. I am an unlikely protagonist, among many other esteemed companions, on an unlikely journey.

'My career as a banker began much like any other. I joined a commercial bank as a management trainee and then became an Executive Assistant to the Executive Vice President. From there I ended up as the head of Human Resources, Corporate Training, Research and Corporate Communications for that bank. This bank is where I met my colleague who is now my CEO, Chairman and friend. Though I had given my heart and soul to what I was doing, he and I faced some dilemmas. We did not agree with the way the bank was being run by the owners, so we made a decision to leave. However, while he went to buy a small bank, the bank we now work for—Plantersbank—with a grand ambition of turning it into a big commercial bank, I took the opposite route.'

Floy Aguenza was disheartened with her experiences, so she decided to retire and focus on her family. During that time, she was able to travel and take up Chinese painting.

A new calling for the bank

'One day, my colleague who bought Plantersbank asked me to join him and head the bank's core business which is the loan side. I knew from working with him that he was a man of character and integrity—he believes that this is the only way to keep good professionals.'

By that time, Floy Aguenza was deeply in touch with her spiritual core. She told us that she found her response to his offer by going within and asking herself what the Lord would do. When she asked herself this question and got her answer, she was revitalized and ready to get back on the road. She accepted the job offer, learned the lending business, and became an Executive Vice President. That was in 1981, 23 years prior to this interview.

'And thus a truly unique and worthwhile journey unfolded!' she exclaims. 'Somewhere along the way, this bank, which was intended and being groomed for the big league, had found a new calling. During the times when it was starting out as a small bank in a provincial town, it had no choice but to cater to the small businessmen of the area. For many of these businesses, this was their first experience with formal banking and they saw that it was a better alternative to paying high interest in the informal market. We worked closely with them, giving them the proper guidance, and their businesses started to flourish. We saw the impact our bank was making within this small community and it touched our hearts in a special way. From then on, we made a decision that we would continue to serve this niche no matter how big we would become.

'Over the years we have begun to earn the respect of the larger banks. The assets of our bank are now about US$670 million. Many of the businesses we financed in those early years have grown with us. For some, we started by giving them small loans like 500,000 pesos (US$10,000), but now we are giving them loans up to 100 million pesos (US$2 million).

'1986 marked the end of a 20-year dictatorship and a new beginning for the Philippines. When the Chairman was offered a position as ambassador to the UK, he took the opportunity to serve the country full-time. When I asked him who would take over, I was surprised with his answer: "You." I told him I would pray about it.

'Once again I had a major decision to make that required me to go beyond my comfort zone. And for the second time, I felt God's leading and decided to accept the offer. My prayer at the time was, "Lord, I really don't want this position, but if you want me to do it, so be it; I know you will provide me with the resources to do it." I truly believe that it is only by God's grace that we accomplish anything. Little did I know, however, that this new path in my career as a banker would run hand in hand with my spiritual growth.'

Discovering what we are here for

'I believe in God the Father and Jesus Christ as the Son of God, and that we were placed on this earth for a purpose. I believe we have been given our life for a reason, that there is a purpose for our life and we need to discover what we are here for. The truth is we are here to do good—to make the world a better place, to be a better person, and to help others to have a better life. This is what I keep trying to do every day.

'When confronted with a situation, I am basically guided by the question, "What would Jesus do?" I read an exercise in a book by a Jesuit writer where he talked about seeing Christ in others and helping others see Christ in you. And I try to do that. All of this helps me to cope as my day unfolds and, most especially, it prepared me for what would be one of the greatest challenges in my life. Challenges are part of life. I know I need God's guidance to go through life's struggles, so I make it a point to start and end my day with prayer.'

Exposing employees to spirituality

'I believe that people who are well balanced and spiritual make better employees. I spend a lot of time thinking about how to help nurture the spiritual growth of our people. So I decided I wanted to see how I could expose the employees of the bank to spirituality. Since they spend most of their waking hours in the bank, we must try to help them without sacrificing the objectives of the bank. We started with letting our people attend spiritual retreats as part of our training activities. The turnouts have been quite good with very positive feedback.

'I was the only woman in the management committee. Typically, Filipino men are not very comfortable about spirituality, as this goes against the Filipino macho culture. But knowing that our Chairman was himself quite open, I suggested we start our meetings with prayers to which he readily agreed. That was the start of our practice of starting all meetings with a prayer and all important initiatives and occasions with the Holy Mass. This is also how an ecumenical Plantersbank family prayer has developed, which includes: "*Lord God, Heavenly King and Father . . . Grant that we may learn to exercise responsible stewardship over all the resources You entrust to us . . . Lord, help us to see in every client an opportunity to be of service and to be a blessing to the life of another; to find in our fellow workers a greater inspiration to give our best in everything we do.*" We also created a prayer and meditation room where the staff can go if they need some time alone or to pray.

'Later on, we began the Wednesday and Friday masses. We asked Fr Armand Robleza, who conducts our retreats, to be our official Chaplain and to guide our spiritual programme. He has been doing this for the last 13 years. To this day, I get letters from some of our staff thanking us for these opportunities for spiritual development. Each year also begins with a grand celebration of thanksgiving to God where officers from our head office and the more than 65 branches all over the country come together to praise and thank God for the blessings, pray, review the past year, recognize people and events, and offer our plans for the coming year.

'Since there is a small minority of our employees who are not Catholic, we have worship services for them. I myself also attend worship services of faiths other than mine because I want the employees to feel that they are not marginalized because they are of a different faith. Any time something happens, such as a death in the family, I consciously go out of my way to show that I am concerned about what has happened. We want our employees to be happy and fulfilled working for us and we want our customers to be happy. We really do mean this.'

Dealing with an organization-wide crisis

'Early on in my presidency, the bank's Treasury Department was unwittingly dragged into a government controversy. By the very nature of our business, it is a no-no to be involved in any controversy, and much more so with anything that tends to put doubt on the capability and stability of the bank. We thought it was unfair to drag the name of the bank into the issue when it was not clear how things happened or who was accountable for it. But we could not do anything as the publicity that accompanied the controversy got out of hand. I had to deal with it head-on.

'When it happened, it felt like the heavens had fallen on my head. I prayed to the Lord to be with me during those difficult times. I feared that, because of the bad publicity, the bank might suffer a run, and no bank, no matter how strong, can survive a run.

'The first thing I did was to find out exactly what happened, the extent of the problem, and the consequences. Within a short time, I knew exactly what the problem was. The controversy dragged on for weeks. Every morning I prayed and intentionally put on a smile because I knew that everyone was watching me.

'It was a tremendous responsibility. I was consoled by our people in the organization who held together and stood strong. From the beginning, we kept our people informed of our actions and decisions, especially the branch managers who were at the forefront, they having direct client contact. They worked very hard to convince our customers that there was nothing to be worried about. And then there were prayers. Everyone was praying. We knew we could not get out of these troubles without the Lord's help.

'The crisis lasted for about a month. Public confidence was soon restored and we emerged as a much stronger organization. In hindsight, I knew there was a purpose for this happening. Without it, we could have been susceptible to even larger disasters. It opened our eyes to the weaknesses of our systems and processes and the need to strengthen further our controls. When the financial crisis hit the Asian region and the Philippine banking industry in 1997, the bank was prepared.'

The bank's role in society

'It is very clear in our minds that our business must be profitable to be sustainable—of course, this bank has been set up by the shareholders and they expect a good return. However, equally clear to us is that it is not profit at all costs. This must be balanced with all of the other concerns of the organization, and its role in society. In our case, profitability and social impact are fundamentally intertwined.

'Sometimes we do face certain dilemmas. From time to time, we have had to foreclose on a customer's property and that is difficult. In some cases we do have to go to court in order to recover assets. Corruption is still a problem in our country and giving bribes is a common practice, but we do our best to remain ethical in these situations and have been able to truly take a stand.

'Even though we are a development bank, we follow commercial objectives and work towards financial and productivity goals and a healthy bottom line. Plantersbank is the seventh most profitable private domestic bank in the country in terms of ROE [return on equity]. In terms of total resources, it is the 21st largest bank today among roughly 950 banks in the country, including 41 universal and commercial banks, about 100 thrift banks, five development banks, and about 800 rural banks. So, although we are larger than half of the commercial banks, we have resisted converting our licence to such because we are committed to our market and our developmental mission of helping small and medium-sized businesses grow. The impact that we have made on the lives of the many small businessmen we have dealt with in the process of doing business has inspired us to continue to deal with this sector. I understand that there are very few banks like ours, and so we are being held up as an example, that a bank, a private one at that, can be a catalyst for growth and development.'

Building a spiritual-based corporate culture

'Changing the culture of an organization requires you to unify the values and to live them. So we have lots of different activities and programmes where we try to embed the values throughout the organization at each level. At one point we could really see the Lord moving through our organization. We came up with an official culture change and transformation programme called "Whole Heart and Mind—the WHAM Way" which embodies our vision and mission, our beliefs and our values, and clearly defines the character that we want for our bank.

'Of course, the best way to develop a culture is to live it out in practice. If our employees see us living what we espouse, it flows down through the organization. A consultant who was an ex-monk who was also doing work with Citibank and other big corporations agreed to work with us to help transform our organization and build a spirit-based corporate culture.

'We also have a technical consultant who had previously worked with the local Jesuit University on their programme on inner healing and the six stages of psycho-spiritual growth. I believe that she too was sent to us at an opportune time, so we sat down with her to see how she could help our people. We realize there are a lot of wounded souls here and we worked with her to bring in her expertise. We also have another consultant who is doing some training with us and is willing to help us build our spiritual culture, without taking any fees.'

Business setting an example

'Businesses have a role to play in nation building and in building the character of the people. If we all do something, we can all gain. Through our work with the small and medium enterprises, we are able to take part in the economic development of the Philippines and set an example for corporate social responsibility.

'One of the Philippine President's major strategies is an SME development programme with the goal of generating about six to ten million jobs in the next six years. Employment is at the heart of her campaign. She is my neighbour and she knows what we do at the bank and the awards we've won, how it serves entrepreneurs and provides jobs.

'I believe the quest for spiritual-based leadership is a continuing journey. The advice I would give to those who want to be spiritual-based leaders would be to look within their hearts because the opportunities are there. The Lord will open up the way; the Spirit will open up the way. If you sincerely want to do something, you can do it no matter what level you are at. Then it can spread from there when other people see what is happening in the group.'

13

John R. Behner

Former Country Manager, Nabisco, El Salvador

John R. Behner was born and raised in the USA. After his graduation from college in California, he worked for some years in his specialty, labour relations, before moving in 1969 to his wife's country, El Salvador, which he described as 'the smallest country in Latin America as well as its most industrialized nation and, due to the strong work ethic of its people, it has a vibrant economy and is often referred to as "the Japan of the Americas". From beautiful beaches on the Pacific Ocean to lush pine forests in the mountains bordering Honduras, and volcanoes, some semi-active, and volcanic lakes, the country is blessed with rich natural beauty. San Salvador, the capital city, is known as "the Valley of the Hammocks" as it is the site of numerous earthquakes which cause the hammocks to swing.' He fell in love with El Salvador and has lived there ever since.

Out of 40 years in leadership positions, John Behner was for 20 years the Country Manager in El Salvador for the USA-based multinational food company Nabisco.[1] He was 66 years old at the time of the interview and has been retired since 1997.

---

1 Nabisco was founded in 1898 as a merger of 114 bakeries in the US. It soon became a major producer of cookies and snacks, and over the years it expanded into many types of food products. Its most recent history tells a story of the role played by greed and the lust for power and represents an extreme opposite to the type of leadership demonstrated by John Behner in El Salvador. In 1981 Nabisco merged with another huge American food company,

Throughout most of his career in El Salvador, spirituality has been the focal point of his leadership. 'Spirituality,' he told us, 'is trying to see God in everyone and trying to interact with everyone on a very loving basis—being humble and trying to help.' Although he sums up his spiritual view of life in the theme 'realizing God by serving others', he adds on that what is most important to him is 'to realize my oneness with God. I see spirituality as having a personal relationship with God. What is my goal? It is to become one with God.'

John Behner's life has been characterized by hard work and always trying to find creative solutions to problems—transforming what appeared to be difficult situations into opportunities. Throughout his career he has drawn upon a natural talent for getting people to work together to solve practical problems. In modern business parlance he would be referred to as 'proactive'. We have known him for some years as a very calm and peaceful person, seeing the positive in the challenges he meets, even when they take the form of unpleasant situations or people. Perhaps this is why he has been able to be so peaceful and content, even in times of great crisis.

Realizing God by serving others

Serving everyone is extremely important to me. The idea of serving— and, for me, trying to see God in everyone—is my cup of tea . . . We were having fun at work. What we were doing was a positive thing, making healthy products for the public. We had a wonderful relationship with our clients, and I had good relationships with my employees. The economic outcome was the result of this philosophy of serving; the employees prospered, the company prospered, and everybody was happy in what they were doing.

According to John R. Behner, he has always been a man of action, driven by a powerful work ethic. 'I was always an honest, hardworking, German-work-

---

Standard Brands, and only four years later was merged again with the tobacco giant, R.J. Reynolds. The resulting company RJR Nabisco was in turn bought out in 1988 in what was the biggest leveraged buyout in history (described in the best-selling book *Barbarians at the Gate: The Fall of RJR Nabisco*, and then in a film based on the book). Just two years later another tobacco giant, Phillip Morris Companies, acquired Nabisco and merged it with the huge food company Kraft Foods.

ethic-type. Even when I was in elementary school, I was doing odd jobs. The idea of deferred gratification was part of my upbringing. It was entrenched in my personal make-up. When I started in seventh grade, I would get up at 4 o'clock in the morning and tend to my paper route. And at 6 o'clock I would go to the golf course and look for golf balls, which had been lost by the players the day before. Then I would go to school, and as soon as I was out of school I would go back to the golf course and collect more balls. I also had a shoeshine business and, during the weekends I carried golf bags for golfers. By the time I started university, I had saved US$5,000, which was a lot of money at that time, so I was able to pay for my own education. I grew up in Southern California, and all the time I went to the University of California at Los Angeles I worked at different jobs.'

After graduation in 1959, John Behner got jobs in his speciality, labour relations, where he gained administrative and negotiating experience. However, reflections on the best environment for his family led to a major decision. 'My wife is an El Salvadorian, and in 1967 we decided to move to El Salvador, because we thought it would be a better place to raise the kids,' he says. 'The first thing I did was to form my own company, a real estate business. But that didn't last too long, because I was approached by some people who took me to the public cold storage area, where a room was filled up to the ceiling with dressed turkeys, and the temperature wasn't that good. They were going to lose them, if somebody didn't do something. I offered to help them on a part-time basis.' This was to be the start of a long career in the food industry.

'In about 60 days, I had sold the whole cold room full of turkeys. The people I worked for were really impressed and asked me if I would like to be their distributor for the whole of Central America. I agreed to give it a try. So I started a frozen-food distribution company. I filled barrels full of water, put the turkeys in them, and then put them in a blast freezer so they came out like a rock. We put them on containers and shipped them to Nicaragua, Honduras and Guatemala in one day and Costa Rica in two days. They arrived perfectly.

'Little by little I started adding other products. It was a booming business, but like most businesses in Latin America, it was not booming enough for you to hire a good, well-educated manager, and to pay him a good salary, so you could sit back and enjoy the fruits of your work.

'After about seven years, someone gave me an offer to buy the business, and I decided to sell it. At that time in 1976, a multinational food company had an opening for a general manager in El Salvador, and I got the job. When I started as manager in this company, which became Nabisco in 1981, it only had 25 employees.'

Serving, being humble and trying to help

Shortly before starting to work for Nabisco, John R. Behner met his spiritual teacher, Sathya Sai Baba, in India. The strong work ethic from his youth now became part of a spiritual quest. 'Realizing God by serving others—and trying to see God in everyone' had become the guiding light on his search for self-realization.

'Spirituality to me is the application of the human values—truth, right conduct, peace, love and non-violence—in your way of doing things. But it's also more than that. It's trying to see God in everyone and trying to interact with everyone on a very loving basis, seeing everything as being perfect, and not pointing your finger at anyone or anything. Each of the human values that you are trying to live and put into practice comes out in reflections of what you are doing. Being spiritual is being humble and trying to help.

'The purpose of business is to make other people happy—serving your customers and making sure that your customers are happy is the reason for your business and the reason for your being there. But not only your customers, also your employees should be happy. There should be a lot of employee enthusiasm and satisfaction, and this should be made part of this energy of trying to do the best they possibly can. I tried to instil in the employees the idea of serving, and that the reason for them to be there was to serve our clients and to do the best possible job. For example, if they were in manufacturing, they were told to look at the quality of the products as if they themselves were going to eat them.'

In his long career at Nabisco, John Behner continually and consciously attempted to integrate his spiritual perspective on service into the company's day-to-day business practice. 'El Salvador is a small country and, in order to make the budget goals, I kept adding products. Everything that happened in 20 years was growing that little nucleus; we were making profits of millions of dollars in the end, and we had 300 people. All of the key ratios were very, very good. First of all, we were having fun. What we were doing was a positive thing, making healthy products for the public. We had a wonderful relationship with our clients, and I had good relationships with my employees. The economic outcome was the result of this philosophy of serving; the employees prospered, the company prospered, and everybody was happy in what they were doing. People stayed for many years; we had very little turnover.

'My experience of working for Nabisco was very good. Besides the visit when I was hired, I was only visited two other times in 20 years by anyone from a higher office. They left me completely on my own, as if it were my own company.'

John Behner also told us about how his spiritual discipline of 'trying to see God in everyone and trying to interact with everyone on a very loving basis— being humble and trying to help' empowered him and his employees to serve the needs of the public during two major crises.

Serving during a guerrilla war

'A guerrilla war was going on in El Salvador for about 12 years. At one time there was a major invasion of the capital, San Salvador, by the guerrilla forces. The war was going on all over the city, which had about 1½ million inhabitants at the time. As we were in the food business, we looked at how we were able to feed the people. Our employees would call us every morning. Since they lived all over the city, we would know where the fighting was going on and where it was calm. So we set up a whole system in which all the salesmen would go to one area of the city where there was no fighting going on that day, and start taking orders as fast as they could. The next day there might be fighting in that neighbourhood, and we couldn't deliver the orders they had taken until later, but then all the salesmen would go to another neighbourhood where there wasn't any fighting. In that way we were covering the whole city little by little.

'We also set up a system of transportation for the employees. For those who could get to the downtown area, we sent vehicles. Then they went up about half way to where the plant and the offices were, stopping at a supervisor's home. From there they would call the office—this was before cell phones— and find out if the coast was clear, because sometimes there would be fighting near the plant or the offices, but most of the time they could come and go to work. We usually had a few employees who couldn't come, but we paid everybody while this war was going on. People were taking risks to get to work, but they all saw their mission as feeding the people.'

Serving after an earthquake

'In 1986, there was a big earthquake in San Salvador, so we got a little experience in dealing with a crisis. One of the first things we saw was that all the supermarkets, which were our biggest clients, were affected; all their merchandise was all over the floor. They had a tremendous job of trying to clean what was saveable and to throw out what was broken and maybe take some kind of inventory of it. We also saw that our production lines were useless, because, if the supermarkets could not put our products on their shelves, what good was it to produce it? So we shut down our production lines and sent the salesmen to all the major supermarkets. We offered them a team of our production people to help them clean up. We did this very successfully, and we were the only company that did it. All the supermarkets were happy to get this kind of service, which didn't cost them anything. It only took about a week of very concentrated effort. It got them on their feet faster, and so we could start selling faster.

'We took stock of our employees, and we had nine employees who had lost their homes. Since we had shut down production, our maintenance department wasn't doing anything. So we asked these guys to go and rebuild the homes of these nine employees. Temporary structures were put up in the nine homes, and the employees were very grateful. El Salvador gets earthquakes periodically. In 1994 when we had another earthquake, we were all prepared, because we had already gone through the big one in 1986.'

Teaching human values in the company

'At a certain time, we decided to do some combined publicity for the company and human values-training. We went to local high schools and offered them an opportunity for the students to come to the plant. We had an auditorium, and I had each of my managers talk about one of the five human values: truth, right conduct, peace, love and non-violence, and how it affected his area.

'The Controller would talk about *truth*, how truth is important in doing the bookkeeping, the accounting, paying the taxes, etc. The Sales Manager would talk about *right conduct*, how you have to treat the customers correctly. The Plant Manager talked about *love,* because he had to keep everybody in harmony, so the production would be good. The Quality Control Manager would talk about *peace*, that if you do your work right you will be tranquil, because you'll know that the quality of all the products is fine. The Maintenance Manager would talk about *non-violence,* that if you weren't polluting and contaminating then you would have non-violence.

'The amazing thing was that the students would come in batches of a hundred, filling the auditorium. The managers were the ones who benefited the most, because they had to learn about these values to talk about them. Then they started seeing how the values worked in their job. The students would also understand the values in relation to a work ethic. As a result, some of the young people would apply to work with us, because they liked what they saw.'

Loving the employees

'You have to have discipline, but at the same time I always tried to protect my employees, and I was a good friend with everybody. Even when I had 300 employees, I would find time to sit down with each one of them and talk to them for three or four minutes. "How are the kids? How far away do you live? Do you have troubles getting here?"

'A lady told me she had a problem getting on the bus to go to work because of troubles with her legs. She only lived about six blocks from the company, so I said, "We'll send a car for you in the morning, don't worry about it." Immediately I asked a salesman, who used to come early in the mornings, to go and pick up the lady, who worked in the accounting department.

'I tried to believe in the people, and I think that 99 per cent were very, very good. But I had some problems, like right after the civil war, which was finished in 1991. There were a lot of armed robberies then. Whenever they would see a truck without a gun on it, ex-guerrillas and ex-soldiers would assault it. In each of the first three years, we had about 36 assaults on our delivery trucks and on the office itself. I was reluctant to put armed guards on the trucks and at the plant, because I didn't like guns around. But then they were going to cancel my insurance, so I had to do it. That stopped the assaults. It only shows, sometimes you have to do something which you don't want to do.

'What do you do in a situation when you get mad at somebody, and then you cool off and figure that maybe you were a little bit wrong? I can remember one day I got really mad at a lady who handled the merchandising in the supermarkets. I don't remember for what reason, but I really got mad at her and told her off. I didn't fire her or anything, just told her that she was doing wrong, and I balled her out for it. Then I thought I was really mistaken. I got into my car and drove to the place where she was working and apologized to her and told her I was sorry. Ever since that day that lady would have done anything for me and for the company. She had been there before me, and when I left she was still there. You have to be humble, even if you are the boss.

'I treated all the employees as if they were my children. I had a really good relationship with them. The people working for me were very appreciative of the love and the way they were treated, and the personal interest that I showed in them and their welfare.'

Consciously growing spiritually

'One of the most important things in my life has been to have a sense of balance, especially in a situation when you have many people who are dependent upon you. You have to have good health, and you have to have your mind always alert. To meditate and exercise was a very important part of my regimen. By 5 o'clock I would be out either jogging or doing yoga.' John Behner told us that he balanced his energetic work with a simple style of living, a limited social life, and vegetarian food. 'In the evenings I was reading good spiritual texts. It kept a real nice balance.'

He also described how this focus on balance and on service permeated not only his work, but also his family life. He told us that when he began his spiritual search with service as the focus, he made sure that he acted so that there was harmony between what he thought, what he said, and what he did. 'We had a beach house that used to be part of our "God". The beaches in El Salvador are very beautiful, and every weekend we were at the beach with the kids at the swimming pool. We sold the beach house, because we realized that weekends were the only times we had when we could do service. So we got rid of it and tried to devote our time to doing service activities.

'I have improved a great deal as a spiritual-based leader. My drive for material accomplishments is much less, and also my desires have come way down. The ability to introspect, to try to see myself, is getting better. My wife and I have been on the same path for 40-odd years. It's good to have someone else on the path with you, someone who understands what you are doing.'

14

G. Narayana

Executive Chairman, Excel Industries Pvt. Ltd, India

When we interviewed G. Narayana he was Executive Chairman of Excel Industries Pvt. Ltd, a highly respected manufacturer of agrochemicals, industrial chemicals and pesticides, providing services in such areas as plant protection and integrated crop and pest management. In recent years the company has received special recognition for its focus on developing environment-friendly bio-pesticides and solid waste management as well as for its spiritual-based leadership. In 2004, it was honoured with the International Spirit at Work Award.

At the time of the interview Narayana had held this position for two years, although he has been associated with the company in various capacities for 15 years. He is also non-executive chairman or director of several other major Indian companies in fields such as paper production, engineering and construction, chemicals and pharmaceuticals, and glassware.[1] He has degrees in electrical and electronics engineering from both India and the UK as well as a postgraduate degree in management studies from India.

---

1   He is Chairman of the Board for: Yash Papers Ltd; Newton Engineering & Construction Co. Ltd; Punjab Chemicals & Pharmaceuticals Ltd. He is a Board Director for: Aryan Paper Mills Pvt. Ltd; Laopala Ltd; Silverlight Nirlepware Industries Pvt. Ltd; and mentor to the Mahavir Group of Enterprises, India. He is also Chairman of the 'Samanvaya' group, which is a council of companies with eight managing directors assisting each other.

An article in the Indian magazine *Life Positive* from 2001 describes his leadership at Excel Industries as follows: 'Warm, exuberant and disarmingly humble, Narayana transcends the persona of the boardroom executive. In fact, he has made the Board an object of worship with a philosophy of management that integrates the scientific principles of the West with the profound thought of Indian scriptures.' Ashwin Schroff, the son of the founder of Excel, has described Narayana in the following manner: 'If you have ever come across an optimist, here is one, ten times over. He has a strong belief that by generating positive thoughts you generate positive vibrations.'

G. Narayana is a prolific writer, having published more than 200 articles and 20 books on themes relating to leadership and spirituality.[2] He travels extensively, also to the West, giving lectures on these subjects. He is also the founder and leader of philanthropic foundations and he is involved in the movement called Indian Ethos, which strives to bring values found in the ancient Indian scriptures into modern management. We have come to be close to G. Narayana and his family. This has allowed us to observe how rich he is in philosophical wisdom, humour, and intuitive and skilled leadership competences—all mixed together like a cake mix, where the binding agent is love. When we asked him to express his spiritual theme, he replied: 'Noble actions, noble feelings, noble thoughts, noble responsibility.'

At the time of the interview, Narayana had already made plans to retire from Excel as its Executive Chairman. He told us: 'After that I will spread light wherever I go. I am already doing this, but I wish to reach more companies. It is our responsibility to take our lamps and light other lamps.' Perhaps the best way to capsulate his present stature is by relating that he is no longer referred to by his name; he is simply called 'Guruji'. This term, ordinarily reserved for spiritual masters, is translated into English as 'honoured preceptor' or 'beloved teacher'.

Work is worship

My concept of business is the harmony of ethics, energy, excellence, economy and ecology with effectiveness and efficiency that leads to

---

2   Among his noteworthy books are these four: *Appropriated Integrated Management; Transformation to Transcendence: Breakthrough Ideas for Leadership in the New Millennium; Stairway to Excellence;* and *Responsible Leadership in the Gita.*

enlightenment. All this occurs through wisdom, coming from purity and beauty. This is my vision of the future of business. The purpose of business is to add value and happiness. If you serve the world, you serve God.

G. Narayana was 60 years old at the time of the interview, with a personality of abundance, overflowing with love, happiness and joy. He is an extremely active and a very generous person, always caring, always giving, never saying no; this also goes for his time. But he has not always been like this. Spiritual growth often requires a turning point. He has a story to illustrate this.

'After I finished my engineering education, I joined an international tele-communications firm. I stood first in their training. Then I saw an advertisement for Voltas, and told my father I wanted to join that electro-mechanical company. He preferred a government job for me and refused to give his consent. I fasted for three days and he allowed me to join,' he tells.

As a young engineer with a postgraduate diploma in operations management, G. Narayana had what he himself terms as 'a fantastic career' at Voltas. In 11 years he received eight promotions. 'Western management was in my blood. Management by objectives, planning, organizing, directing and controlling were absorbed by me. That's why my rise was so high. I had engineering plus management, but spirituality was missing.' At Voltas, his ego was rising. 'I was an angry man and I used to break cups,' he told us.

The rise and fall of the ego

'Then I went to Baroda in Gujarat in the North West of India and joined New India, a joint venture company with Germans as partners, producing and exporting large numbers of cameras. I was trained in Germany and became the first Indian General Manager. There also, I produced fantastic results and my ego further rose. Then I thought I was the greatest man on earth.

'One day, my colleague who was a dear friend and also a noble contributor to the company, was asked to leave the company due to internal conflicts at the top level. As a result, I resigned too, which created a chaotic state for me. I was without a job and my three children were very young. Within one week, we started a data centre called Procon. I was the proprietor and made it an all-woman organization. All the supervisors and operators were taught about quality teamwork and leadership and we became a top data preparation organization. All the ideas that I could not implement in the large corporations I worked for were implemented here.'

Procon became an experimental leadership development workshop for G. Narayana. While it was on the way to becoming self-sufficient, he also did management consultancy, as well as starting a computer services company called Prism, which specialized in information systems.

'In Prism, we purchased a hard-disk computer. I invested all of my savings in Prism and my friends invested 50 per cent of the capital. Within six months of our purchasing the hard-disk computer, the personal computers (PCs) came into the market. PCs were much less expensive and had much more capability. Our then outdated system could not compete with PCs and the people whom we trained had many opportunities outside because of the IT boom. As a result, people started leaving Prism.

'Prism had yet to pay a considerable amount of loans and, at this point, my ego started melting. I realized that it was not my greatness that made things successful at Voltas and New India, it was the greatness of those organizations.'

The miracle of the Gita

G. Narayana was in great confusion, and so he went to his native village. 'The situation at Prism was so critical that suicide became one of the alternatives,' he tells. 'But because our children were very young, that alternative was not correct. While at my native place, we went to the Godavari River, and there was an old temple nearby. While my wife and I, my cousin and his wife were in the waters of the river Godavari, I asked my cousin if we could go to the temple and get a memento from the ruins of the old temple. He said, "Wait! Something is touching me in the river!" He reached down and brought out two Shivalingams (elliptical stones representing the cosmos and that are worshipped as the "form" of Lord Shiva in the Hindu religion) attached to a common base. He gave them to me. The two lingams represented Kaleshwar (death) and Mukteshwar (liberation). The message was clear: liberation from my death-like situation was in the offing! I thought it was a fantastic day.

'In the afternoon, my wife Sujana and I reached her parents' home where my brother-in-law was reading a book. I asked him, "What is that book?" He showed it to me and it was the *Gita* Makarandam, which is a commentary on the *Bhagavad Gita*.[3] Till that time, I had not read even the first three verses of the *Gita* and I did not know Sanskrit. I always thought, "What is the need for *Gita*, when one is working 14 hours a day? In 18 chapters *Gita* is teaching

---

3 *Bhagavad Gita*, The Song of God, is one of the world's major spiritual and philosophical literary works, often referred to in the West as the 'Gospel' of India. It is considered by many to be part of the 2–5,000-year-old epic poem *Mahabharata*.

about karma yoga (the spiritual practice of selfless work) and that's what I am already doing!" I was about to return the book to my brother-in-law; then I remembered the good omen of the Shivalingams in the morning. I thought this book, the *Gita*, was another blessing and I should not lose the opportunity. I opened the book at random and the following verse was present.'

G. Narayana quotes from memory: ' *"Whoever works with full dedication and offers everything to me, who works relentlessly, him, I will take out of the river of death and put him on the bank."* This was the best guarantee I had ever heard!' he exclaims.[4]

He then took the book home and studied the *Gita* for 18 days. 'Now, I had the *Gita*. Since the guru [teacher] did not come, but only the book came, I took the book to Baroda where I lived. The author was a well-respected Swami, so I thought of him as my guru and I did an 18-day yoga (spiritual exercise) of studying the *Gita*. What I did then, I now call "*Gita* yoga". I read one chapter every day, eating only one time a day, and completely avoiding alcohol, non-vegetarian food (which I was not taking anyway), tobacco . . . I observed silence while studying the *Gita* and I underlined whatever appeared wonderful, although everything looked wonderful in the *Gita*! I practised celibacy during all those 18 days.

'It was a fantastic experience. At the end of 18 days, I stood up and the world stood up along with me. I went back to the bank and assured them that I would pay back every rupee of the loan. I told my partners that I would pay back their investment. During those 18 days, new understandings flowed in my thought and consciousness. My fear was gone.

'When I took responsibility with this new spirit, things started occurring that turned around my situation. Prism was closed after paying all the loans and Procon did better and better. With the new confidence and consciousness, solutions were shining and problems were dissolving. Then companies approached me and I became a management and turnaround advisor.

'In 1985 I got the *Gita* yoga and the rest all flowed from that. My mind-frame changed. Then I did Vipassana yoga (a special type of prolonged meditation) and it helped me to further develop my qualities. Before 1985 my wife

---

4 In G. Narayana's own poetic translation of the Gita, done several years later, after he had taught himself Sanskrit, these lines read (Chapter XII—verses 6 and 7):

XII-6: *But who dedicates his work in 'Me'*
And who considers as Supreme 'Me'
Concentrates on 'Me' in none-other way
Contemplates on 'Me' in determined way.

XII-7: *He shall be taken up by 'Me', see!*
From this world, a deathful Sea
His deliverer, becomes 'Me' soon
With mind on 'Me', this boon.
Free from fear.

and I were enemies. My children would not give me a birthday card. They would give to my wife, but not to me. After 1985 everything changed with my family, it was the change in me, not in them. We now have a fantastic relationship.'

Today spirituality permeates G. Narayana's entire being. 'Spirituality is experiencing divinity in others and self. Spirituality is inspired responsibility towards people, other living beings, and the world . . . seeing and relating with divinity in every aspect. Being responsible is being divine,' he says. 'Self-improvement plus world service equals spirituality.'

Showing GOD

Gradually his reputation as a wise and inspiring leader spread and the top management of an increasing number of companies started to seek his advice on leadership issues; one of these was Excel Industries in Mumbai.

In particular, G. Narayana became known for his ability to get people to focus and to work together, even if the starting point is one of chaos or even conflict. He forms groups of people and motivates them to create a particular result. This collective group energy is said to work wonders. He told us about this process at Excel. 'When I first came to Excel in 1987 the company was losing money. There was no direction. The founders of the company were spiritual, so the culture here already had a spiritual base; they did a lot of service. But a booster dose was required for the business. So I joined them to advise them and they called me Guruji, "beloved teacher".'

This title sticks to him, not only at Excel, but wherever he goes. We observed that no matter whether it is the union leaders or the management, they equally regard him as Guruji. In talks the management has with the union leaders, they don't see him as management; they see him as the guru taking care of both sides, helping them to come to the best possible solutions together.

He told us, 'That first year was critical. I showed them "GOD". What is "GOD"? Group plus Organization plus Direction equals "GOD". Leadership is a process of participation (in a group), decision (for the organization) and initiation (of the direction). When you have shared vision, shared mission and shared plan, you must have shared success. When success comes, credit must be shared and then fruits must be shared. We did all of this, like partnerships with trust and responsibility.

'Then also, rewards were required. There was no systematic salary structure, so we made the first salary and reward structure. We offered well and received the work; we offered and received. This is my spirit. We did not take and give, or give and take. Position people, and give them challenges. Share the success. When you practise it, it is fantastic.'

During the first six months of G. Narayana's first year at Excel there was a loss. 'Then we all joined together as a spirited team and turned around the situation, and profits occurred in the next six months. Then Excel had a wonderful growth.[5] Last year, 14 years later, we had a downturn and had to turn things around again, which we did.

'In my management consulting I've also had the opportunity to assist people to bring out the latent energies within them. The people and the companies brought out their inner potentials and excellencies; people became leaders and heroes. Then I became a hero builder and GOD is with me. G.O.D. is also Group–Organization–Direction.'

Work is worship beyond time limits

Life has taught G. Narayana that man can be what he chooses to be. According to him, this freedom to choose opens the door to the immense potential within each of us. 'The first measure of success is the happiness of all stakeholders. Happiness is the measure. The customers must be happy, the suppliers must be happy, employees must be happy, all must be happy. The *Gita* says, "If you do good work, you will get the returns, so do not worry about them." If you go for the returns, the work will not get done. You must do excellent work and not worry about your individual return.' In this connection Narayana tells us that his spiritual purpose is: 'to return added value to the world; to be a being of love; to contribute, endeavour, excel, and assist others to excel.

'To grow spiritually, I follow and give the following advice: never say "no". Offer, offer, offer. Work is worship beyond the time limits. Be available. Assist always. If you love, you give time. If you do not love, you will not give time. If you look at the Divinity in the other man, then you can inspire. That is inspiring leadership.

'We have formed a "Samanvaya" group, which is a council of companies with eight managing directors helping each other,' he says. Not only is G. Narayana chairman of that group serving all of the companies in the group,

---

5 From 1989 to 1997, Excel Industries' sales increased tenfold from Rs 400 million to Rs 4.1 billion (from roughly US$9 million to roughly US$90 million at a 2006 rate of exchange). In 2005, Excel Industries Ltd was demerged into two companies: Excel Industries Ltd and Excel Crop Care Ltd. As of 2005, the combined revenue was Rs 6 billion (US$130 million) with 2,100 employees.

he is also non-executive director or chairman of several other major companies, as well as an honorary guide to a number of medium and small-scale industries and voluntary organizations. In addition to all these leadership activities, he also finds time for writing. 'I have written 220 articles and have 20 books published. There are still 200 books waiting.

'In giving continuous love, I do not get tired, even though I travel all the time. My wife thinks that I will be coming home tired and she gets tired waiting for me. But I come running and she wants to know how that can be. But then everyone gives me love back, so I receive more than I give. Love energizes. No matter where I go, I give love, even more than information.

'Whenever any person comes to me, in each transaction I evaluate: "When he leaves from my office, has he become small or has he become tall?" I measure. If he has become small, I will not let him go; I make him sit. Only when he becomes tall he can go. Only when he becomes happy he can go. An unhappy man cannot leave my room. I may fight with him for eight hours, but I keep at it until he is happy. Only a happy man can escape from me. And everyone can judge whether the man is happy or not.'

15

Niran Jiang

CEO, Institute of Human Excellence, Australia

Niran Jiang is the CEO of the Institute of Human Excellence, a small Business Training and Consulting company in Sydney, Australia. In her own words, 'The institute serves coaches and organizations who wish to develop their people to the highest levels of performance at work, to have greater fulfilment in their personal lives and to make a contribution to the wider community.'

She was 40 years old when we interviewed her in 2004 and a 'world citizen'. She was born and raised in Inner Mongolia, studied at universities in China and the USA, and has had leadership positions in China, USA and Australia.

This multicultural background has had a strong influence on her spiritual purpose in life. The ideology that pervaded her upbringing during the Cultural Revolution in China (1966–76) was not only iconoclastic; she also presented it as being idealistic. 'When I grew up in China during the Cultural Revolution, religion was torn down. The slogan of the Cultural Revolution was, "Tear down the old and build the new". Idols were destroyed, and all the different churches were closed down because of the communist idea of collectively building an ideal society that works for everyone,' she says. Today, Niran Jiang combines the utopian teachings of her youth to 'build an ideal society' with her spiritual motivation to serve all embodied souls: 'For me, spirituality is everything; I don't put it in a separate compartment. As I was created with a soul, for me life is life-force, the connection with the universe. It's where we come from, what we are carrying, and where we are going. Spirituality for me is what makes everything shine. I want to contribute what I can in a process of "whole-system change" to create a world that works for everyone—not just humans, but for all species, plants, everything that has a soul. I think this has been an indirect result of growing up in China, where you grew up with a strong sense of collectiveness that's above individuality.'

Niran Jiang started her career as an assistant professor in international finance and trade, which led to her becoming director at the International Business Centre in China's first special economic zone. She received a fellowship to do research in the USA and, after taking an MBA there, she had leadership positions in two huge international companies, S.C. Johnson and Coca-Cola. After giving birth to her child, she made a major shift in her career, leaving large corporations and starting her own consulting business in Australia, where she then founded the Institute of Human Excellence. She underscores that her peripatetic behaviour is not only a journey on the physical level; it is primarily a spiritual process: 'These past years have been a "journey", bringing more and more spirituality into my work.'

She has a bachelor's degree in Genetic Engineering and a master's degree in Organization Management from Nankai University, China, as well as an MBA degree in Marketing Strategy from the University of California in Los Angeles, USA.

~

Co-creating a world that works for everyone

The business agenda is about the bottom line—for example, selling more Coke—but I don't care about that. I care about the processes that touch people and get them to shift. Everything has a soul for me. I think this has been an indirect result of growing up in China, where you grew up with a strong sense of collectiveness that's above individuality . . . The most important thing for me is the interconnectedness of everything; I believe in true equality because of this interconnectedness.

Although an expatriate, Niran Jiang is proud of the deep roots that keep her in contact with her 'tribe': 'I am a native of Inner Mongolia, an autonomous region of China, where I was born in a small town. I am currently living in Sydney, Australia. I never had a strong affinity with nations, but if I were forced into choosing my identity, I would choose Chinese. I connect with my "tribe", the like-minded, like-hearted and like-spirited people,' she tells. Yet her spiritual orientation is not local, it is inclusive of all. 'My spiritual theme,' she told us, is 'interconnectedness, wonderment and compassion.

'Wonderment is a big part of my spiritual feeling in the sense of a curiosity, a life force. I wonder about the world. When you want to understand the universe there is cosmology, the big, and there is quantum or particle physics, the small. Both can allow the mystery of the universe, but my orientation is from the small. The most important thing for me is the interconnectedness of everything, of all of us people, of different ethnic groups; I believe in true equality because of this interconnectedness. Based on the interconnectedness and equality that I see, love and compassion naturally come.'

Working for 'a better tomorrow'

After completing her bachelor's degree in Genetic Engineering and her master's degree in Organization Management from Nankai University, China, Niran Jiang began to work in the academic world. 'In 1987, I went to the south of China, to Shenzhen, which is next to Hong Kong. I was fairly young, 23, when I began to teach at Shenzhen University as an assistant professor in the International Finance and Trade Department. This university in China's first special economic zone was the first reformed business school in China after the Cultural Revolution. Because Shenzhen became a booming economic zone, a kind of new reform place, a lot of things were happening, and in business a lot of foreign investments and joint ventures were coming in. I was pretty active then. As the Director of the International Business Centre I was practising entrepreneurial leadership at an early age.

'Three years later, I got a research fellowship and went to the USA for my research and further postgraduate studies, obtaining an MBA in Marketing Strategy from the University of California in Los Angeles. I also toured the USA, travelling and working, in order to experience the culture of the country.

'I then got a job at the large international company, S.C. Johnson, which is the third largest privately owned company in the world, producing household products. It's a company with very strong values, run by the third generation of the Johnsons. The family has always been working for "a better tomorrow", and the company is doing environmental studies across the world, monitoring its activities and environmental impact.'

Niran Jiang was sent to Australia in 1993, where she spent three years as a Marketing Manager, and then returned to the company headquarters to work with innovation. She says, 'My leadership there centred very much around defining new visions. My strategic focus and my team's breakthrough incubation of new concepts at S.C. Johnson resulted in the largest acquisition in the company's history.'

Changing the thinking of the company

'I used the same approach at S.C. Johnson as I did later on at Coca-Cola with regard to creating an opening for this large acquisition. The company was experiencing stagnant growth. We invited a consulting group to do a major study of where growth could come from. Based on that study we were ready to look for radical changes for the business.'

Niran Jiang speaks of how her spirituality influenced her in this search for change. 'What stimulates wonderment is when you truly connect the inner life forces. Three of us, who connected really well, said, "Let's take this project." We went into hiding and identified the target for a new acquisition. It was Ziploc—a small plastic storage bag. Everybody said "no", as it was not in our traditional category of household cleaning products; we didn't have the manufacturing capability, and we didn't have any knowledge about making bags. Looking at acquisition criteria, everything said "no, no, no!" But intuitively this felt really right for the three of us, and we were amazed at the power of the brand, as a US brand magazine had listed Ziploc as number 17 on a list of 100 top brands, together with names like Disney and Harley David-son. We knew all the "noes", but we felt a lot of wonderment about this, almost a passion; it was not just about valuation, but about future potentials.

'After doing the traditional marketing research, we kept on brainstorming ideas, though not in a way according to the manual of S.C. Johnson. This was pure idea flow because of the passion and the life force, the wonderment and the mystery of why we were so attracted to this brand. We were joking, having fun, a lot of humour, and all the ideas became very visual and graphic. We opened up to tremendous creativity. We put everything beautifully on the board for the CEO and said, "This is your future business." After ten minutes he said, "I got it, we're buying it!" All the senior management committee members' jaws dropped. They said, "But what about manufacturing? We don't know how to . . ." "We'll learn," the CEO said. The company paid US$1.1 billion in 1996–97, and that became their largest acquisition. Today that business has provided the largest growth of the company. I got head-hunted away, but I still got the credit for what had happened and I was told that it was amazing how I had been able to shift the thinking of the company.

'My spirituality brought to this exciting project a true respect for and feeling of equality on the soul level with everybody in the small team; nobody was afraid of opening up. We were passionate. We had a strong curiosity, which I see as spirituality, as a life force. We got connected to a universal power, and we all felt a great commitment. This is why we succeeded.'

Shifting people's level of consciousness

'In 1997, after leaving S.C. Johnson, I went to work for Coca-Cola in the USA for three years. I worked on USA–Australian stuff as a Senior Trends Manager, where I concentrated on strategic planning. I could see the opportunity for using trend intelligence to drive business and innovation in order to make people feel more connected with what they do.

'I was given the job of building business models and delivering brand, channel and organization innovation, so I developed the first Future Trends function for USA. When you are the number one market leader in the world in the soft drinks industry, you have to be alert. My way of creating things there came from my spiritual orientation and ideas about co-creation. I decided to interview 30 top leaders at Coca-Cola, both domestically in the USA and internationally, to take into consideration the bigger picture. I spent roughly 45 minutes with each business leader in order to learn and understand the business scenario: What drove and motivated them? But it was also about engaging them by developing what I call a co-creating process.

'A lot of difficult issues were coming up which the top management knew about, but were not willing to face. By making one-to-one interviews and coming from a space of pure respect, I created a very safe environment for a lot of stuff to come out. Also I set very clear boundaries, and I was trusted. Of course, all the interviews were anonymous. I summarized my findings in a non-confrontational document and presented it to the Senior VP. At first he said, "I have ten minutes for you." ' Niran Jiang paused and thought back to that experience, remarking, 'The power they have in large American corporations and the way they treat people . . . it's worse than in communist China! They treat you like a peanut. But I refuse to feel like a peanut. I treat people below me with dignity, I treat people above me with dignity, and I don't take a confrontational style. So he said, "Ten minutes", and I said, "Fine", and went straight to the heart of the issue, bringing up the truth in a calm and gentle way, not criticizing him. This turned into a two hours' meeting.

'The Senior VP obviously got confronted with a lot of issues about how people truly felt, and that they were not able to speak the truth. I brought out issues that he could connect to from his level of consciousness and which could motivate him to create change. Therefore, from then on I got a tremendous amount of support in creating initiatives that were very new and very challenging for the company. Out of the work we were able to accomplish, via Future Trends, there were major costs saving initiatives in a number of departments at Coca-Cola. In one project we actually quantified a cost saving of over a million US dollars.

'This is how I see consciousness shifting; it's not just a piece of work. The business agenda is about the bottom line—for example, selling more Coke—but I don't care about that. I care about the processes that touch people and get them to shift.'

Interconnectedness and storytelling

Niran Jiang's spiritual view of life is strongly shaped by her belief in 'the interconnectedness of everything, of all of us people'. This is reflected in her spiritual purpose of personal growth and individual transformation. She says that this 'affects how you relate to and interact with your work colleagues day in and day out—from how you greet them, and how you look them in the eyes, to how you make a change in the world.'

She told us that it is therefore natural for her to collaborate, to share and to give credit to others, and gave an example of how her spiritual focus on interconnectedness and interaction was expressed in her work at Coca-Cola.

'I started an Urban Teen Connection Project, bringing teenagers to the company, doing a lot of storytelling, and learning from their stories. Also in business, stories teach in magic ways, and they don't preach. We tried to understand teens, to build a brand with teens and to bring this into the process of initiating new PR and new advertising activities in a most competitive landscape.

'I started the process by doing strategic planning differently from what they had been doing, and a year later it led to and created good business results. It was a chain effect. I gave everyone the credit along the way as a result of the interconnectedness I felt. I had people collaborate rather than compete for credit so they could get a promotion. It was a little cultural change in the company.'

Human excellence

'I see myself as an emerging leader; there is a major leadership call for me. These past years have been a journey, bringing more and more spirituality into my work. Up until the year 2000, my life had been all about career. After I had my child, my priorities shifted dramatically. So I started my own consulting business, Star Venture. For about four years I worked as a consultant in Australia and the USA. With two other partners and five expert associates, a year ago I started this new business called Institute of Human Excellence.

'We are building it on a whole new business model based on collaboration and transparency. Business should be a home, a vehicle for individuals to operate at the maximum of their potentials. The vision is to really help organizations in their transformation process, to create a more meaningful, purpose and values-driven and happier environment, and to contribute to society.

'After we are well established in Australia, I see part of our business going into Asia-Pacific. That will be where we contribute to the world.'

Prayer as co-creation

'I enjoy going into my inner space and meditating. I remember a story of the Buddha and a disciple. The disciple asked, "What is your advice?" Buddha's answer in Chinese is four characters. Translated word by word into English it is: "As if I hear it". The meaning of this is: "Listen inside to the higher Self for truth". What does my inside say? This has always been a good piece of advice for me.

'I have a certain resistance to prayer because of the cultural connotation that is carried by it—that the person who is praying is lower than the God prayed to. In my spiritual practice it is very important that the relationship is equal. Prayer for me is a co-creation; I do ask for what I need, but also I do give what is asked, so it is equal. To whom do I pray? The "universal mystery". I pray for "all that is". I pray to the "work-god", to the "spirit of the soul", to the "four directions", to the "going-in", to the ancestors, the wise men and women, and the wise teachers in history. So when I start praying it takes a long time.

'I believe that the teacher always comes when I am ready for the journey. That teacher for me can be a person, a daily event, my reflections, or my studies. I am very interested in different religions, and I go to different churches once in a while to experience them. Sometimes I go to a Christian Baptist church, a Unitarian church or a temple. I go to meditation retreats, and I practise chi gong which is the physical dimension of meditation, practising the heart power. I also study Buddhism with a group of teachers, but I wouldn't call myself a Buddhist. Meditation for me is throughout the day. It is being mindful, staying connected with what is around me: people and the universe. When I am out of place—being busy, shutting my door—I know that I am also out of place with my spirituality. When I am connected, I am practising spirituality.'

In this section

Although many of the spiritual-based leaders we have interviewed have used the word 'compassion' at one time or another, in this section you will meet five top leaders from four continents, all of whom have a particular focus on 'compassion' when they reflect on their spiritual view of life and how it affects their leadership. You will meet the Chairman and former CEO of one of the world's major manufacturers of pumps in Denmark; a former Senior Managing Director in one of the largest banks in the USA; a former HR director of a major international re-insurance company, later the CEO of the Swiss operations of an international foundation oriented towards protecting the environment; the President and CEO of a small American consulting company; and the Executive Director of a major Indian manufacturer of machine tools and engineering products. Here you will meet:

Niels Due Jensen, Group Chairman, Grundfos Management A/S, Denmark

In *Leading with compassion and responsibility,* Niels Due Jensen says, 'Having employees with a mental or physical handicap working for Grundfos has become a natural part of the company's life and behaviour.' He tells how this is a natural reflection of his spiritual theme of 'empathy, compassion and love for my neighbour'.

Rajan Govindan, former Senior Managing Director, Bankers Trust, USA

In *Becoming a better human being,* Rajan Govindan tells of the growth in his compassion. 'The challenge for me was what to do with a person who made the same mistakes over and over again. For years, I simply let people go the first time they made a mistake. I was looking out for the customer and that is what justified my actions. Today it would be very painful for me to fire a person. Today I would try to help them not make the mistake again. If they did make a mistake a second time, then I would try to help them find another place in the company where they would be better suited.'

Carol Franklin, former HR Director, Swiss Re and former CEO, World Wide Fund for Nature (WWF), Switzerland

In *Caring for and being responsible for the earth and its inhabitants*, Dr Carol Franklin says, 'For me, spirituality and ethical behaviour are very similar. Spirituality may be defined as "caring for and being responsible for the earth and its inhabitants". It's like the Hippocratic oath taken by doctors. It deals with not doing harm.' Her spiritual perspective formed the basis for a new strategy at WWF: 'The strategy was to change people's behaviour—to show them that you have to change your own behaviour if you want to change the world.'

Nilofer Merchant, President, Rubicon Consultants, USA

In *Moving from fear to love,* Nilofer Merchant tells the story of a difficult meeting she led with one of her clients. 'It was one of those moments where I just offered to the group the gift from my heart that happened to be there. I just happened to be the one who could help them find the truth that was already there. I think this process drew upon people's goodness. Sometimes we forget that most people really do want to live in alignment with their values, but they just don't know how. So often it's up to the leader to create the environment where people can live their values.'

S.K. Welling, Executive Director, HMT International Ltd, India

In *A leader must have concern for others,* S.K. Welling says, 'You may have the world's best strategies, but they must be implemented with people. If you want your business strategy to succeed, you should address the root cause of success: the people themselves. The results follow by themselves. In this spirit, we have doubled the profits and doubled the dividends. The roots—the people—have been watered using spirituality. But I don't announce the spirituality. I never use the word "spirituality" when I talk about it.'

16

Niels Due Jensen

Group Chairman, Grundfos Management A/S, Denmark

Niels Due Jensen retired as CEO of Grundfos in 2003 and is now Group Chairman, Grundfos Management A/S in Denmark. He was 60 years of age at the time of the interview. With a background in engineering, he has for 30 years been the leader of the pump manufacturing business started by his father in 1945. Grundfos consists of about 50 companies, including 15 production companies in major regions of the world, not least in Asia. It is the world's largest producer of circulation pumps with a share of roughly 50 per cent of the total world market, and its market share of all kinds of pumps is roughly 15 per cent. The company has more than 11,000 employees.

In 2004, shortly after we interviewed Niels Due Jensen, Grundfos received an award for designing a pump that can run on sun and wind energy, and which is designed to assure water collection in poor and hard-to-access areas throughout the world. At that time, Niels Due Jensen stated: 'Our ambition with the SQFlex pump is to increase the quality of life for people who live in areas where it is difficult to live. The income from such a pump will most likely never be anything special for Grundfos—but it is an important part of our responsibility to develop and produce that kind of pump,' he underlined.

This is in keeping with Grundfos's reputation as a world leader in corporate social and environmental responsibility. For example, it has a large number of employees who would otherwise find it very difficult to secure regular employment. These include people who are physically or mentally handicapped, have chronic health problems, have a prison record, are recent immigrants, or are alcohol/drug addicts. According to Niels Due Jensen, 'The main goal of our inputs here is to provide people in need with working conditions so they can help themselves. My starting point is that each person has a right to a meaningful existence—and, for most, that means a meaningful job. It all boils down to compassion.'

When asked if he could express his spiritual view of life in a concise theme, he replied: 'Empathy, compassion, and love for my neighbour.' He continued by saying, 'My spiritual view of life is based on being a Lutheran Christian, and I try my best to live up to the basic rules from the New Testament in the Bible. However, it is not something that I am conscious about every day. It is kind of in the back of my mind all the time, and therefore I instinctively base my decisions on these ground rules from the New Testament, although, of course, like any other person, I am a number of times failing on the way; that's for sure. I should note that I don't try to separate the way I think and decide and act in my private life as compared to my business life. It all goes together.'

Leading with compassion and responsibility

It is clearly with high pride that we in Grundfos are manufacturing pumps and pump systems, because these products really are helping society to grow, helping millions of people all over the world to fulfil certain very basic needs. We are in a business which does not do damage to others, does not contribute to creating wars, but which is really helpful for human beings all over the world. It may be for people in Africa with simple needs for clean water, or it may be for people in highly developed societies where they need a lot of pumps in order for everything to be functioning.

Reflecting on the position of Grundfos in the world pump industry, Niels Due Jensen told us: 'Over the past 20–25 years, we have been able to develop Grundfos so that it has become probably the most successful pump company in the world. This year [2004] we will reach an annual sale of approximately

11.5 billion Danish crowns. With the current exchange rate, that is around US$2 billion. Grundfos has definitely reached a respectable position within the pump industry.'

This development is supported by the social orientation of its major shareholder, the Poul Due Jensen Foundation, named after Niels Due Jensen's father, who was the founder of the company. As Niels Due Jensen says, 'Purely achieving high financial goals and productivity goals is not a target for Grundfos. It is more important for us to focus on the growth and development of our business instead of just optimizing financial results. It has always been a part of our policies, and particularly a major principle of The Poul Due Jensen Foundation, that profit is not a target in itself. Money and a good profitability are necessary for us to maintain a successful growing company, which is a good place for people to work in.'

This social orientation is also strongly supported by Niels Due Jensen's own personal values and his spiritual view of life: 'What is success for me in my private life is first of all to have a good life in harmony with my family . . . Money has never been a target in itself; it is simply a means for being able to do things and for achieving various goals in life. My major spiritual principle and value is first of all honesty. Honesty and openness and also trying to "love your neighbour", which I try to practise also in my business life.

'I was born in this little town of Bjerringbro as one of four children,' he told us. 'My father, Poul Due Jensen, came out of a farmer's family, but he wanted to break away from that way of life, so he became an apprentice in a machine shop. Later on he attended a school of engineering here in Denmark, and based his career on designing machines for this little machine shop. When I was born in 1943, my father was already a foreman. He was a very entrepreneurial person, very innovative, and, after the end of World War II, he started his own machine shop in Bjerringbro, and called it Grundfos.

'So I grew up with such a small machine shop, and of course got acquainted with and fell in love with machine work and the design of machinery. I quickly got in touch with many of my father's workers, and very early in my childhood I decided to go for a career in engineering and machining. I became a mechanical engineer and had different work experiences. Back at Grundfos in 1974, I worked here until my father suddenly passed away in 1977. At that time I got the enormous challenge of taking over the chairmanship of the Grundfos Group, which already consisted of 10–15 companies with the main company here in Bjerringbro. There were approximately 2,000 employees, spread all over the world, about half of them working in Denmark.

'I was 34 years old and had an interesting but also rather demanding job of trying, so to say, to take my father's company and make sure that it continued to develop. Now, about 25 years later, I can lean back and say I succeeded, not alone, but together with many, many good employees.'

A deeper meaning of life

Niels Due Jensen is one of the few leaders we interviewed who equated spirituality and religion. 'I think that spirituality is the same as religion,' he told us. 'Spirituality gives me a deeper meaning of life, and therefore also regulates the way I behave on a regular daily basis in my private life as well as in my work life. I grew up in a Lutheran-Christian family. I married a woman who has the same basic opinions about living a respectable Christian life as I have always had. This background has influenced my whole life and therefore also the way I behave. As I see it, you can not really separate what you do in your private life and what you do in your job; it all "hangs together"; you use the same feelings and the same background for taking your decisions.

'Since there is quite a bit of discussion going on in Denmark and other European countries as to religion at the workplace, I should add on that I feel that the question of religion is something which you want to keep to yourself.

'Prayer is part of my daily life. My childhood Christianity is still with me. I frequently go to church. I like to sit in the church, to follow the ceremony, and thereby have time to think a little bit, to reflect upon my life and also sometimes upon business questions. I do not always follow the preacher's sermon closely: I sit there thinking by myself; that gives room for considering things, which I like; it gives time for reflection.'

Social responsibility

'My principle of trying to "love your neighbour" has guided me in the direction of developing what we call "social responsibility" at Grundfos. It wasn't something I started; it was in fact my father who already in the late 1960s began our tradition of practising social responsibility. Because of my spiritual background I have always had this activity within Grundfos high on my agenda. Over the years it has developed in such a way that today we have a considerable number of employees who would probably not be able to be with us without a certain support and attention from our company. Out of about 4,500 employees in our Danish factories and companies we have about 150 who are employed under what we call "special conditions".

'Having employees with a mental or physical handicap working for Grundfos has become a natural part of the company's life and behaviour. We in the management have made it clear that this is our responsibility; this is our policy, and these are conditions you have to accept as an employee, if you want to work for Grundfos. People have accepted that over the years and they are more and more proud of Grundfos having this tradition. They are also increasingly accepting that it is a natural and right thing for a company like

Grundfos to acknowledge and act in accord with our responsibility towards society.

'If I had not had my Christian background, including the desire to do something for such unfortunate people, we would not have had this tradition at Grundfos. You may call it the need to love your neighbour, and this means your neighbour in this local society, but first of all your employees in the company.

'I have been able to spread this message out to many other Danish companies over the years, not only as an example through the way I have behaved, but also through the way I have spoken about social responsibility. Since 1997 we have a "Danish National Network of Business Leaders working with Corporate Social Responsibility." This network was founded in 1997 by the then Minister for Social Affairs. I became a member of the board; later I became the chairman. We now have about 700 Danish companies as members of this network through six regional networks. It has spread, and I think that Denmark is one of the nations in Europe that is at the very forefront in exercising social responsibility on a daily basis, first of all focused on the employees.

'About a year ago we introduced a new policy for what we call corporate social responsibility within Grundfos. We have laid down some major framework and policies as to how we would like to see the foreign Grundfos companies be active in living up to a social responsibility. We do not demand that they do exactly as we do in Denmark, as the cultural environments differ from country to country, and therefore the way you execute this corporate social responsibility on a daily basis is very different. We allow and encourage our local companies to lead the activities, which they feel are most helpful to them in being socially responsible towards their employees and their local community.'

Values in leadership

'We try to develop an organization of people who take responsibility not only for their job, but also for the company. Over time we have tried and continue to try to implement some core values.

'We have eight basic values, which we try to promote and exercise on a daily basis, not only in top management, but the whole way through the company, hopefully this means by each employee. Of course, it takes a long time to get this perspective in the backbone of every employee, and for new employees it takes several years to understand the real meaning of these basic values. They are described as [here Niels Due Jensen recited from memory, although he from time to time looked at a brochure he had on his desk]:

- *Sustainability.* We will act in a way that minimizes our negative effect on the natural environment and our work environment.

- *Focusing on people.* We respect human rights and operate in an ethical manner wherever we operate—and treat our employees as we treat our families and friends.

- *Global thinking.* Not only will we operate internationally, but we will respect local values, cultures and societal conditions, while living up to international norms.

- *Open and honest conduct.* We will be a trustworthy and reliable company with a high level of transparency with respect to our stakeholders, with our employees having top priority, and where dialogue is in focus.

- *Leadership.* We will be a world leader in the production of pumps, with a high degree of self-reliance, respected for the quality, design, longevity and value of our products.

- *Partnership.* Our customers shall consider us to be their stable and long-term partner, not just a supplier.

- *Responsibility.* We will be respected for our responsible behaviour with respect to our employees, customers, suppliers, the local societies where we operate, and the environment.

- *Independence.* We will continue to develop Grundfos by primarily investing our own means and maintaining our independence, in accord with the wishes of the founder; high profits are a means for the concern's continued development, not a goal in their own right.

'Within the last four or five years, we have tried systematically to work on the introduction of these basic values throughout the organization, but it takes time. Hopefully, we will end up with an organization which is not managed from the top through a lot of instructions and orders, but rather managed in a way, so that every employee feels related to these values and exercises these values in the actual situations they meet in their jobs. We hope this will make the people more motivated, more engaged and "pull" much more in the same direction.

'The way we work with these values is first of all to try to demonstrate through our own behaviour that we live up to them. Management has to take its own medicine, so to speak. Living up to the values is an exercise on a daily basis.

'We have put all the eight basic values together with our mission and vision in a small pamphlet, which has now been published in 24 languages.

Each new employee gets this booklet, but this is only the beginning. In each company and in each department we discuss these values with the employees. It is important that the man or woman working in production knows exactly how he or she should exercise and practise these values in their job. That is why we have a very long and careful dialogue with employees over the years in group meetings and on an individual basis.'

Openness and honesty

'The basic rules of my own life, like openness, honesty and a feeling of high responsibility, as well as "love your neighbour", are good for any organization to practise. If these principles are honestly practised, they will always lead to an organization that demonstrates high responsibility, and which is therefore in many ways successful in the way it does its business.'

To illustrate his point, Niels Due Jensen told us the following story: 'About three years ago we had a situation where we had far too many "wild strikes". People stopped working for a day or two or three, just to demonstrate what they would like to see, or even just to protest towards the way things were run. What I did then was to write an open letter to all employees, telling them in a really straightforward way that Grundfos was not able to continue with this behaviour from some groups of employees, because it would simply ruin our company.

'To begin with, this openness and honesty with our people was taken very badly by quite a few, but, as time has gone by, people realize that I was right in telling the truth about what our company needed from them. Today I believe that my openness and honesty to our employees at that time really has changed the agenda for our whole company, when it comes to working more in harmony and in dialogue with each other on a daily basis instead of confronting each other with problems.

'My philosophy is clearly that it is important to inform in due time about the things which you as a top manager are aware of, as to what might happen in the company, and first of all to tell about unpleasant things before the more pleasant things. Be open in your dialogue, and be very honest. In this way you will be able to create a dialogue and understanding, also for those unpopular decisions which now and then necessarily must be taken. If I should advise potential leaders, I would advise them to manage in a highly responsible way: always be honest in the way you do business.'

17

Rajan Govindan

Former Senior Managing Director, Bankers Trust, USA

At the time of the interview Rajan Govindan was 56 years old. Although he has held several important leadership positions before and after his time with Bankers Trust, this interview centres mainly on the 18 years, from 1981 until 1999, when he had leadership positions in this major American bank. He ended his career there as Senior Managing Director. Together with many others, he left the bank when it was taken over by Deutsche Bank, the major German-based international finance house, after major attacks on Bankers Trust's reputation and severe economic losses in 1998.[1]

When he speaks of his spiritual view of life, Rajan Govindan continually refers to the concept of being a good human being. 'To me, spirituality in the workplace means two things: one is you have to be "correct and righteous". To me, being a human being means to act with right conduct, to act with moral char-

---

1   Bankers Trust is a historic US bank founded in 1903. In the 1990s it began moving from tra-
     ditional loan operations to trading on various markets and became a leader in risk manage-
     ment. In spite of its expertise in managing risk in the trading room, its reputation suffered
     great damage when some of its very complex so-called 'derivative transactions' led to huge
     losses at several of its major corporate clients and to ensuing lawsuits against the bank which
     received considerable media attention. The loss of trust and reputation, combined with
     leadership problems, led to very heavy losses and to the bank being taken over by Deutsche
     Bank in 1998.

acter in everything that I do. The second is more personal to me, and that is that God has given me the work to do and I must leave the results up to God. It has taken me 35 years to really understand this. Work is an activity that has been given to me to do by God and I must do it well. I think we all have two kinds of karma, both a spiritual and a physical debit/credit book that we carry. I believe that we are born to pay off this karmic debt. To me, paying off this karma means that you live your life the best you can and keep doing what it takes to make you a better human being.'

Rajan Govindan has a bachelor's degree in engineering from Birla Institute of Science and Technology (ranked by UNESCO in its 2005 list of Asia's top 20 universities) in Rajasthan, India, and a master's degree in Operations Research from New York University in the USA.

As of today, the summer of 2006, Rajan Govindan is Chief Operating Officer at another major American financial institution, Bear Stearns Asset Management in New York.[2]

Becoming a better human being

The purpose of business is to make money through proper values. There is so much corruption today in business and all of it represents an absence of values and character. Spirituality is clearly needed in business today. I think it is the business leaders' purpose to ensure that the employees do things well for the company; it is their job to develop these values and character in people. You need to lead them so that they behave properly toward their customers and co-workers and so that the company is a wholesome place. When a company environment is wholesome it will be quite productive.

After his postgraduate studies in New York, Rajan Govindan stayed in the USA and has worked and lived there ever since, although he still has strong ties to India. 'I've worked for about 32 years and was an engineer by education. My first job was in the systems technology field at a company called EDS (Elec-

---

2   Bear Stearns Asset Management currently employs approximately 12,000 people worldwide. It has a total capital of US$57.6 billion (2006) and total assets of US$292.6 billion.

tronic Data Systems) in Dallas, Texas, USA,' he says. Later on he worked in the management consulting group of what is now known as Deloitte & Touche.

'In 1981, I joined Bankers Trust and spent 18 years with them. At Bankers Trust I did all kinds of things,' he tells. For example, for almost five years Rajan Govindan ran the 401K department which managed corporate retirement accounts. At the time he started with this department, it was losing a million dollars a year. Within three and a half years it was making US$100 million and became the number one provider of retirement plans in the USA, he explained. During the following years Rajan Govindan was running different functions, including marketing, for all of the retirement services, the domestic private banking department, and the centralization of the bank's technology. When Deutsche Bank bought Bankers Trust in 1998, he, along with many other employees, left the bank. 'I thought I wanted to try working for a small company because I had always worked for a huge company. So I went to work for a company named Lord Abbott with only 400 people, as opposed to 20,000 people at Bankers Trust. I was the Chief Administrative Officer, so I had technology, operations and finance, everything, reporting to me. I was there for four years. I found that working for a small, family company was okay but, since I was not part of its founding members, it was hard for me.'

Working without worrying about the result

After leaving Lord Abbott, Rajan Govindan then found that working independently, doing strategic management consulting with several men he knew from the past, gave him a wonderful opportunity to try something new and different. 'It took us four years to build credibility and begin earning a steady income. We were able to recruit a team and finally began to see the fruits of many years of investment. At that time I was hoping to get myself organized to where I could do consulting a few days a week and put some balance into my life,' he states.

However, as he told us in 2006, several years after the original interview, 'Out of the blue, late one night I got a call from the CEO of Bear Stearns Asset Management asking me to consider coming to work for them.' Before making a decision, he went to India to spend some time at an ashram he has frequented, hoping to get inspiration from the spiritual master there. 'Being in the ashram in India,' he told us, 'I felt strongly that nothing happens unless willed by God.

'I concluded from that visit that I had not completed my "karmic" obligations of working in a corporate environment and that is why I needed to go back into the competitive stressful environment.' Rajan Govindan explained what he meant by such obligations: 'My understanding of "karmic debt" is that each one of us gets exactly what we deserve based on what we have done in this life or previous lives. God orchestrates this perfect cause-and-effect phenomenon through nature and natural processes.'

He continued: 'But, after taking the Chief Operating Officer position of Bear Stearns, I have realized that the only reason I am in this job is because God wanted me to be here and now I am not worried or stressed out. I work hard and do my best, but now, for the first time in my life, I am not worried about the results.'

Acting from love each day

'To me, spirituality in the workplace means two things: one is you have to be "correct and righteous". I hesitate to use the word "righteous" because it has many connotations, but you have to be very correct in how you conduct yourself at work. I think this is one of the most important things and it can apply to everyone. The second is more personal to me and that is that God has given me the work to do and I must leave the results up to God. It has taken me 35 years to really understand this. Work is an activity that has been given to me to do by God and I must do it well.

'Spirituality to me is also that people should behave as human beings; this is actually what I mean when I say "correct and righteous", or "correct behaviour". To me this means that you must be honest, fair and objective. My personal goal is to become more human. To me a human being means to act with right conduct, to act with moral character in everything that I do. Being here in the USA for 36 years, it has taken all of this time to continuously focus on "How do I become a better human being?"

'All of my spiritual exercises are about how I spent my day. I think that, when it comes to determining how well a job you have done, you must ask yourself, "Did I do the best I could?" The only person who really knows whether I did a good job or not is me. I don't have the ability or desire to do all of the things that other more spiritually evolved people do. My path is to focus on acting from love each day, each moment, and not reacting. When I pray in the morning and at night, I do not ask for things for myself or my family. Instead, I ask to be able to think of love towards all. I try to think about the times that I have not spoken with love or when I got upset, so that I can learn from them. If I know I have something tough I am going to face that day, I pray that I will not lose control. Then in the evening, I look at what happened and see if I lost control or not and most importantly thank God for a wonderful day and a great life.'

Improving, not firing people

'I feel as if only in the last ten years or so have I internalized the spiritual prin-ciples that I've learned. Before that time, it was more superficial, although it was always important for me to be honest with a customer and to admit a mistake if I made one. If I did not act this way, it would really bother me. And I tried to get everyone around me to be the same way. I made it a rule with anyone who worked for me that if we made a mistake we must call the cus-tomers and tell them.

'The challenge in all of this for me was what to do with a person who made the same mistakes over and over again. You have to realize that at Bankers Trust our retirement account customers were huge corporations like IBM and General Motors, so, if we made the same mistake even twice, we were running the risk that they would fire us. Also, we would, from time to time, have to write off millions of dollars due to these mistakes and that would affect every person's salary and bonus pool. So there were major consequences if we did not do our job correctly.

'For years, I simply let people go the first time they made a mistake. Today it would be very painful for me to fire a person. I was looking out for the cus-tomer and that is what justified my actions. Today, looking back, I feel much differently and would try to help them not make the mistake again. If they did make a mistake a second time, then I would try to help them find another place in the company where they would be better suited.

'At Bankers Trust, ultimately I was responsible for the managers who had to let people go. Unfortunately, I was not strong enough spiritually to help them see this from a spiritual perspective. I am aware of the suffering that these decisions have caused others and their families. Previously, I felt it was their problem, not mine. Today, I feel their pain and it bothers me; that is why my outlook on these situations has changed.

'I think it is most important to evaluate people properly according to what they are capable of doing and then promoting them accordingly. I feel that this will keep them from getting hurt later in their career. And this will keep the company from getting hurt as well. To me this is what I am talking about when I talk about acting with a righteous attitude.'

Doing things differently

Rajan Govindan told us about how this reflection on 'acting with a righteous attitude' affected his choice of job after leaving Bankers Trust. 'Throughout my career at Bankers Trust, we had a tremendous focus on results. People were secondary. After I left, I would have thoughts back to all of the people that I had fired; it was a very tough game there. I felt overwhelmed by the fact that in some way I would have to pay for all of that. So, when I joined Lord & Abbott, I decided that I was not going to work in this way anymore; I wanted to see how I could do things differently.

'This was difficult at first, because they wanted me to let people go who were not performing well from the very start. However, in the four years I was there, we didn't fire a single person. Some people fit in organizations and some people don't. I think that when you work for a corporation you do need to have certain attributes. Even knowing all of this, I was determined not to fire anyone.

'So I tried very hard to coach the people and help them to improve. It wasn't easy because so many of them did not want to change. I had a lot of pressure to fire the people who were not productive, but I was not willing to do that. Now I sit back and wonder if that was right or wrong. I did it because I thought, rightly or wrongly, that is what a spiritual person should do. My guess is that 80 per cent of the people were willing to change and embrace new things and 20 per cent were not.

'I cannot say for sure that they would not have been happier if they had been let go. Maybe they could have found something better for them. I wished I had tried this experiment ten years earlier in my life and could have learned what I have learned now.'

Ethical dilemmas

'I think that in all of my work I have had to make ethical choices. In the banking business the rule is that if the bank made a mistake, then the bank had to pay for it. However, sometimes when an error was made, it was in the bank's favour. For example, maybe you were supposed to sell 500 shares of stock and you sold 5,000 shares instead. If the market was moving down, then the sell of 5,000 shares could mean that the customer made money. Most of the time the customer wasn't even aware that something like this had happened. So how we handled something like this was always an ethical dilemma.

'My feeling, however, is that once you go down the path to try to cover up your mistake, even if it was in the customers' favour, you can not gain the true respect of your customer. You must set clear rules and they must be followed. The moment you are wishy-washy you set a trend.

'I have also always told the people who worked for me to be honest when they filled out their expense report. I told them, "Don't try to add a $5 tip just because you can get away with it." To me even these little things will always haunt you. I always taught the people to be clean in everything they did. This way you don't have to look over your shoulder and worry about what might happen to you.

'In the last one and a half years I worked for Bankers Trust, I was working with someone where we made presentations to the board on projections we felt we could meet. But then when we got into the actual work, he instead wanted to manipulate the financial numbers in order to show that we achieved the projected results, rather than working toward actually obtaining the results themselves. He would continually approve projects, but then put pressure on us to eliminate costs. One way he wanted to deal with this was to capitalize the costs, so they wouldn't show up as current expenses. I felt this was not correct and so I had to end the relationship.'

The analytical mind and the compassionate heart

'I sometimes feel that there is an inherent conflict between spirituality and being an investor: most investors want maximum return on their investments as quickly as possible while spirituality aims at the greater good for all. But without investors there are no opportunities for anyone!

'Decision-making that can be done using black and white analytical facts, mostly having to do with economic impact, is what our minds do best. But the best visionary leaders have been those who can integrate their analytical mind with their heart where the spirit resides—the spirit that always seeks the greater good for society and not personal gain; the spirit that is our moral compass and never lets us stray too far. It is the spiritual heart that enables us to make decisions that we will never be sorry about; it is the compassionate heart that makes our priorities right.

'In the tough impersonal business world, it is very easy to become hardened by our analytical mind—the challenge is to remain softened by our heart so that we can lead our lives as God would want us to. We've all become experts in rationalization and we have become so good at suppressing our inner world. To become a better person, the first thing one has to do is start listening to the inner voice and stop rationalizing. When you stop rationalizing, slowly but surely the inner voice starts to speak up. Every time you do something, ask yourself, "Is this right? Is it the correct behaviour?" In doing this you will start to see many things. When you stop rationalizing, your inner voice will tell you right away when you have done something that was not correct. Instantly you will feel it.

'As I have matured, I have started to realize that it is not management that decides my destiny, but rather God. Unfortunately, it is only when you get

18

Carol Franklin

Former HR Director, Swiss Re and former CEO, World Wide Fund for Nature (WWF), Switzerland

When we interviewed Dr Carol Franklin she did not use her married name, Engler. She was born in the UK in 1951 but has lived in Switzerland since she was nine years old. She has held leadership positions there for more than 20 years, mainly at Swiss Re, the major international re-insurance company. Here she has been Head of the Aviation Department (re-insurance), Head of HR, and a member of the executive team of the European division responsible for Scandinavia, Great Britain and the Eastern Mediterranean. Upon resigning from Swiss Re in 1999, she accepted a position as CEO of WWF, the World Wide Fund for Nature (formerly World Wildlife Fund), Switzerland, an organization with 250,000 members and 150,000 sponsors. In 2002 when her very active strategic leadership led to conflicts at the organization's grass-roots level, she was fired. For the following almost two years Dr Franklin was the manager of 'In the Spirit of Davos', a Swiss Foundation aimed at promoting constructive dialogue regarding globalization between politicians, business leaders and representatives of civil society.

As an ecologist, Carol Franklin defines spirituality as 'caring for the earth in the widest sense', a perspective that includes 'not doing harm, making sure that when you leave the earth it is not in a worse condition than when you got here'.

'But,' she says, 'that is not enough. Caring for the earth means not only caring for the environment; it also means caring for people. It's a sense of responsibility.'

Together with her husband she now runs a consulting company called 'Vorausdenken', meaning 'Thinking ahead', which works on promoting ethics and sustainability in business. When we interviewed her in November 2004, Carol Franklin had also just accepted to be the COO at the Swiss National Museums (consisting of eight museums) for a limited time.[1]

Her leadership positions have not only been in business. In Switzerland, where military service for men is obligatory, service for women is voluntary, but identical. During the period 1975–2003, Carol Franklin served the Swiss military, both as a commanding officer of a transport unit and as a judge at the martial court. In 2005 Carol Franklin also accepted the role as 'Ombudsfrau', the Swiss term for a female Ombudsman, for the telecommunication branch in Switzerland. Along with a team of lawyers she treats conflicts between consumers and the telecommunication companies.

$\sim$

Caring for and being responsible for the earth and its inhabitants

I will only work for a company that has good products that make the world a better place. The idea is that the product itself has to be worthwhile; it has to be in alignment with my spiritual view of life, which is caring for and being responsible for the earth and its inhabitants.

Throughout her career Dr Carol Franklin has actively sought positions of responsibility—not to be able to exert authority, but to be able to compas-

---

1   In addition to these leadership positions, Dr Franklin is on the board of companies engaged in: plantation and marketing of FSC-certified teak tree (Prime Forestry Group), insurance (London-based Hiscox, £1 billion/US$1.8 billion premiums), and recycling (Citron, listed on a Swiss stock exchange with its factory in France). She has board/leadership positions in foundations and not-for-profit organizations such as Pestalozzi Children's Foundation in Switzerland, Spirit in Business Switzerland, the Prime-Value Ethics Committee of the Dr Höller Vermögensverwaltung & Anlageberatung AG (investment management), Committee for Further Education at the University of St Gallen, and the Lassalle-Institute in Switzerland (serves leaders in business, politics and other sectors of society based on perspectives from Zen Buddhism and ethics).

sionately serve and to live up to her sense of duty. This is not only clear from her career path, but also from the way she reflects on her personal life.

'I was brought up a Protestant Christian, but I am not active in the church. My spiritual view of life includes being personally responsible for the earth, including people. It's like the "Hippocratic oath" taken by doctors. It deals with not doing harm, making sure that when you leave the earth it is not in a worse condition than when you got here, enabling future generations to live in similar if not better conditions. I am an ecologist. I don't think there are any hardcore ecologists who are not spiritual. Caring for the earth means not only caring for the environment; it also means caring for people. It's a sense of responsibility. I am more pragmatic—more "hands-on" spiritual—than transcendental.

'*My* purpose is to be responsible for what I do, and to do whatever I do the best that I can. Be the change you want to see in the world. Help move the world forward. The purpose of *business* is to make the world a better place for our children. I do *not* think that the business of business is business. You can say that the purpose is to make a profit, but it must be an ethical profit, profiting the employees and the communities they are in, making products that are worthwhile and that do not harm the world. Only sustainable businesses that care for people, the planet and profit will survive.

'I think spirituality is broader than religion. All religions must be spiritual, but not all spirituality must be religious. For me, spirituality and ethical behaviour are very similar. Spirituality may be defined as "caring for and being responsible for the earth and its inhabitants".

'Possibly you have two types of spiritually inclined people: there are the ones that go their own route in trying to transcend their own person; and there are people like me who focus on their responsibility, on how they impact others and the world. I think it is typically European not to use big words or to talk about God, although people from a lot of different cultures do that.'

In spite of her strong grounding in 'European' culture, Carol Franklin's spirituality also contains elements of a more Eastern, mystical tradition: 'I believe that we will reincarnate after death, and that we are responsible for what we do—and that we probably will have to live with the results of our actions at some other time: a kind of karma concept.' Once again, the concept of 'responsibility' is at the fore.

Caring for people

'I was born in Bradford, England; my father was English and my mother Swiss. We lived in England till I was nine, then the family moved to Switzerland. I grew up with a strong sense of justice, fairness, and responsibility. My father had a great influence upon me. His sense of fairness and justice had a very strong impact on me.

'I studied English language and literature at the University of Zürich and then wrote a thesis on women in the novels of three contemporary British novelists. In 1979 I completed my PhD In 1992 I attended an Executive Management Course at Yale University, USA.

'When I was 28, I joined Swiss Re, the largest or the second largest re-insurance company worldwide. I started off in the aviation re-insurance department as a normal trainee and worked there for 16 years, working my way through the ranks, moving around basically from one part of the world to the other. The last three years of the 16 years, I was head of the department, responsible for all the aviation re-insurance for Swiss Re worldwide.

'I was asked whether I wanted to take over the Human Resources department, and I did that for three years. I was responsible for both the operational human resources at Swiss Re Zürich, which employs 3,000 people, and on a strategic level for Swiss Re global, which employs 8,000 people. Before I went into Human Resources I said that I didn't want to remain in a staff position for a long period of time. So after three years as head of the HR department I went back into the re-insurance business and did that for a year. Finally I decided that it was time to move on.'

Carol Franklin told us how while she was at the HR department she promoted the policy of employing handicapped people. In addition, she worked to improve the opportunities for young people in the firm, and, in particular, to improve the opportunities for women. 'That was easy,' she said. 'When I took over HR we had 15 women in middle management, and when I left three years later we had 45. On the senior management level we had two when I took over, and when I left we had 12. This was all part of my established policies based on my spiritual orientation of caring for people. And I think it is good for the business, too. If you do business on an ethical basis, you'll make more profit and get better employees.'

Not working for money alone

'In 1996 everything was changing at Swiss Re. As the head of the Human Resources Department, I introduced training on a worldwide basis for developing our employees' potentials. I had to introduce many changes in the way things were run. I introduced a new remuneration system, which included a bonus. At the time, I thought this was a good idea.

'However, after about two years I realized that we were giving the wrong people the wrong bonuses, and that the way it was being done was not really fair. We said we would compensate teamwork, but we compensated individual performance—as if there is any such thing within such a large company. We were rewarding people to work against the interests of the company.

'If you measure performance on the basis of figures in such a business as reinsurance, which is a long-term business based on trust and confidence in your business partners and your employees, and you give them a bonus on an individual annual basis, it's going in the wrong direction. People used to feel—and Swiss Re was known for this—that "we like to work for the company, because we're part of the family", "we're part of a good company", or whatever. But now it was going in the direction of purely making money. A department would say, "This is ours, not yours." They didn't work together any more.

'I started off believing that bonuses were good, but then I came to the conclusion that bonuses in general lead to corruption, because they assume that people only work for money and not for intrinsic values or because of intrinsic motivations. If you assume that people do that, then they become like that, and then they will only work for money, and you lose the best part of the people. That's why I said, I can't agree with this any more, and I have to leave. My superiors were very much in favour of this bonus system. Greed was getting to them. And that is why I left.'

Be the change you want to see in the world

'In the beginning of 1999 I told everybody I was looking for a job, and I was offered the job of CEO of WWF, the World Wide Fund for Nature (previously World Wildlife Fund) in Switzerland. This was a difficult and very high-profile job. It was also a very political job, though I didn't realize at the time how political it was. WWF has 250,000 members in Switzerland and about 150,000 sponsors, so you have 400,000 who pay and help WWF Switzerland, which for a country with 7 million people is quite a lot. It's a very powerful organization; it has more sponsors, partners and members than all the political parties put together. I worked there for three years.

'Within the ten years before I joined WWF, nine CEOs had left, and the year before I joined they did not even have a CEO. When I joined they had especially been looking for somebody from business, but the employees were not so happy with this, because they thought it was a different culture; and so it was.

'We went into a new strategy, the conception of which I was able to participate in from the beginning, which was very lucky for me. The strategy was to change people's behaviour—to show them that you have to change your own behaviour if you want to change the world. It was kind of Gandhian: "Be the change you want to see in the world". If you want to change the world, you also have to find the longest lever, and that is business, because, if you get business on your side, it is easier to change people's behaviour.

'That meant that on the one hand we wanted to work with business, we wanted to "green" business. On the other hand we wanted to change the consumers' behaviour—which meant that we were showing them the ways and means to change their behaviour. By doing that, they could influence politics, and they could influence business, because obviously business does what the consumers want it to do. That was very successful. We had partnerships; we introduced the first and only real "green" electricity at the time and worked well with lots of corporations. We had an excellent image, and were constantly present in the media, always on a very positive note.

'It all worked relatively well for about two to two and a half years, but then again, as with my predecessors, we ran into a structural problem. There was a gap between the professional way that 180 people worked in the national administration, and the way the chapters in each of the 26 cantons (Swiss "states") were run with more or less grass-roots people who had great local interests. The difficulty was trying to guide them into accepting the strategy, recognizing that what they did was very important, but had to be the same as what we were doing on a national level and what we were doing on an international level.

'So we had the international, the national and the local level, but in these 26 chapters they had always been able to do whatever they wanted and had not been really integrated into the overall strategy. They felt we were curtailing their rights. These chapters elected over half of the members of the board. So people from the chapters went to the board and said, "We don't like what the professional part is doing, because WWF is the local part", and some of the board members, having been elected by the chapters, agreed.'

Working for a cause

'So what happened? They fired me! But because the employees had accepted this strategy and supported it, and because the media was very positive about the changes, the employees as well as the media stood up and said, "You can't do this, you can't fire her." So WWF was again all over the media and the organization lost an awful lot of members. Practically all of Switzerland and all the employees stood up and said, "You have to fire the board and not her", which they didn't do, of course; the board won. I knew exactly what I was doing. I was not there to work for myself; I was there to work for a cause. That's why, for me, being fired was not such a bad experience. It was for me one of the most important points of my life. It was simply a matter of principle—if you believe in something, if you believe in something good for the cause, you stick to it.

'Our membership grew by ten per cent, which is a lot because we had a very big membership. When I left, it dropped again. We also grew the income from 30 million to 45 million Swiss Francs (US$23 million to US$35 million) within the three years I led the WWF. When I left, the board was split, and many people had to leave the board as well. WWF was essentially non-existent for two years, which was very, very bad for the organization. This made me wonder, of course, if I had acted correctly, but the organization probably needed the crash to be able to rise out of the ashes.'

Building bridges

'In November 2004, I joined the Executive Board of the Swiss National Museum. There is one main museum in the middle of Zurich and seven smaller museums. I have taken the position of COO for 18 months in this national museum, which is going through a change of structure.

'I declined a lot of jobs before accepting the position of COO at the museum. A multinational pharmaceutical company asked me to work for them, but I said: no, thank you. They produce a lot of things that I don't think are good. A grand casino asked me to be on their board, and I said no, it is not going to be in my portfolio. I will only work for a company that has good products that make the world a better place. The idea is that the product itself has to be worthwhile; it has to be in alignment with my spiritual view of life, which is caring for and being responsible for the earth and its inhabitants.

'The museum wanted someone for such a time-limited contract in order to find out whether they need an entrepreneur or an accountant. The accountants can't deal with the insecurities, and the entrepreneurs can't deal with the bureaucracy at the moment. They asked me to do this because of the experience I had with WWF. There will probably be antagonism between the large central museum and the smaller ones, similar to what I experienced at WWF between the central office and the many local units. I want to help them with the change management—they have gone through so many change processes. I think I can coach them quite well, and they need bridges—and my speciality is building bridges.

'The idea is to develop the vision using a process that engages the employees, where we agree on the milestones. My job as COO of this organization is to make sure that people then do what they say they will do. On the one hand it is organizational, but it's also spiritual in the sense that you are responsible for your own behaviour. If you say yes, then you do it.'

A question of courage

'My advice for aspiring spiritual-based leaders is to be the same person at work as you are in your family life. You have to be able to live with the values that you have as an individual in your work life, because otherwise things won't work, at least for me. You have to have your thoughts, words and deeds work together. I think it is well worth saying that it is fine to accept a job that is not well paid; if you are in the right place, and you are comfortable with the values, then the career will happen by itself. My advice is: (1) Get the fun job. (2) Don't split your values. (3) If you don't like what you are doing, get out of it; you won't be good at it.

'You should lead by example, and then you can explain why you have done what you did. If the employees, the clients and the customers see that by doing something in a spiritual way gives you better results, then you can explain why and how you have done it. Then you can talk about spirituality, because then they will see that it is more successful, also from a business point of view. The courage of doing things that people haven't thought about is something that will get you further. Do first and tell afterwards.'

19

Nilofer Merchant

President, Rubicon Consultants, USA

Nilofer Merchant, President and CEO of the marketing consulting firm Rubicon Consultants in the USA, was 34 years of age at the time of the interview and one of the youngest leaders profiled in this book. She is a market strategist who founded Rubicon Consulting in 1999 after ten years of operational experience in notable technology firms such as Apple (doing market research), GoLive (Vice President of Sales and Channel Marketing) and Autodesk (Revenue Manager). Rubicon Consulting helps high-tech firms, both start-ups and global brands, to define, design, defend and optimize their operations.

She had her first board role at the age of 19 while she was working on her BS in economics from the University of San Francisco in the USA (she also holds an MBA from Santa Clara University in California). While at college she became involved in student governance issues, which eventually led to her being a member of the State Board of Governors, the leading governance organization for 106 community colleges in California. So, early on at the age of 19, without any real work experience, she was sitting across from senators and writing legislation about student governance. At the age of 25 she held her first executive role—and in spite of her relatively young age she has now for years been a coach and mentor to directors and VPs of high-tech firms.

Nilofer Merchant was born into Islam, but as a married woman converted into Christianity. 'I do not consider myself a religious person,' she says. 'I consider myself to be a spiritual person and I use my religion as a way to express and nurture my spirituality.'

Reflecting on her compassionate nature, she tells of how this nurturing of her spirituality empowers her to be authentic: 'I think it is so clear that we were each born with our own unique essences, but we get distracted. We look in the mirror or to the outside world and think, "This is it. It's not easy to hear and feel that inner voice. I've never found that the answer comes from outside, even from a spiritual teacher. The answer is truly within you, and all of the spiritual methods and processes are designed to help you get quiet enough, fearless enough, courageous enough, compassionate enough, loving enough to discover who you really are.'

~

Moving from fear to love

To me, success means that I get a chance to use the gifts that God has given me every day. I get a chance to serve other people with those gifts and I help other people to feel heard and cared about and help them to use their gifts. It's so easy to think that success is about the work that's getting done, but to me it is not about that. It is entirely about how people connect and the process by which you live your life. You show up, you are fully present, you offer up your gifts fully, and you collaborate with other people. When you do this, the rest takes care of itself.

Nilofer Merchant has held leadership positions for eight years. For the past three years, she is the President and CEO of Rubicon Consultants, in Cupertino, California, USA. She tells about how quickly she became involved in complex leadership issues in high-tech firms. 'After I left college, I worked for Apple Computers and ultimately ended up running a channel (marketing) programme. At that time I was in my mid-20s and was the youngest manager on the VP staff. While I was head of this programme, our small team won an award for the best VAR (value-added reseller) programme. Apple had not won this award for eight years.'

After she left Apple, Nilofer Merchant worked for GoLive Systems, which was later acquired by Adobe Products, and was their Vice President of Sales and Channel Marketing. 'I set up worldwide distribution systems and did some direct sales. I wanted the experience in direct sales because I only had experience at that time in marketing. I had a disagreement about ethics while in that position and was fired.'

She then went to Autodesk, Inc., which is a technology company that developed CAD (computer-aided design) software, where she reported to the Vice President and had cross-functional responsibilities. 'My role was of a Business Development Manager. I had lots of influence, but no power really, because I had no technical skills.

'In 1999 I started my own consulting practice, Rubicon Consulting. I am pleased with the growth of the company, and now, in the third year, we will have over US$500,000 in revenues. This has also been done during a major recession in the technology industry. We have a good stable client base and are doing well in the area of market strategies. I manage all of the client interfaces and then contract with other consultants when the need arises.

'In choosing the name Rubicon, I was looking for a name that would reflect my own personal transformation. The story of Rubicon has to do with Julius Caesar before he became the ruler of ancient Rome. Caesar crossed a river called the Rubicon along the northern part of Italy. The river was unprotected, so he took a huge army and crossed the river, which was something he had never been able to do. So the phrase "crossing the Rubicon" came to me and I realized that there was no turning back. At that time, this was certainly the case in my personal life as well as my professional life. This concept of "crossing the river" or "crossing a chasm" also really works in my business.'

Using your gifts to the fullest

'I met a professor named André Delbecq during my MBA programme at Santa Clara University. He taught two courses: one on Innovation Leadership and Management and the other on Spirituality for Organizational Leaders. I was very impressed with how he taught people to be fully integrated and how to use and work from their gifts. He also taught how to build teams using other people's gifts. I cannot imagine doing the work that I do now without that experience.

'I am a practising Christian and go to church every Sunday. I use my religion as a way to express and nurture my spirituality. My own personal spiritual purpose is to figure out who I am and live that out authentically and to help other people to do the same. To me this means creating a climate where I help someone to discover his or her calling and to seek and hear God's will in it . . . The answer is truly within you, and all of the spiritual methods and processes are designed to help you get quiet enough, fearless enough, coura-geous enough, compassionate enough, loving enough to discover who you really are.

'I have a phrase I really like and that I feel best defines spirituality for me: "Living fully the glory of God is being fully alive". To me this means using your gifts to the fullest, working in a position that is using all of you, and being in true, intimate relationships with other people in the community—all of those things that bring you fully alive. The second element is the aspect of being present. To me this means that, when you are there, you are really there.

'I am looking outside at that beautiful tree and thinking about how spiri-tuality helps me to draw strength from the roots of life. The tree doesn't get nourishment from the leaves. And yet what do we see when we look at the tree? We see the branches and leaves and not the root system. So I think spir-ituality is about defining where our true strength comes from as the root sys-tem. We have a chance to consciously change the wellspring from which we draw our nourishment.'

Praying is one of the ways Nilofer Merchant consciously changes that well-spring. Every morning she prays, *God please shed your light on the work I am to do today and show me what it is you want done. Please help me to serve and act as You with all of the people that I touch.* 'This really does set my priorities in order,' she says.

Raised Islamic—baptized Christian

'At the age of 18, I started living away from my family. I thought at that time that life was just up to me. I was going through a very difficult marital time, and since my husband was raised as a Christian, I thought maybe we should go to church and see if that would help. As a result I had an incredible expe-rience of healing.

'I had been abused as a child, and one of the sermons at my husband's church was based on a book called *A Child Called It*. In a few words, the author described what a wounded person feels like: alienation, separation, etc. I had never so succinctly heard anyone express my experience of life before. Inside I thought, "This is me!" I began to cry and then I heard her say another thing that is still a transforming notion of who I am today: "We can move from a place of fear to a place of love. The things that caused us to be wounded today are things that human people did. But God doesn't do this, and God can love you fully."

'I really did have the self-belief that I deserved the abuse that happened to me, and that I would be wounded for the rest of my life. So you can imagine how powerful these words were to me. It was in those moments that I realized I could live a different life, and I made a choice to do that. I think that I had always wanted a different life, but I had never understood that I would have to give some part of myself up in order to have it. I had to give up being that wounded person, even though at some levels "being wounded" was somewhat comforting and reinforcing. And somehow it always gave me permission to fail.

'I ended up being baptized in an Episcopalian Church, which is highly unusual for someone with an Islamic heritage. I believe that Christianity is one way that I can develop my spirituality, but I don't rely on it entirely.'

Saying what we are afraid to say at work

'I do believe in people's goodness and in the redemption quality of people—that even if they do make a mistake, they can come back tomorrow and do it right. And I think I am often the voice of truth in a group, so that whatever is unsaid I am usually the person who can articulate that. This is how I use my gifts in my work. Many people are afraid to speak their underlying fears, and so I help create a safe environment for them to do that. Once people are able to name these fears, they are able to address them in a whole new way.

'Not long ago, one of my clients with whom I was doing marketing strategy work was at the same time going through an organizational change. The ramifications of the decisions on marketing strategy they were about to make were also going to make a quantum shift in their organization. We were in a group discussion with the Senior Directors, Executive VPs and VPs where everyone was talking about this in a very intellectual way, the way you normally proceed in business. I was well aware that there was lots of tension, which no one was addressing.

'I had really prayed that morning that the group could come to a consensus and use their decision as a positive move forward. I was very quiet for some time as I watched the group, even though I was actually leading the group. I was fully present, and I kept feeling as if there was an important question that needed to be asked. I closed my eyes for a second and when I came back I said, "What is it we are *not* saying? What is it we are *not* addressing?" Because of the way I asked the questions, it created a sense of safety and people were able to respond and say what was true in their hearts.

'Someone who had been very reluctant the whole time spoke up and said, "I am really afraid about what this will mean for my people." It brought the whole group together and people began to step forward and say, "I'll take 50 of your people" and "I can really see your people transitioning into this new organization; we'll take care of them."

'For the first time in that discussion, that Vice President was able to agree to the new organizational structure even though it meant he would be sacrificing his organization. He was able to offer his organization for the benefit of the whole team.'

Looking back on the outcome, Nilofer Merchant reflected: 'I thought about it later I realized that I had no idea those questions were going to come out of my mouth. It was one of those moments where I just offered to the group the gift from my heart that happened to be there. I just happened to be the one who could help them find the truth that was already there. I think this process drew upon people's goodness. I think sometimes we forget that most people really do want to live in alignment with their values, but they just don't know how. So often it's up to the leader to create the environment where people can live their values.'

Helping people manifest their gifts

'When I was managing people while leading in my corporate positions, I always wanted to find a way to use their gifts well. So I often spent time with them personally, rather than on their job duties, and talked to them about what they personally most wanted to do. I would ask them what they felt their natural gifts were. I would then tailor their jobs so that they could use these skills and strengths optimally. In places where their job required them to do something that they just did not really have the gifts to do, I would find someone else on the team to help them. I would create a team around the responsibility, so that they would not fail. I never wanted to spend any energy trying to get a person to do something that they did not want to do. I always wanted to find a way to bring out the person's essence. This has been an important part of my own spiritual development, and I have tried to pass that on as a leader.

'I feel that the greatest thing a leader can do is to help people manifest their gifts fully. Finding out what those gifts are, and helping people to match up well to the job they have, is an important process to me. I also took a long-term view of this and tried to find the best place for the employees in the organization, which sometimes meant that they would not stay in the job they were in. Sometimes I had to create a new role for them and sometimes I helped them to acquire new skills so they could find a new job outside of the company that would be better for them.

'I believe that businesses have the most amount of influence on causing transformational change in society. And then, because there are so many people working in companies, if they were all using their gifts well and serving one another well, just imagine how transforming the organization could be, not only to the employees, but to everyone they touch. I believe that, when people are working to their fullest capacity, they naturally go out and serve society well. Business naturally creates wealth, and I believe it can also naturally create positive social change.'

Nilofer Merchant also spoke about how she herself, at a very personal level, contributes to serving society. 'I go on a regular basis to a homeless shelter and do service. Now I do not think of any separation between me and them. I feel like we are just here together and I can look them in the eye and speak with them with a respect that I would not have had earlier. Before, I would have felt the desire to solve their problems and be of use to them as if I were separate.'

Learning from failure

'I think that the greatest conversion I have had spiritually in my work has to do with the many times in my career where I thought that I was responsible for finding and convincing others of the right answer, and that everything that happened was based on my sheer intelligence. In other words, it was up to me to figure it all out.

'Now that I look back I can see that this type of attitude and behaviour is what caused me to fail the most. Yes, I might have made it through the project okay, but did I really contribute to the organization? Did I really help people to unite around a common vision? To me, this way of operating was not what I would consider to be good leadership on my part.

'Today, I feel that it is much more about working together in a collaborative way. It is much more about inspiring others to use their gifts well. It is really not about me at all; I am just a vehicle. I may be the person with the most resident knowledge, so I will offer that, but I do not own it as if it is solely mine. I no longer feel that I am the one who has to have the right answer. When we all work together and apply our gifts, we will manifest what is right. And whatever it is that I need to learn and offer will manifest itself as well.'

Risk and faith

'Being a spiritual-based leader is much like falling off a cliff. It takes a certain act of faith to believe that you can lead differently than what the outside world might reward. So even though you may feel as if you are falling off a cliff, the arms of God will catch you. However, there will be moments of absolute fear and trepidation, and yet everything will be okay.

'In the past I had never defined myself as a big risk taker. However, as I have walked the path of becoming a spiritual-based leader, I can see the courage that it has taken. To me the greatest definition of courage is to be willing, without any prior knowledge or experience, to take the risk to transform yourself into someone that you have no idea how to become.'

20

S.K. Welling

Executive Director, HMT International Ltd, India

S.K. Welling has been a leader at HMT (Hindustan Machine Tools Ltd) for 32 years, having worked in production engineering, production technology, marketing, business planning, management information systems, restructuring, consumer marketing and international marketing. HMT was founded in 1953 in a technical collaboration with a Swiss engineering company, Derlikon, as a public sector (Indian government owned and regulated) corporation manufacturing machine tools. Since then it has diversified into other fields including watches, tractors, printing machines and other engineering products. Today it is a holding company that comprises six subsidiaries and also manages the tractor business directly; it has 18 manufacturing units in India.

When members of the research group met S.K. Welling in 2002, he was Executive Director of corporate planning and policies at HMT International in Bangalore. This is one of HMT's subsidiaries and is wholly owned by HMT. It markets, manufactures and exports HMT's products, as well as machine tools and other engineering products from firms in India and internationally. S.K. Welling was 55 at the time of the interview.

With regard to his spiritual search, S.K. Welling says, 'My spiritual purpose in life is self-satisfaction. This means I love to be happy and I would like to see the people around me happy, and the community happy. From day one in my career, I have felt love and affection for people. Even as a young man of 23 straight from college, I had nearly 110 workers under me, and that love and affection was already embodied in my system. I got into human relations from this very young age.'

S.K. Welling has a degree in mechanical engineering from India and an MBA from Leeds University in the UK, having been one of only five people selected by the government of India at that time for a Queen Elizabeth scholarship which covered the costs of his studies in England.

S.K. Welling retired in 2004. Since retiring he has carried out international consulting and is a member of the Board of Directors of four companies. In speaking about his retirement, he told us, 'Post-retirement, I am peaceful, happy and contented.'

A leader must have concern for others

I think the ultimate game of business is that we should have happiness for all stakeholders of the business: employees, customers, suppliers and shareholders. The happiness I am talking about is the faith and commitment you must have to achieve something together. The totality of all this happiness is what business is.

Happiness is a key concept in S.K. Welling's perspective on business and success. On a superficial level it includes traditional notions of comfort and wealth: 'A shareholder looks at getting a dividend. Employees are happy when they get some bonuses. A supplier is happy when he is getting a better price from the company or getting payment on time. So each one has that one very narrow circle around them, which gives them happiness.' But it is primarily a concept of happiness based on his spiritual view of life. 'So many leaders try to get the work done by terrorizing people, by shouting at them and by putting fear into them. I am just the opposite of this. I am a people-oriented man,' he says. 'I don't trust sitting in a chair and going on pressing buttons. That is not my style. My style is to care for people in a warm way. I do not care to hurt anyone. As a result, often people will work very hard for me; they will even happily stay and work late.'

'I used to go to the factories and sit with the workers and the union representatives. If there were problems, I would go to that spot and sit there for hours and sort it out, as the General Manager. That is my style—hands-on and a personal touch. I love people. This is one thing that I have that has taken me to this level.

'I have always had an inner feeling that I must do something for people. I feel so much for people that I am willing to sacrifice for others. It comes very natural for me. This feeling has come I am sure from my earlier association with spiritual teachers and the way I was brought up.'

Just as he relates his idea of happiness and satisfaction to his relationships with his employees, when he speaks of his leadership, S.K. Welling frequently uses words seldom heard in the boardroom—words like faith, trust and purity.

Faith and trust and purity

'To me, spirituality is actually purity, and for all this you ultimately have to have devotion. And first of all you must have faith as a leader. I have tremendous faith. And when I say that I have faith I am not just saying faith for faith's sake. So what do I mean by faith? Take for instance a work situation. We have a plan for this company presently. As an individual and as a leader of this company, I must be totally committed to it, and I must totally have faith that the plan will be successfully implemented. That is what I call faith.

'Another thing—I don't know if this comes naturally to me or if I developed it—is that I have tremendous trust. The word mistrust is missing in my dictionary. That is why even sometimes my wife tells me, "Look, any Tom, Dick and Harry you meet, you say he is good." I reply, "I just don't see any negative thing about anybody and that is probably why I can sometimes get in trouble."

'I firmly believe I must improve myself. First of all I have to refine my character, which leads to purity of mind and thoughts. I've been striving all my life to curtail selfishness, jealousy and hatred. All these don't ever come in my mind at all now. This self-effort, which I have developed in myself, has brought me to this platform.

'Ultimately as a human being you like to achieve higher levels of self. I am still not satisfied about where I am with the question which I always ask, "Who am I?" I see the light, but I do not see the full light. I can see a pinhole. That hunger is still there in me. That urge is still there in me. As I look at it, the deeper you get into it, the further you feel you have to go. I do not know where the end is. And I strive for spiritual leadership. Spirituality, in my opinion, is identifying myself with others. It gives me immense strength to be calm and cool with the many problems I have had, especially for the past two years. People and union officers come and bang on the tables and I stay calm.'

Downsizing

Before the liberalization of India's economic structure started in 1991, S.K. Welling as the General Manager of corporate planning at HMT prepared the organization for a major restructuring. This was needed in order to be able to meet the competition that could be expected when Indian firms were to become exposed to an open market economy. Being government owned and regulated, this also meant dealing with a parliamentary committee and many agencies of the government.

'In 1987, I was picked up by the Chairman to head up a small management "think-tank" in his office. We were only about three or four people, who were the eyes and ears of the Chairman. The whole company was massive, with a revenue of around Rs 10 billion (approximately US$750 million at that time) and employing, in those days, 23,000 people. In one of the brainstorming sessions, the Chairman, who was a great visionary, said to me, "Look Mr Welling, it is going on well now, but the environment is not going to be the same for us. Sooner or later, the government has to liberalize. Sooner or later, we have to get into the market economy. You need to prepare this organization for that competition. Today, we are in a closed market; whatever we produce we sell, because it is a seller's market. Tomorrow when it becomes a buyer's market, this company will not be able to address the needs of the market economy." That was three or four years before the liberalization of India's economic structure.'

S.K. Welling then told us about his leadership of the painful transition phase that followed when liberalization led to previously unknown competition. 'The company was in extremely bad shape. Losses were mounting. Net worth had eroded. There was absolutely no money in the company. I said to myself, "The only thing to do now is to again rise from the dust and make a turnaround plan for the whole company." Since my spiritual basis is seeking purity of character for myself and for others, in the turnaround plan I was looking to "purify" every area that I addressed. This purification was required in the company because of the complacency of operating in a closed economy and the refusal of the top people to change their mind-sets.'

As General Manager, S.K. Welling formulated a plan where a major aspect was manpower rationalization. Looking back on what happened, he recalls the personal dilemma he faced. 'With a very heavy heart I had to reduce our manpower. Sending people home without a security net, in a country like India, is something that really touched my heart. I was not totally convinced about sending people home knowing fully well that they would be in trouble. Even today as a Director I still believe that we should create more jobs by doing something rather than sending people home. This downsizing, I must admit, caused a big conflict between my inner self and my outer self, but, in order to keep the whole, I had to accept that we had to let a part of it go. We made a voluntary retirement scheme to reduce manpower. We identified 6,500 people to receive the golden handshake and leave the company.'

'It took me 14 months to do a total turnaround plan for this company—to get the whole thing formulated and to get it through the management, the board and the government. When the turnaround plan was implemented, even though I was the architect and author I didn't project myself as the main person. I never said that I did it. I always do things and withdraw to the back. This is what has happened throughout my career in this company.'

Competition and confidence in difficult times

'In 1994, the watch business group was doing very badly, and I was asked to take over. We had started with hand-wound watches in the 1960s and had absolutely no competition. People used to line up in queues when the new watches arrived in stores. Only Indian watches were available in the country, and ours were among the best. When competition came in during the 1990s, we started losing focus, and the whole thing was choked up when I took over. If something wasn't done, people might lose their jobs and this part of the company might even be shut down.

'I really had a tough time. First of all, I was new to marketing and watches. I had to spend 16 to 18 hours a day for the first six months to get the whole thing going, virtually taking a broom and sweeping the whole thing clean. From shambles it came up to a very high level. In three years, the sales picked up considerably, the product range improved and sales doubled. We sold nearly ten million watches in three years.'

'In the first year after I took over (as Executive Director in HMT International in 1998), the financial measure of "value added per employee" doubled. The people increased the productivity by three times. So I tackled the root part of it. It is the people who have to be focused on. You may have the world's best strategies, but they must be implemented with people. If you want your business strategy to succeed, you should address the seed cause or the root cause of success: the people themselves. The results follow by themselves. In this spirit, we doubled the profits and doubled the dividends. The roots—the people—have been watered using spirituality. But I don't announce the spirituality. I never use the word spirituality when I talk about it.'

Pressure from two sides

'While I've been the Executive Director of HMT International, there has been an internal advertisement put out to recruit and fill some open positions within the international division. There were several people whom the Chairman wanted to have placed into these positions as a favour to him.

'The day the interviews were called, the union leaders came to my office, about 20 of them, in order to put pressure on me not to hire these specific people. I called them all into my office, and they began to shout and tell me why two of these people should not be hired because of pressure from the Chairman.

'I first told them: "You should leave this to me. I will not accept these two just because there is pressure from the Chairman. Nor will I not take these two fellows just because you are saying that I should not take them. I will apply my own judgement, and I will only go by the merits in each case. I will see how they fare in the interview and where they stand and I will take my decision from that. If you think that I am going to take them based on pressure from the Chairman, you are wrong. I am the last one to do that. I would resign and go away instead. And just because you are saying that I should not take these two fellows, I will not bow to your pressure either. I will not work under pressure from either of you."

'Once I said this, they all calmed down. Then I invited them to sit and have coffee, and we were able to talk harmoniously.

'When they first came loudly and agitatedly to my office, I knew I didn't need a personnel man to help me with this. Instead, I needed to clear their doubts myself. Because of the spiritual feelings I have inside, I knew immediately when they came that they didn't mean anything against me; they just wanted to show their strength, *vis-à-vis* what they were feeling against the Chairman. They could not go and do this show with the Chairman, so they came to me.

'I knew this very well in my heart, and as such, I could anticipate what was about to happen. Without this perspective, most people in my position would have been very frightened by this display from about 20 union leaders, and likely would have called for the security officer and the personnel manager before going to meet with them. But since I had the inner feeling that they meant no harm to me, I had no reason to be concerned.'

Spiritual confidence

'I have often thought about how I became successful, or appear to have become successful, when I have been shifted to so many areas within the company that I did not know anything about. I have always believed that spiritual confidence has augmented my professional competence.

'My spiritual vision for business is to convert resources into goods and services that benefit the larger interest of society and mankind. We must view our business from a larger sense: we have employees who also have families; we have suppliers who have their own factories and employees; then we have the customers who also have their own families. We are all touching each other and interacting.

'In the past, we as a company have spent a large amount of money on our people. Sometimes we may have even overdone it. But now, if we add this cost to our products, we cannot be competitive. This question of how we view our business in an open market economy has become very challenging and I have not found the answers that I want as of yet. This is the problem I am now facing and looking into: doing business in today's context and doing business in the true context of spiritual values.'

Section 5

Divinity

In this section

In this section you will meet four spiritual-based leaders, two each from the USA and India, all of whom underscore the role of surrendering their will to that of 'God', the 'Divine', the 'Transcendent'. You will meet a mentor on spirituality and leadership to Silicon Valley CEOs; the HR Director of a major Indian media group; a Senior Partner at one of India's largest providers of professional services (accounting, auditing, taxation, governance, risk management . . .); and the Vice President of Spiritual Care and Values Integration at a major hospital in the USA. Here you will meet:

André L. Delbecq, Director, Institute for Spirituality and Organizational Leadership, Santa Clara University, USA

In *Willing to be God's fool*, Dr André Delbecq explains the difficulties he faced in preparing the first programme on Spirituality in Business Leadership and of his 'prior arrogance born of defensiveness. Your whole sense of self builds on your expertise developed over years of scholarly effort. Fortunately, I had begun to understand that this spiritual path required me to give up the need to be the expert. Once having accepted this truth, everything I needed was given to me. People whom I had never met found out about my efforts and provided constant new resources.'

Ashoke Maitra, HR Director, Bennett, Coleman & Co. Ltd (The Times of India Group), India

In *Manifestation of latent divinity*, Ashoke Maitra tells about experiences from the *Times of India* as well as about leading the merger of two petrochemical companies that for years had fought each other. 'I knew my job was to take people out of grief. Throughout the merger process, I chose to create a spiritual connection so that they could learn to relate with each other as divine beings, rather than employees of two different companies. This resulted in integration at the spiritual level. We had one of the smoothest mergers of two competitive petrochemical companies in the history of India.'

V.V. Ranganathan, Senior Partner, Ernst & Young, India

In *Seeing God in everyone*, V.V. Ranganathan says, 'I heard someone telling me this a long, long time ago: The first thing to realize is: "There is God, God is on earth, God is in you, and God is in everyone." If you are able to work in that context, it completely changes the way you look at people and then you start sharing that invisible bond.' He used that perspective at Ernst & Young, India in handling a grievous employee error as well as in coaching clients and colleagues.

Thomas Daugherty, Vice President of Spiritual Care and Values Integration, Methodist Health Care System, USA

In *Connecting with the Divine*, Dr Thomas Daugherty explains, 'I conceptualize spirituality as the connection among myself, other people and the Divine. Spirituality is also staying connected with my own spiritual centre, my connection with the Divine and then listening to what I hear there. I do believe that the Divine is both transcendent and immanent.' That spirit of transcendence plus immanence shaped how he overtly brought spirituality into the corporate culture of the health care system.

21

André L. Delbecq

Director, Institute for Spirituality and Organizational Leadership, Santa Clara University, USA

Since this book is about spiritual-based leadership in business, it may at first glance appear to be inconsistent to present a professor. But Dr André L. Delbecq is no ordinary professor. He is also Director of the Institute for Spirituality and Organizational Leadership at Santa Clara University, California, USA. He is probably the most influential academic in the USA (and perhaps in the rest of the West) with respect to teaching and lecturing on spirituality for business leadership. Twice a year he runs a seminar called 'Spirituality for Business Leadership' where the students are both MBA students and leaders of hi-tech firms from Silicon Valley.

His teachings have strongly influenced leaders who have searched for a way to integrate their spirituality with their business practices; two of the leaders profiled in this book have referred to the inspiration and knowledge he provided:

This course offered me a wonderful opportunity for deep immersion into spirituality. It had an enormous syllabus; I read for about a year and am still reading today. My spiritual studies are the best moments of my day.

—Ricardo B. Levy

I was very impressed with how he taught people to be fully integrated and how to use and work from their gifts. He also taught how to build teams using other people's gifts. I cannot imagine doing the work that I do now without that experience.

—Nilofer Merchant

When asked about how he nurtures his spirituality, Professor Delbecq spoke about turning everything into prayer: 'In the Christian tradition, there is the discipline referred to as "living in the presence of God". It is the belief that one should commence each task conscious of God's presence, much as a Buddhist seeks to enter each task "with a beginner's mind". The intent is to be fully present to the next task, to be fully present to the next person one meets, and to be present with purity of intention that by doing so the task or relationship is turned into prayer.'

André Delbecq not only talks about leadership as a professor; from 1979 until 1989 he was Dean of the university's School of Business. Santa Clara University, with more than 8,000 students, is a Jesuit Catholic university located in California's Silicon Valley. He told us: 'I think God makes good use of each of us. The fact that I—a former Dean of the Fellows of the Academy of Management, (the oldest and largest scholarly management association in the world), a former member of the Board of Directors of the Academy, a former president of both the Mid-West and Western Divisions of the Academy of Management, a former Executive Director of the Organizational Behavior Teaching Society, a senior scholar with a reputation for rigorous conceptualization—was entering this new field did provide courage to others.'

Willing to be God's fool

We need to study the lives of noble and good business leaders to inspire the next generation of business leaders. That the spiritual can be integrated with, is not separate from, the secular is an important affirmation for the MBA students and executives who spend time with me at Santa Clara University. They begin to understand with greater certitude that it is in the 'now' of the everyday-ness of their leadership efforts that the spiritual journey is lived and unfolds, if being an orga-

nizational leader is their vocational calling. The spiritual journey is engaged as they struggle with their daily tasks including the boring, the mundane, the frustrating, the agonising and the rewarding.

André Delbecq recalls: 'I was 26 years old when I received my doctorate from the Indiana University School of Business, which is very young for completing a PhD My interest has always been how innovation can be introduced in complex systems.' He told us that his efforts to understand innovation were predominantly oriented towards the public sector so that 'when I came to Northern California in 1979, to an area now known as Silicon Valley, I had had very little prior contact with private sector business. I now found myself in the most dynamic business region in the world.'

'The business leaders in Silicon Valley obviously knew something about managing change that other organizational scholars and I didn't understand. Consequently, I arrived accepting the position as the Dean of the Business School at Santa Clara University with humility. My continued scholarship during the decade I served as Dean would be devoted to discovering how Silicon Valley organizations created structures and processes that allowed such exceptional rates of innovation.

'It was only in 1998 that I began to engage in a systematic study of spirituality. Prior to that, I had been teaching a seminar where senior leaders came to the campus and entered into dialogue with the MBAs. These and other leaders continued to ask why our university did not have a course that probed the inner life of the leader. Because of their insistent request for such an offering, and inspired by some colleagues who had earlier been engaged in the study of spirituality within the Academy of Management, I finally accepted the "call" to examine the emerging interest in workplace spirituality. I devoted a sabbatical in 1999 to studying at the Graduate Theological Union in Berkeley, California.

'As part of my sabbatical, because so many of our students at Santa Clara were from the East, I knew it would be important to study Buddhism, Hinduism, and Taoism, and not simply my own Christian tradition. I had never read in depth about any of these Eastern traditions. So I began reading both Eastern and Western literature.

'As my understanding grew, I began to put together an outline for a seminar for business leaders. I certainly was not operating out of confidence, but at this point I had discovered what it meant to surrender. Anything I was going to do had to depend on God and not me. I don't remember where I first read the phrase "willing to be God's fool", but, for the first time in my life, I was willing to be God's fool. Now this is a tough thing for a senior academic.

Your whole sense of self builds on your expertise developed over years of scholarly effort. Yet here I was preparing to teach in a new arena of knowledge where I was still a novice. To understand this you would have had to know of my prior arrogance born of defensiveness; of all the psychic walls I had built to avoid ever being an intellectual fool. I was really stepping off a high cliff, where I knew I could completely fail in this new endeavour.'

Everything I needed was given to me

'Fortunately, I had begun to understand that this spiritual path required me to give up the need to be the expert. Once having accepted this truth, preparation for teaching the seminar unfolded with constant surprises. Everything I needed was given to me. People whom I had never met found out about my efforts and provided constant new resources. So the knowledge I needed began to arrive through others.

'When I had finished my year-and-a-half of study and preparation, I invited nine of the very best CEOs that I knew in Silicon Valley together with nine MBA students. They were to participate in an initial test of the spirituality seminar for organizational leaders. Twelve individuals, equally distributed between the two groups, accepted the invitation.

'The night before I was to deliver my first seminar session, my wife asked me if I was afraid. I told her I wasn't afraid—I was terrified. I had never said "God" before in a public place, and here I was about to commence teaching a seminar where God must be the centre of what the seminar was all about.

'This initial alpha test of the seminar was very successful. Although I was not aware that it would be the case when I began this programme of teaching and scholarship, there was clearly great readiness on the part of both practising professionals and academics to commence addressing matters of spirituality.

'Today I continue to teach a seminar called "Spirituality for Business Leadership" twice a year at Santa Clara University. I also lead an institute that facilitates dialogue between executives, theologians and management scholars. I am active in the Management, Spirituality and Religion Interest Group of the Academy of Management. But it is important to note that this focus on spirituality constituted a major career shift.'

Reflecting on his reluctance to use the "G" word in public, André Delbecq thinks back on his experience at the American Academy of Management; he told us: 'There are two things I never thought I would see in my lifetime: one was the fall of the Russian empire, and the other was hearing the word God spoken of in the Academy of Management.'

Inner peace in trying times

'The path that unfolds as I teach the spirituality seminar at the university flows out of my own deep beliefs regarding the spiritual path of leadership integrated with a Christian perspective. The seminar commences by examining the presence of God in all things. So we reflect and meditate on the way in which God acts in the contemporary organization. We consider its role in providing products and services that are needed by human kind; how human gifts and talents are energized within the organization, the presence or absence of a supportive community within its culture, the experience of justice or injustice, the charisma of wealth creation, and the manner in which society is supported through both taxes and philanthropy that is a fruit of wealth creation. We also look at potential or real darkness in organizations, without giving power to the darkness.

'We then turn to the notion of leadership as a calling. We reflect on each person's unique gifts, and affirm who they are in their "essential *be*-ing", and what they feel calling in "*do*-ing" through the expression of their leadership. Participants begin to listen gently without being overly scrutinizing and compulsive to the presence of God in the day-to-day-ness of their organizational leadership. Even if they have a sense that they may be moving to another organizational setting in the future, they discover that their spiritual journey is in the "now" of their present work setting.

'We later look at the great temptations of organizational leadership: hubris (exaggerated pride) and greed. We study the spiritual disciplines and virtues that offset these darknesses.

'The only way I have found to deepen the consciousness of self and organization within the context of leadership is through meditative/contemplative practice. If you grow in awareness without simultaneously being able to surrender to the Divine, the experience is too overwhelming. I think that a leader cannot be a leader very long without turning to prayer, however one defines it. I believe we need contemplative communities that pray for organizational leaders. At Santa Clara we have formed a meditation community, The Community of Joseph, and we meet for three hours every week for intense prayer on behalf of organizational leaders. Members of the community are primarily executives.

'It is wonderful to watch the increased inner peace of the MBA students and executives who spend time with me at Santa Clara University, even when they have a day that in the past they would have considered to be a day of misery. They develop the capacity to see that even struggles have meaning. They find that there is something to learn in every moment, and, by remaining in touch with their inner peace even during trials, they are able to bring a different presence to the challenges. They know all too well that without spiritual awareness such challenges would lead to burnout and dysfunction. So spirituality is no longer a separate part of their lives; it is no longer peripheral to their leadership.'

Spiritual view of life

Having spoken so eloquently on the path that led him to where he is now, we asked André Delbecq to reflect on his own understanding of spirituality. 'Spirituality,' he says, 'is particular to the individual. The journey is undertaken in light of your own personality, life history, education, spiritual tradition or non-tradition. It is that personal journey of entering into becoming the true self. The fruit of becoming is always a change in what you do. The test of spirituality is increased compassion and a new way of being present to and touching others.

'So, for me, spirituality is less a matter of definition; it is more a matter of sharing our deep, lived inner experience that one taps into and draws from in every aspect of life, including professional/organizational efforts. The spiritual journey includes the choices you make in the unfolding inner journey. True spirituality seeks to avoid any dualism between the inner self and outer action. Our actions dealing with the secular and mundane are part of the spiritual journey.'

We asked André Delbecq, coming as he does from a Jesuit University, if he distinguished between spirituality and religion. He replied: 'Spirituality and religion are, of course, not the same. Religion encompasses the belief system associated with a world view, patterns of worship and ritual prayer, and brings together a community that shares a particular spiritual path and disciplines. Spirituality, in contrast, is specific to the individual, and encompasses each person's lived experience. Each individual's world view is never exactly the same as another's, even if they share the same "religion", since no two individuals have the same DNA, parents, life experiences, etc.'

When we asked him if he could concisely express his spiritual view of life in a theme, he replied: ' "Wonder" is the theme that naturally comes to me. I have always loved innovation because I am continuously thrilled to see what was once only imagined emerge as an institutionalized reality. I have always had and continue to retain a great excitement associated with building collaboration between bright minds seeking to understand a complex problem and engaged in the discovery of a creative solution. But now my sense of wonder is enlarged. My eyes are opened to how the unimaginable emerges in all of creation—for example, in nature in a blossoming flower, in the movements of the tides and the mysteries of the sea. The world is filled with wonder, echoing the limitlessness of the transcendent.

'I have always had a good sense of adventure,' he continued. 'I love boating, motorcycling and travel and I am willing to take risks. But in the past these activities have been something that I felt I had to work hard at, something I mistakenly thought depended primarily on me. Now I see such efforts as tapping into a mysterious abundance. I realize how little I do. This is not to diminish the importance of what each person does, but rather to increasingly see how God, the transcendent mystery that bears a thousand names, is at work in people and in nature.

'This allows for increased inner joy even in the midst of the greatest difficulties. Of course I still have days of great unknowing; I still sometimes experience desolation and anguish. Yet even these experiences don't disturb a deep core sense of peace and wonder as my spiritual journey unfolds. It's as if the fire just gets brighter and brighter as my life unfolds.

'In the past, I would have talked about my spiritual purpose in the context of my profession. I love being an academic. But, in these more senior years, I am much more content to let God be God, and am increasingly content to simply be in the presence of God without feeling that I always need to be doing something for Him, or anyone else. Yes, I am invited to play a part, but I increasingly realize I am not such a major player as I once thought I was. I feel privileged to be a modest contributor, but I know the world isn't awaiting my every word and accomplishment. I now understand God is the master builder so to speak. So I am able to both "be" and "do", whereas I would have defined myself mostly in terms of "*do*-ing" and less in terms of "*be*-ing" before my spiritual journey deepened.

'This has also changed the way I teach. I know who is truly in charge of the universe now. It is actually very liberating, because I do appreciate what I am called to do and I still have a great sense of joy in it; but I have much less of a concern about being the symphony leader and am simply happy to play my instrument when it is appropriate.'

Purpose of business

Professor Delbecq reflected on the purpose of business as seen from a worldly, commercial perspective, and from a spiritual perspective. 'I think a business exists to provide an innovative and compelling answer to a societal need in the form of a needed service or product. The successful "solution" encompassed by the product or service must be innovative in the sense that it continually seeks a solution at the edge of unfolding technology, and/or is efficient in a solution that encompasses high quality at a low price avoiding waste. So to me this is the discipline of business. This is what we ask of the business organization, and this is how we should judge business organizations.

'When this purpose is approached through a spiritual lens, it will be shaped differently in many ways. The needs you start becoming attentive to shift. You become willing to let go of many trivial and opportunistic concerns, and instead increasingly put energy into important challenges. The transformational system you create to receive inputs and transform outputs will also shift, allowing greater attention to stewardship, justice and inclusiveness of the concerns of all stakeholders. The character of the organization's culture will shift. The relational culture of the organization will be more attentive to the gifts of all, and compassionate regarding each person's needs. Your own willingness as a business leader to endure the mystery of suffering will shift. For example, your tolerance regarding the discipline of having to meet Wall Street's expectations about profitability will shift. You will see all the elements of business challenges as part of a calling to service.

'Because of this deeper perspective regarding the nature of business, a sense of patience and a greater willingness to endure hardship unfolds. All of the struggles of business leadership as a form of societal service take on a very different coloration when they are seen from a spiritual perspective. Servant leadership now becomes a reality.'

22

Ashoke Maitra

HR Director, Bennett, Coleman & Co. Ltd (The Times of India Group), India

Ashoke Maitra, head of Human Resources at the Times of India Group, was 45 at the time of the interview. As a youngster he grew up with a spiritual focus to his life, keeping the company of sages, studying the world's well-known spiritual texts, and performing service activities. At 17, his life's mission was to become a monk. However, after a year and a half in the Ramakrishna Mission—where the training period to be a monk is nine years—one of the priests advised him to go back to his scholastic career: 'You are not fully convinced that you want to lead this life; you are partly convinced, but this is not a matured reaction.'

So he left the mission to attend to his university studies. After getting his degrees he entered the world of business, all the while nurturing the deep roots of his spirituality; he can best be described as a monk in a corporate setting.

Almost seven years prior to the interview, he joined Bennett, Coleman & Co. Ltd, known as the Times of India Group. This is a private company owned by a spiritually inclined family. He is not only head of Human Resources for the entire group (comprising 7,000 employees, 12 factories, 10 retail shops, 12 radio stations, Internet, Times Music, Multi-Media and related media enterprises), he also heads up the Times Foundation, the goal of which is to create consciousness for building an effective civil society and to act as a point of convergence for NGOs, industries and the government to bring policy-level changes in the government.

The purpose that has permeated his career in HR is 'promoting human excellence'—which for him means spiritual fulfilment. He says, 'My goal in life is to manifest the Divinity in myself and in every person. I may do it by yoga—karma yoga (path of action), bhakti yoga (path of devotion) or jnana yoga (path of wisdom). Or, I may do it by teaching, training or being a carpenter. What matters to me spiritually is to give expression to the Divinity that is perceived as dormant, but is actually alive in each person.'

Ashoke Maitra has a bachelor's degree in history from Delhi University and a master's degree in social sciences from Tata Institute of Social Sciences in India. Before he joined the Times of India Group he held leadership positions at major Indian corporations: the Tata Group, Mudra Communications and NOCIL. In 2003, due to an employee training programme that Ashoke Maitra developed and conducted on 'Self Mastery', the *Times of India* received one of the International Spirit at Work Awards.

We were in contact with Mr Maitra again in summer of 2006. He informed us that he left the Times of India Group in 2004 to dedicate his life to his chosen gurus, Sri Ramakrishna Paramahamsa and Swami Vivekananda, and to conduct work based on their teachings. In 2005 he founded the Centre for Human Resource Development providing consulting services in Human Capital Management and Organizational Development, and in 2006 he founded Sri Ramakrishna International Institute of Management, which he describes as a 'movement in Holistic Management Education and Training for working professionals.'

Manifestation of latent divinity

The Times of India Group is the market leader in every product that we are in, by huge margins. We are making huge profits, and in our debt–equity ratio there is no debt, only equity. How has all of this happened? It has happened because we are concerned about the human beings and their happiness. We are helping them, through spiritual methods, to know their latent divinity and they are feeling much happier with themselves, with their work, and with their lives.

Ashoke Maitra has had a fast-track career. After his one and a half years of training in the Ramakrishna Mission to be a priest, and after completing his bachelor's and master's degrees, he chose to work in Human Resources 'because that was closest to me: I love teaching, training, being with human beings, and working with human beings.'

His first position was with the Tata Group, and during the ten years he spent there, he quickly climbed the corporate ladder, becoming a General Manager at the age of 29. While at Tata he was also the executive assistant to the legendary J.R.D. Tata. When he left Tata he became General Manager (Corporate) at Mudra Communications Ltd (the third largest advertising agency in India at the time), looking after corporate affairs and organization development. After Mudra, and before joining The Times of India Group, Ashoke Maitra was head of Human Resources at NOCIL, a Royal Dutch Shell company.

Increasing bliss

Ashoke Maitra is clearly proud of his leadership at The Times of India Group, where he has been for almost seven years. 'My name is Ashoke,' he says, 'which means "one without grief", so I made my name our "core" value. We said that the only thing we will do is to create "grieflessness" or "increase bliss". To my mind if a person is joyful, happy and inspired, then only can that person reach the highest level of productivity and performance.

'A business house fulfils a very important need for human beings to live an active life; it provides a job, prestige and a status in society. If this business house also helps them to realize their ultimate purpose in life, their true worth and a new self-concept, then I think it is doing a lot of good for them. As we help each employee realize his or her own potential, then their productivity goes up and they themselves get the benefit.

'The old Western school of management that prescribed control as a major function has given way to leadership through mentoring, coaching, developing and counselling. You can only do your best when you are in a state of equipoise; when you are composed, happy and willing to give to others.

'In our company anyone who joins goes through a programme, where we basically de-school them. We provide them with inputs to manage themselves by teaching them how to control their body and mind, how to be detached, and how to present themselves powerfully.

'We tell them that the ego that you have, the degrees which you have received, are fine as long as you use them as instruments to give you some level of comfort, which all of us need. But if you get married to them and think that is what life is all about, then that is the greatest foolishness, because you are not that. Those are instruments that you need, just like you need food to survive; however, you are not the food.

'So our work is completely experiential; we do not give any lectures. We do exercise after exercise after exercise to help people analyse and understand the meaning of "true joy". We are telling people that, "Yes, you have joined an industry. Yes, you need your children, family, a certain amount of technology, and money to survive in life. Yes, you must have that, but this is not all there is. Your true joy will come in your own spiritual realization."

'The first level of orientation we do is on "bliss" and "self-perfection". The second level that we do is to control and integrate our body and mind. The third level of work we do is to examine the values and mental balance. All of this has to do with your original self. We tell them, do not bother about this industry; the *Times of India* will exist even without you. It has existed for 164 years; it may exist another 164 years with or without you. You look at yourself. If you are happy, not by the cars and houses you have, but by your own self, then anywhere you go you will be happy. We are not even telling them to stay in this company. We are saying that you be happy, not by material rewards, you be happy internally.'

Seeing your divinity

'My definition of spirituality is that each soul is potentially divine. I believe that I am not the body, I am the soul. Spirituality is all about introspection. It is a process, a process of awakening. God is the source of spirituality and society makes us un-spiritual. Our regular worldly education process does not allow you to see your divinity. Its goal is to cram lots of knowledge into you. To me, this kind of system has lost consciousness.

'Spirituality is only a going-back to where we started. We go from purity to impurity in life and, if consciousness dawns, then we go back to purity.

'I don't try to analyse myself, because for me life is a journey. I only know that one day I will die and before that I want to do as much good as I can for the society. What is the need for me to analyse where I am, because I don't want to gain anything in the first place? I am very happy with what I already have. I have never wanted anything and whatever has happened to me is by God's grace.

'To my mind, religion is a reflection of spirituality. It is a comment on spirituality. It is like the way we comment about things in the newspaper. It is a comment piece about a self-realized soul. There was a person who was self-realized, who said something that someone found to be intrinsically true.

Then they did a knowledge management job and captured it as an expert system and it became a religion. Then the self-realized followers went and spread it. And it became a community or a religion.'

Profitability and purity

Speaking of the experiential learning that characterizes the work of the HR department, he says: 'I am conducting these workshops in order to increase human productivity, which for me means increasing human excellence. While I do have to promise the owner of the Times Group that this programme will increase productivity and performance, resulting in profitability, that is not the focus of my goal. That is a by-product; it is going to happen in any case. My goal for each individual is that they manifest their latent divinity and become happier. I know that when an individual is happier and more joyful, his/her productivity is bound to go up.

'It is also our goal to make our readers' lives more meaningful and give some benefit to their life. Different levels of people have different levels of consciousness; therefore we have to straddle across many different audiences. We are using the Khajuraho temple as a model for our newspaper layout. If you go to the Khajuraho temple there are a lot of erotic statues outside, but once you go inside to the sanctum sanatorium there is no eroticism. So in our newspaper we take people from the gross to the subtle. This is why we have the *Speaking Tree* and *Inner Voice* as spiritual columns in the centre of our newspaper. We have also started a *Goodwill* column on the second page that reports all of the good things that are happening in society.

'People are born pure, then they travel to impurity because of our society and its education. Now, in our organization we are trying to get them back to the purity they had at birth.

'When we have a reputation for being a good corporate citizen, it reduces our costs. When we are seen as philanthropists, when we are seen as spiritual, when we are good to this world, our own costs go down. The image works as currency. As a newspaper, if we increase literacy, we have more people to buy and read our newspaper. For us to include society makes business sense.

'We went into the Internet business in a big way and the whole dotcom market crashed. However, we did not sack a single person. We put them into other ventures. When the government closed down our radio channel, we didn't sack anyone. We put them into our retailing shops where they did announcements, talked to customers, all kinds of hand-holding exercises. We knew that we would start a radio station again in the future and that these employees would be useful.

'Now we have some of the best radio jockeys from the old team and today when competition is offering them three times the salary, those very employees are refusing the offers. Why? Because we stood by them when they needed us most.'

Creating alignment

'When I came to the Times Group, there was a big fight between the journalists and the management and they each had major criticisms of each other. I knew I had to create a clear alignment and integration of these two groups as we were all working for the same paper and for the same purpose.

'The first thing I did was to come and sit here in the editor's cabin. This is the journalist area of the *Times of India*; this is not the management floor. When I came and sat here, the first thing they asked me was, "How can you come and sit here? You are from the other side." I said, "But I thought we were all on the same side." They said, "No." So I said, "Fine, I am sitting here and if you hate me I will go away. But it is your choice. I have made my first move to show you that we are all one, because that is what I believe." After 15 days I asked them whether I should stay or go. They asked me to stay. They were very happy that a management man was there because, if nothing else, I would at least make sure the bathrooms were clean. I have now been on this floor for over six years.

'During the early days I held a strategic planning workshop. Because there was a lot of misunderstanding between the journalists and management, I felt there was an acute need to bring them together through a participatory process to create a sense of well-being, understanding and camaraderie between them. After all, all of us worked for the same cause.

'My colleagues, who are Directors, in fact were very critical. They opined I was wasting my time trying to change the behaviour of journalists, based on their past record. Even the owner of the Times Group warned me that the journalists would not attend. The first person to walk into the workshop was the resident editor of the *Times of India* and then came the *Economic Times* editor. Someone asked one of the editors why she came and she said, "I came because Ashoke called me and I know Ashoke doesn't see any difference between the management and journalists. If anyone else had called, I would not have come." All the editors came and all the managers came and we had a three-day workshop to decide the future of the company. It worked. I am happy.'

Merging competitive companies

From 1988 to 1994, prior to joining the Times of India Group, Ashoke Maitra was head of Human Resources for the Indian petrochemical company NOCIL which was partly owned by Royal Dutch Shell. Due to a lack of trust between Shell and NOCIL, their ways parted. When NOCIL was merged with another petrochemical company, PIL, Ashoke Maitra stayed with this newly merged company.

'The two companies were culturally very different and were organized very differently,' he says. 'One had seven levels of management and the other had 19. There was a lot of hatred between these two companies because for years they had fought each other to prove who was better. Now one of the companies was merging into the other and would be losing their identity. I was the HR person for NOCIL, which was the surviving company, and I had to lead this merger.

'The structure, systems, staffing, style of management, etc., were widely different in both of the companies. The people in NOCIL were angry and wrote "NO PIL" instead of NOCIL: They replaced the letter "C" with "P". Similarly PIL employees were losing their identity; therefore, they were also equally upset.

'The first thing I realized was that I must not identify myself with either company, while at the same time taking full ownership of my HR position and responsibilities. You see, I knew my job, even back then, was to take people out of grief. I knew I had to be involved in it, but out of it. I began to read the spiritual texts as much as possible in order to school myself on being detached with equipoise.

'Throughout the merger process, I chose to create a spiritual connection so that they could learn to relate with each other as divine beings, rather than employees of two different companies. We created 44 task force teams and with each team did a retreat-style workshop for two days in which we taught self-mastery: the art and science of taking responsibility for oneself and learning to stay at equipoise, centred in one's existence.

'The retreat had a tremendous healing effect and allowed people to detach themselves from the current reality and look at life from a fresh positive perspective. This resulted in integration at the spirit level, and after that individuals from both sides started working together and were able to evolve a new vision, mission and values policy for the company.

'I think the reason they accepted what I said is because they saw I was not concerned about the company; I was concerned about them and their grief. I managed to get people together through a participatory process, to develop respect and positive feelings for each other. I believe that if I had not been detached and acted with equipoise, I could never have achieved this. My transparency and credibility had to be grounded on my spiritual foundation because people knew I was a spiritual person.

'We had one of the smoothest mergers of two competitive petrochemical companies in the history of India. We had no press reference, even though we could have been the centre of attention in the news at that time.'

23

V.V. Ranganathan

Senior Partner, Ernst & Young, India

At the time of the interview, V.V. Ranganathan was 53 years old and Senior Partner in the India branch of Ernst & Young[1] in New Delhi. He told us of the many
'hats' he wore there: 'I started as an audit partner with a large number of clients,
and an equally large number of people working for me. But slowly I was drawn
into the overall management of the firm wearing a lot of hats. Today I handle
only a very few clients, who are mostly international and multinational companies. I am a member of the executive team that helps manage the firm. I am
also the national risk management partner for the firm. I spend a large part of
my time as the National Director for the Entrepreneur-of-the-Year programme.
I am also a member of the team that runs the World Entrepreneur programme.

'Yes,' he said, 'this is quite a handful, but I have learned, over a period of time,
not to panic. I have a firm belief that God Almighty will take care of things and
that things will happen with or without me. I feel that my spiritual purpose is to
be a person who performs selfless actions. Yes, God has given me the equipment to pursue my desires, but I must do so in such a manner that I remember
the principles of karma (cause and effect) and that my decisions are not fuelled
by selfishness or egoism. What I mean is that my effort and involvement in

---

1 Ernst & Young is a global provider of professional services (including accounting and auditing, tax reporting and advisory, business risk services, etc.). In fiscal year 2005 it had 107,000
employees at 700 locations in 140 countries, and revenues of US$16.9 billion.

doing something is not determined or driven by what I get in return. And I know from my own experience that this works.'

We were in contact with V.V. Ranganathan again in summer 2006, and he told us, 'I recently stepped down as a Senior Partner of the firm to give more time to matters that are closer to my heart.' These include founding Pinnacle Opportunities, a non-profit organization that helps build capacities and accreditation to non-profits that run projects in rural education, health and employment, and chairing a product-incubation company, Compassites, designed to help budding entrepreneurs to develop and grow their ideas into products or solutions.

Prior to his time at Ernst & Young, India, V.V. Ranganathan had leadership positions for about 15 years, including six years as Manager at Arthur Young & Co. (one of the eight global accounting firms at that time), in the Middle East, and four years as Partner and Director of an accounting firm in South Africa. He has a Bachelor of Commerce degree from Sacred Heart College, India, and he is a Fellow of the Institute of Chartered Accountants of India.

Seeing God in everyone

I heard someone telling me this a long, long time ago: 'The first thing to realize is: There is God, God is on earth, God is in you, and God is in everyone.' To me this is a wonderful way of looking at humanity. If you are able to work in that context, it completely changes the way you look at people and then you start sharing that invisible bond. The realization that the personality is different from the power that drives the personality started gaining ground in me.

After qualifying for his accounting exam in 1978, V.V. Ranganathan went to work for a large steel plant in India. Later he worked for a large accounting company, Arthur Young & Co., in Kuwait. 'I was 26 years old at that time and had quite a wonderful experience with this very large firm. I was able to work with seven different nationalities in various countries and began to understand the Arab way of life. I went to their university and learned a little bit of Arabic. Then I started reading the Quran to understand what it was all about. While in the Middle East, I did a lot of work in Europe, the UK, the USA, the

Far East, and all around the world. I reached a stage in the organization where I should have been given more responsibilities, but they had a policy in those days that only Arabs or Whites could be partners in the firm. Since there wasn't the possibility for my career to progress in the firm, I returned to India in 1986. I had been in the Middle East for six years.

'I married, and we began to set up our life in Bangalore. Companies began to invite me to be on their boards. In the midst of all of this, my younger brother, who was just 32 years old, suddenly died. So I dropped everything and left Bangalore to be with my parents in Kerala (state in the south of India). I stayed with them for six months. This gave me a lot of space to do introspection and to look into the mysteries of life. I had a lot of ambitions, and this experience of my brother's death put a lot of things into perspective. Then I said that I must carry on with my life.

'In 1990 my wife and I left India and went to live in a little town in South Africa. There, I formed a partnership with a friend and was a public accountant. After four years, we reached a stage where I said that it was time for me to go, and I bid him farewell.' V.V. Ranganathan returned to India in 1994 and ran a small business for three years. He then decided to go back into the accounting profession and joined Ernst & Young. 'During these eventful years in New Delhi,' he says, 'I was at the core and in the thick of the firm's meteoric rise to fame and fortune.'

Selfless action

'Because I was born into a Brahmin (priestly class) Hindu family, the atmosphere at home was quite charged with religious ceremonies, and I attended a number of these religious functions. Sometimes I was even made to perform some of these ceremonies without understanding what they were, because in those days it was sacrilegious to even question anything that was religious. So I used to think that spirituality and religion were one and the same; I did not understand the subtle differences. So anything that had to do with some priests surrounding a fire and performing some rituals was spirituality to me. It has been very difficult to un-programme myself and think differently. Today, spirituality to me is an intangible, subjective experience. By subjective I mean it is beyond the senses.

'Having said that, I think the real understanding of the difference between religion and spirituality came to me when I met and listened to Swami Ranganathananda at the Ramakrishna Mission. In those early days when I had listened to the Swami it struck me that God doesn't reside only in temples. The temples here in India are like national flags: the flags evoke a lot of pride and consciousness in people. But the national flag is not the nation; it only represents the nation. In the same way, temples are not God, or the only place God is; they represent God. It is a place where you can go and get the concentration to transform yourself to that plane above the normal sensory perceptions.'

V.V. Ranganathan told us he believes that 'there is nothing wrong with leading an active life and following desires as long as you believe in the concept of "nishkama karma", which means "selfless actions".

'I feel that my spiritual purpose is to be a karma yogi, a person who performs selfless actions. Yes, God has given me the equipment to pursue my desires, but I must do so in such a manner that I remember the principles of karma (cause and effect) and that my decisions are not fuelled by selfishness or egoism. In my mind, being a yogi means to immerse myself in the work that I have been entrusted to do and perform it with devotion, without being driven by expectations and calculations of something in return. What I mean is that my effort and involvement in doing something is not determined or driven by what I get in return. And I know from my own experience that this works. I believe that anyone who is moving towards this path of being a karma yogi will get more than they deserve.'

Responding to an unethical partner

'In South Africa I had formed a partnership with my friend as a public accountant. My friend and I were also partners in a larger partnership. He began to complain of their unethical practices and said he wanted to extricate himself from them. So I helped him organize our de-linking from that firm and we set up our own partnership. The practice was going very well and we were working with small and medium enterprises, giving them a lot of advice on how to run their business and manage their finances. We also helped them manage their personal wealth and did a lot of personal estate planning.

'We travelled all across Africa, and I really enjoyed this time. It was during this time that I realized that my friend was in fact slowly and perhaps unconsciously following in the footsteps of the other firm. I told him once or twice about this and that I did not believe this was any way to establish our firm. He knew better and we reached a stage where I said that it was time for me to go, so I bid him farewell.

'I must admit, thinking back to all of this, today I would have done things differently. I would connect with his spiritual being and reason with him. Today, I would seek to strike a chord with him on a different plane. I would bring a consciousness to the situation that did not have a right or wrong judgement. I would not bicker or argue with him; I would ask him to see my point of view and try to understand the merits of what I am saying. I would have given him the space and time to digest this and I would have been patient.

'But at that time, I did not do that. I left the partnership and moved out of the country. At some point after I left, my friend did finally realize that he must turn his clients over to a professional firm, and now he is a big industrialist. Today we are still friends.'

Handling a major mistake

Ernst & Young has a worldwide practice called Environment Management Services which helps governments and industries to address pollution and other environmental problems. 'In one project, there was a preliminary environmental management report that was submitted to the consulate authorities in order to clear a project that involved the construction of a dam. In a study like this, you must study the flora and fauna to determine what would happen to the environment if the dam were built in this area. You must also study the people to determine the social consequences of building this dam. Based on the report that we submitted, it then had to go on to a national board before permission could be given to start the project.

'Unfortunately, an overenthusiastic young man, who had only been in our firm for about six months, was working in this area. He had been trained as an environmental engineer in the USA. He cleared an environmental report in less than a week; this was something impossible to do within our firm's normal review process. What he actually did was to use a draft from another report without going through our review process. Then he sent the report to the state board on our letterhead, and they adopted it.

'There were a lot of environmental activists who wanted the building of the dam to be stopped and they suspected that this clearance had been done to please the company which was going to build the dam there. So the press picked it up and said that Ernst & Young was a big fraud in how they cleared this large environmental project report.

'I got a lot of calls from the press because they saw this as a very juicy story. When a journalist came to my office we had a totally different conversation. I asked him, "If someone brought you a story and you published it in good faith, and then you found out it was completely wrong, what would you do? You would come with an apology the next day. This is exactly what has happened here. The firm has not done anything wrong. It is unfortunate that a very immature person who was in his position for less than six months did this. We are very sorry that this has happened. We have officially withdrawn the report and we have agreed to not handle this assignment for our client."

'We got many emails from environmental groups in the USA, Canada and Europe. I would patiently take each one of them and reply. My spiritual theme of "seeing God in everyone" helped me in this situation a lot. It allowed me to come out with the truth and to put it into perspective. It helped me to speak from a conscious mind with no ulterior motives whatsoever. It helped me to not get mentally agitated at all. I believe that it is only because of this spiritual basis that I could be so tranquil inside.'

Spirituality and a balanced scorecard

'If you are able to run any enterprise without selfish motives and with selfless service then I believe that success will fall into place. When the motive of running an operation is selfless service, that does not mean you are running a charitable institution. It does not mean you give things away free and people come and go. It also does not mean that you cannot make profits. At an organizational level, success must be measured by the wealth that is created for all people.

'Yes, we must make a profit; but, most importantly, we must ask, "How did we make this profit?" The various perspectives and shared values of the people, the clients and financial growth processes are all an important part of a "balanced scorecard" process.

'If you were to look behind the work that was done to come up with this concept of a balanced scorecard, you will see a lot of spiritual thoughts in the process. The reason is that the balanced scorecard moves away from the usual measures of performance, which are financial in nature and places an emphasis on the importance of people, clients and processes. We have even added another dimension to our scorecard called "shared values and cultures".

'The organization is built on the talents of many people. If you take care of them, then everything else will be taken care of. People have different skill sets: some are marketing people, some are professionally oriented (such as the consultants), and some are the workers. We can group them as "the grinders, the minders and the finders". We don't expect a grinder to be a finder, nor a minder to be a grinder. But the sum total of all these people is what brings growth to the firm.

'So, throughout the organization people have different skills and cannot be expected to function equally. Therefore, we have personal scorecards that are not necessarily balanced taken separately; this process recognizes the capability of the people where they are and shows the training and mentoring they need to move into other areas.

'I have found that this balanced scorecard approach is actually a tool that I can use to measure the presence and application of spirituality in our organization.

'Some people are afraid to contaminate their careers with ideas that do not have a scientific basis. So it is important to articulate spirituality very carefully in the business world. If you are going to bring spirituality into the balanced scorecard concept, you would need to frame the questions very carefully. If you do this, then I believe it is possible to touch an inner nerve and "reach the roots that bear the fruits", so to speak.

'Consider this in the context of the ancient Indian values of *kama, artha, dharma* and *moksha*. These are the four major goals of life. *Kama*, desire, is the entire range of human cravings for family, home, career, status, etc; *artha*, wealth, is the instrument for fulfilling desires; *dharma*, ethical sense, is living in harmony with creation; and *moksha* is experiencing spiritual fulfilment.

'Therefore, a balanced scorecard approach to business should have all these four cornerstones to create a healthy, wealthy, happy and sustainable organization.'

Developing as a spiritual-based leader

'The difficult question that often arises for a tax professional is: are we the taxman who makes sure that the organization's officers follow the form and letter of the law? Or, are we the ombudsman who makes sure that the organization's officers follow the substance and purpose of the law? The substance is the motive: "What is the motive behind what the client is doing?" Even if actions seem to be within the law, the motives should be subject to question. This change in consciousness is what I am trying to bring out in the work we are doing in the practices of our organization as well as with our clients.

'I have always used the spiritual context to develop relationships with my colleagues and other employees. I am particularly interested in people who do not readily respond to my approach. I work on them and get them to realize the merits of my method. I would like to help those people who believe that their careers can be contaminated by spiritual ideas that are not associated with scientific models. They, unfortunately, do not understand what they are missing. I would like to reach out to these people and articulate these thoughts in a manner that will subtly evoke their consciousness. When my colleagues and team recognize the truths of the spiritual plane and practise them, they come and tell me how differently they feel and how fearless they have become.

'As an auditor of large multinational companies, I have been confronted on almost a daily basis with situations where I have to pass transactions through my internal "ethics" system and see if they pass my litmus test: the *lakshman rekha*. This is the imaginary boundary line that every individual has that he will not cross.

'I think the current boundary line that has been dictated by ethics is driven largely by human knowledge, meaning that somebody tells you this is not right or that is not right. This is something you usually get from your childhood. When I refer to the *lakshman rekha*, I am talking about the invisible line that is within everyone's system that is driven by consciousness. This is a consciousness that has its own existence. It comes into the mind; it is not a product of the mind or societal influences. It is something that can stand on its own. It has an independent standing of its own and is capable of influencing you. It is like a direct knowing, rather than a belief system.

'I am very careful and particular that I do not breach the trust I have developed with an individual when I relate to him at the spiritual level. You see a reflection of yourself in that other person and connect with him with utmost trust and truth. So never ever use this trust and confidence you have gained in that other person in the same way you use your ability or skill for achieving your ends or someone else's.'

24

Thomas Daugherty

Vice President of Spiritual Care and Values Integration, Methodist Health Care System, USA

When interviewed, Thomas Daugherty was Vice President of Spiritual Care and Values Integration at Methodist Health Care System, Houston, Texas, USA. He had held this position for the past four years and was 61 years of age. The hospital where he works is one of many hospitals in the Texas Medical Center, which is the largest conglomeration of hospitals and health care facilities in the world.

In addition to the hospital where he works, Methodist Health Care System has three satellite hospitals in the metropolitan area of Houston. In total, it employs roughly 8,000 employees. According to Thomas Daugherty, 'It has always been a leader in medicine locally, nationally and internationally. It has also been a leader in all the major fields of research and medical education . . . and it has been and is one of the strongest health care organizations in America from a financial standpoint.' In 2003 Methodist Health Care System was a recipient of the International Spirit at Work Award.

However, the type of leadership that Thomas Daugherty is dedicated to has little to do with medicine, research, medical education or finances: 'My work is about cultivating a holistic, comprehensive spiritual environment where caring can take place. I think the spiritual and the material aspects of health care and healing were once connected. I want to reconnect the aspects of this environment that have been so long disconnected . . . Success for me is to make a difference and to try to do it in a manner where I can stay connected with people, with myself and with the Divine.'

Prior to coming to Methodist Health Care System, Thomas Daugherty was Director, Chaplaincy Services at Methodist Hospital System, also in Texas, for 24 years. He has a bachelor's degree in Business Administration from Louisiana Technical University, a master's degree in theology from Southern Methodist University in Texas, and a master's degree in Pastoral Care and Counselling from Texas Christian University, all in the USA.

Since the interview with him, Thomas Daugherty has retired from Methodist Health Care System, but continues to work with the Methodist Board of Ordained Ministry of the Texas Conference.

Connecting with the Divine

The difference I hope to make here at Methodist Health Care System is to enhance the quality of care and the spiritual environments in which that care is given. Spiritual care refers to a quality of caring that we provide—it is a quality that connects us with the spirit of the organization and with the spirit of the Divine, which is in our midst. It is comprehensive and inclusive.

Thomas Daugherty's original aims were far removed from a career of service in major hospital systems associated with the Methodist Church in the USA.[1] 'My undergraduate degree was in business. I only took those types of courses because I was planning to go to law school and I thought they would help prepare me for that. I went to law school for one year and had the most miserable time of my life, so as a result I didn't do well. But I did have a highly graceful encounter with the dean as I was having my exit interview from law

---

1   Methodism refers to a group of denominations of Protestant Christianity that originated in England in the 18th century. Due to its strong emphasis on missionary activity it spread to many parts of the world including the USA. By 2006 it had 75 million members worldwide. From the beginning it emphasized education and social services. Among its more prominent members in the USA are President George W. Bush and Senator Hillary Clinton.

school. The dean said, "Tom, you didn't really want to be here in law school, did you?" I said, "No sir, I don't think I really did, but how did you know?" He said, "Well, we had all of your grade point average, we had your test scores, and we knew you could do this if you wanted." Then he said something that really stayed with me: "You will be successful when you decide what it is you really want to do and focus on that." And this has been so true throughout my career.

'Flunking out of law school was the first time I realized that I was living my life in order to fulfil someone else's expectations. My stepfather, who had been the only father I had ever known since the age of six, had always wanted me to be a lawyer. I had tried to be a dutiful son and to make everyone else happy. I had not given much thought to what I really wanted to do in life. That experience in law school was a very important lesson in living and in growing up,' he tells.

After leaving law school, Thomas Daugherty worked in the life insurance business. It was during this time that he got involved in the Methodist Church. 'I became involved in the church,' he says, 'and found my work there to be deeply meaningful. I decided to become a minister in the United Methodist Church and so I went to the Perkins School of Theology at Southern Methodist University; that was between the ages of 26 and 30. There is a part of this period that's very important to where I am today. When I was working as a volunteer in my church and considering being a minister, one of the things that attracted me to the ministry was a desire to help people bridge the gap between what they heard during the Sunday morning worship and what they experienced, and especially lived out during the rest of the week. I wanted to help them make the connection between the two.

'The other thing I realized early on was my natural skills in and gifts for pastoral care. I was very interested in helping people find access to their inner spiritual resources, the things they had learned during their years of religious development in their community of faith.'

Integrating spiritual care and spiritual values

'After I finished my seminary studies, I went on to do Clinical Pastoral Education (CPE). CPE is an extension of the theological education that people receive in seminary or theology school. It is an inter-faith educational programme available to people of any Christian denomination. It places heavy emphasis upon the integration of the head and the heart. That is, it has to do with helping those in ministry, whether a minister or person of the church, learn how to serve out of the context of who they are as a whole person, and not just out of what they have learned from an academic perspective.

'I was certified as a CPE Supervisor in 1974. My first appointment after my academic and clinical work was to the Methodist Hospital in Lubbock, Texas. They hired me to be director and to set up a CPE programme. Initially I was a chaplain and spent most of my time out on the patient floors extending pastoral care to patients, their families, and to the hospital staff. As the size of the hospital increased, and as my chaplaincy staff grew, the demands of my director role became greater, and I was in more of a management role. I stayed there for 24 years.

'As I was coming up through my career—working as a hospital chaplain and teaching other clergy CPE—one of the things that always bothered me was the gap that existed between the administrative staff and the nurses and physicians. While I was visiting the floors in the hospital, I would find nurses and physicians whose hearts really seemed to be in the right place and who felt a great compassion for their patients. They were genuinely concerned about the suffering that was taking place and were concerned about intervening in a way that would bring about healing and curing. Then I would go to a department director meeting and I would hear the managers and directors talking about the business side of running a hospital and there just didn't seem to be any connection. There seemed to be a great disconnection between what was happening in the clinical areas and what was happening in the administrative circles.

'I reported to the CEO of the hospital, and so we did talk about these types of things. But, yet, I still didn't seem to have the leverage that was needed to have my ideas be taken seriously. So, when I heard that the Methodist Health Care System in Houston wanted to integrate spiritual care and spiritual values throughout their organization, I knew this was a chance for me to bring about many of the ideas that I had had for many years. So I interviewed with them and was accepted for this position as Vice President of Spiritual Care and Values Integration beginning in October 1998.

'My responsibility here is to implement the part of our mission statement that says we provide our services in a spiritual environment of caring, and cultivate that environment through a process we call "values integration". Over the last months we've been through an extensive and intensive process to identify our core values, which are summarized by "I CARE". This is an acronym that stands for our five core values: integrity, compassion, accountability, respect and excellence.

'We have been through an evolutionary process as an organization in the last three and a half years. We have a new CEO and there has been a change in my reporting relationship; I now report directly to the CEO and I also have a seat on his CEO council. So I have a place where I am able to be a part of the major decisions that are being made with the senior management team. This is also a place where we can coordinate and implement this cultural transformation that we are trying to bring about.

'I feel that the supportive relationships I have in my life have contributed to my strength in carrying out my responsibilities here. Besides spurring my spiritual growth, my wife, my spiritual teachers, my therapists, and even some of the consultants we have working with us have also provided an invaluable support to me for doing my job. These are people who really believe that I can do what I am doing and help me to stay in touch with what I really do have to offer this organization.'

Spiritual care for the patients

'I conceptualize spirituality as the connection among myself, other people and the Divine. It is the common linkage between these three aspects of existence for me. Spirituality is also staying connected with my own spiritual centre, my connection with the Divine, and then listening to what I hear there. To me the Divine both lives within me and apart from me. I do believe that the Divine is both transcendent and immanent.

'The God within me is that part of me which calls me to deal with my ego and be accountable and responsible for my behaviour. God calls me to live my life with a strong sense of caring, compassion, and love for my fellow human beings. I realize I live to serve and help make the world a better place for having been here. I try to stay connected with this motivation, even though I realize that there is no such thing as a pure motivation.

'I believe that there is a reason that I am here in this position as Vice President of Spiritual Care and Values Integration, and I am well aware that this is a big responsibility. I also recognize that getting this job done—transforming this organizational culture to one of spiritual care and values—is bigger than my own individual talents and gifts. So the challenges of this job—working with the dynamics of the organization, and the resistance to these types of changes that is always present—has pushed me to go deeper and deeper inside, and to deal with my own spiritual understanding of who I am.

'During a recent workshop, a consultant asked us: "If you were writing a book about your life, what would the title of that book be?" For me, this would be: "He made a difference in Methodist Health Care". The difference I hope to make here at Methodist Health Care System is to enhance the quality of care and the spiritual environments in which that care is given. Spiritual care refers to a quality of caring that we provide in this environment. It is a quality that connects us with the spirit of the organization and with the spirit of the Divine, which is in our midst. For me, it is something that involves everyone—our administration, our board members, our housekeeping personnel, our nurses, our physicians, everyone. I am hoping to influence the environment where everyone receiving care in any of our hospitals can feel there is a difference in their care and on some level realize they are receiving spiritual care.

'So my work is about cultivating a holistic, comprehensive environment where this caring can take place. I want to reconnect the spiritual and material aspects of health care that have been so long disconnected. In my view, success for Methodist Health Care System would be connecting the world of spirit with the world of productivity in such a way that there is a blending, a "wholeness" that emerges.'

Finding strength from within

'There has been resistance to the kind of spiritual change we are working to bring about here in our organization. I have encountered people who I fully expected to be supportive of this spiritual approach and I have been surprised to discover that some were not supportive, and in some ways were actually acting counter to what we are trying to do.

'This has really caused me to come to terms with myself and realize that this whole endeavour is not about me personally. When I have taken these types of experiences personally, I have become immobilized, discouraged and depressed. But when I step back and look inside and listen to that still small voice, I remember why I am here and why God called me here. I realize that God didn't call me here because this effort was always going to be peaceful and harmonious. It is from this inner place that I can stay the course and persist. It is this kind of struggle with others that has caused me to access this spiritual centre within me.'

Integrating values in everyone's day-to-day work

'As we move forward with our values integration effort, one of the things we are trying to do is to integrate these values into every aspect of the employee's life cycle: from the application process to the hiring interviews, all the way through the evaluation processes and exit interviews. We want to hire people who are the kind of people who will live these values and will fit with this environment. While we expect people to have the best clinical and technical competence, we feel that this alone is not enough—a person can be competent and capable; however, he or she may not fit into this culture. Living these

values, which will in turn cultivate a spiritual environment, is just as important. The way our employees treat each other in their workgroup, the way
they treat their internal customers, the way they treat people who come here
to be served—the way they go about treating people is just as important as
what they do in their job.

'The training process we currently have in progress will continue. It will
take us 12 months just to train our current 8,000 employees. I, myself, will
start this process with the CEO Council. The next phase we will be introducing in the next couple of months is called the "workgroup commitment
process". This is a process in which we ask all executives, managers, directors
and supervisors to engage the people who report to them in a process of looking at and integrating the five core values.

'One of the things I like to share with other executives is: "Every figure we
see on our financials has behind it another human being that had the mis-
fortune of needing our services. We literally have no funds to operate with
unless someone is sick, injured, suffering or dying." I hope we can come to
this kind of merger between spirit and the world. To me this in no way dimin-
ishes the importance of taking a hard look at the numbers. However, spirituality enriches the process and gives it a deeper meaning.

'Beyond the steps we are taking to start our organizational change from the
top and moving forward in phases, for me the most important way that I
communicate about spirituality is through my direct relationships with people. This involves listening to people and sincerely hearing the fear behind
their concerns.

'In terms of our making a contribution to the rest of the world, literally we
do serve people from all over the world; we have a very large international
clientele. As we are able to serve people from the frame of reference that we
care, hopefully they will take away from here a feeling that the quality of service they received not only took care of the physical concern they had, but
also left them with a sense of wholeness, beyond what they even expected to
receive.'

Guidance on spiritual-based leadership

'One of the things I worked on last year is developing a model of coaching for
spiritual leadership. So this is what I would draw upon if someone came to me
asking for guidance in being a spiritual-based leader. Most of this comes from
my background in teaching and supervising clinical pastoral education. I
would first want to listen and then ask them:

What does spirituality mean to you?

What does leadership mean to you?

What are you aware of, right now, about the disconnection between leadership as you now provide it and the spirituality that you've just described?

'I would then encourage them to think about which places of disconnection are most important for them to deal with right now and talk about why this is an issue for them. I would also ask them to share examples of how this disconnection has played out in their relationships with other people. I would help them think about and design some alternative ways of handling people and situations that would reflect the spirituality that they described in order to connect their spirituality with their work. Then, over time, I would work with them on the issues as they emerge.

'One question that continually comes up is: "How can I be tough and exercise discipline with people and at the same time be spiritual?" The assumption is that if you are spiritual, then you must be nice. So I ask them, "Has this always been true? Have you always experienced people who care about you and let you get away with things that are unproductive or self-defeating? Have you ever experienced someone who cared enough to talk frankly and honestly with you about what they were observing and to hold out bigger expectations for you to perform differently?" Most people can identify with these questions and can see the value of looking at discipline from this perspective.'

In this section

When we interviewed the leaders presented in this book, one of the questions we asked them was: 'How would you describe your consciously held spiritual purpose for your life and your work?' In this section, you will meet six business leaders from four continents (Europe, South and North America, and Asia) who emphasized this notion of 'purpose' during their interviews. The one woman and five men are: the Chairperson and CEO of equity investment companies in France; the Chairman of the world's largest producer of bullet-proof glass for vehicles in Peru; the Strategy Director at the major mobile telephone operator in the Czech Republic; a General Manager at the Indian location of a major international hi-tech company; the Chairman of an American company manufacturing electronic equipment; and the former President of the consumer division of a Swedish paper products company located in Switzerland and of a flooring company in the UK. You will meet:

Hélène Ploix, Chairman & Managing Director, Pechel Industries & Pechel Industries Partenaires, France

In *Giving your talents without counting,* Hélène Ploix reflects: 'I think the purpose of business is to create wealth to the company and to create wealth for a larger number of people without harming the others. This should not be done just for yourself or for a few others, such as managers or owners. I think that the purpose of my own organization and for business in general is creating wealth for the largest number of people—to contribute!'

Federico Cuneo, Chairman, American Glass Products, Peru

In *Sharing spirituality in business,* Federico Cuneo puts business activities into a broader perspective: 'I think my spiritual journey is really the essence of my life. I now find that my life has a purpose. I try to help people see their problems from a more spiritual perspective. Sometimes I tell them, "We've come from eternity and we'll return to eternity. Don't lose your perspective of what is most important." I don't mind saying this even in our management meetings. Sometimes they even say that they need more of this kind of attitude.'

Parantha Narendran, Strategy Director, Eurotel Telecom, Czech Republic

In *Pushing beyond limits and fear,* Parantha Narendran shares how he works to actualize the potential of each person as well as the organization: 'I try to help the people I work with to achieve their best potential. This is an area where spirituality and the objectives of an organization happily coincide. When a leader believes in empowering individuals, he has the best interests of the company at heart. Having the individual realize his potentials along with the spiritual aspects, and having the organization develop itself at the same time, are my primary and secondary goals.'

Deependra Moitra, former General Manager, Engineering, Lucent Technologies, India

In *An approach to fulfilment,* Deependra Moitra defines his spiritual theme as 'living with a purpose' where 'true fulfilment' is then the outcome. 'Living with a purpose is something that is very important to me—it is an issue of passion and emotion. My fundamental goal is to help others succeed, so I am willing to sacrifice a lot to do that. I help a lot of people without feeling any selfish motive. But I still have struggles from time to time between my own self-interest and a larger purpose that I should focus on.'

Ananth Raman, Chairman, Graphtex, Inc., USA

In *Adding value,* Dr Ananth Raman relates, 'I believe that everyone's life has a purpose and that that purpose must add some value. Even if it is a simple matter like soothing a fevered brow or wiping a tear from a child's eye. For this you must first set a personal example. As a business leader I must set an example which others can follow.' Following his spiritual views, he sets an example for his employees in matters extending from quality improvement to financial responsibility.

Magnus Vrethammar, President, Finess, Switzerland and Pergo, UK

In *Opening up*, Magnus Vrethammar says: 'When I look at the world of business, I have never seen so much constructive work being done, so many open collaborations, and so much constructive opening up. So I feel that business is one of the best playgrounds you can have in life for your spiritual development. Looking back on my own career path, I realize that it was also a highly spiritual exercise.'

25

Hélène Ploix

Chairman and Managing Director, Pechel Industries & Pechel Industries Partenaires, France

Madame Hélène Ploix, a most humble leader, has held a long list of highly impressive leadership positions in major financial institutions and businesses, primarily in France but also in the USA and UK.[1] And she has received honours and recognition that few business leaders could dream of receiving. Yet we experienced Madame Ploix as the epitome of modesty. It was with reluctance and a lowered voice that she told us about her contributions, even though she is ded-

---

1 Prior to her present position, her leadership positions have included:

KPMG Peat Marwick, 1995–96, Special advisor for the single currency (for replacing French Francs with the Euro);

Caisse des Dépôts et Consignations (CDC), 1989–95, Deputy Managing Director in charge of finance and banking; Chairman of CDC Participations; Chairman of the Advisory Board of CDC Gestion (€60 billion/US$75 billion portfolio); Chairman of the Caisse Autonome de Refinancement (US$14 billion balance sheet);

International Monetary Fund (IMF) and *The World Bank*, Washington DC, 1986–89, Executive Director;

Cabinet of the Prime Minister, Special Advisor for Economic and Financial Affairs to the Prime Minister, 1984–86;

Banque Industrielle et Mobilière Privée (BIMP), Chairman and Chief Executive Officer, Paris, 1982–84

icated to contributing to the well-being of others. And when we asked her about the difficulties she faced as a woman in reaching her top-leadership positions, she replied: 'My answer is very simple: When people were looking for a woman, there were not that many women around, so they would ask me.'

The first part of her spiritual theme is 'to contribute to society'. In her stories from her childhood of the prayer she learned as a girl scout (of 'giving without counting') and of the parable of the talents from the New Testament, she metaphorically describes what guided her on her career path in business: she invests her abundant talents without counting so as to contribute to the well-being of others.

The second part of her spiritual theme is 'to be attentive to others and have a better understanding of them'. This finds expression in much of her non-business activity. 'I have been participating in organizations where people meet to improve their ability to understand each other better. For example, I am active in the French-American Foundation, and I was part of the founding group of the Aspen Institute in France.[2] I spent my evenings through more than a year preparing a seminar for the Aspen Institute on "The Influence of Culture on Business Ethics", taking examples from Japan, the USA and Europe.'

The following are just a few of her notable achievements outside the domain of business: recipient of the prestigious awards by the French state: 'Chevalier de la Légion d'Honneur' and 'Officier de l'Ordre National du Mérite'; author of books on corporate governance; and director of CEDEP, an executive education centre run by and for a consortium of large international companies ranging from L'Oréal, HSBC and Renault to the Tata Group.

Giving your talents without counting

As a girl scout I learned one prayer that says that you have to give without counting. These are words which express what is deeply important for me. I was told that I should do this, I should manage my gifts well, and that we must give, and do so without counting. This is what I have been trying to do in my life. This is the best way I can describe my spirituality and how it affects my work.

---

2 Institut Aspen France, founded in 1994, is a non-partisan, international forum designed to promote the exchange of ideas on economic, social and political issues.

Hélène Ploix is Chairman and Managing Director of Pechel Industries (since 1997) and of Pechel Industries Partenaires (since 2003). Pechel Industries is a private equity investment firm (a holding company of non-listed companies) while Pechel Industries Partenaires is a management company that manages the portfolio of Pechel Industries, and in addition has its own fund that invests in private equity—mainly in medium-sized, privately owned industrial and service companies. At the time of the interview (summer 2006) she was 62 years old and living in Paris, France.

'I was born in 1944 in the eastern part of France as the sixth child out of eight in a Catholic family,' she told us. 'What made me what I am is being from a large family—coming from a large family you are used to looking after the others, you are used to thinking of the others, and to making sure that everybody gets a fair share of what there is on the table. Another thing which influenced me is that my oldest sister was disabled, so maybe we sisters and brothers stuck more together and paid more attention to each other than was normally done.'

As a young girl, Hélène Ploix was a girl scout. As a scout she not only wanted to demonstrate her natural talents as a leader, she also learned the maxim which has stayed with her all of her life: 'You should give without counting'.

Multiplying your gifts

Madame Ploix's spiritual view of life has to some extent been affected by her religion's more formal aspects, but primarily by its wisdom and moral codices. 'My understanding of spirituality, being from a Catholic family, is much linked to religion, to prayers, to belief in God. As Christians we are told that we have to distinguish between the spiritual and the temporal; the spiritual is about the church. In my opinion, the Catholic religion is very much about appearance and about rituals. I think that it can become much too narrow.'

But she referred as well to the wisdom contained in the teachings of the Church: 'As a child I was struck by a story in the New Testament: the parable of the talents (Matthew 25: 14–30). A man was leaving on a journey. To one of his servants he gave five talents (a monetary unit at the time of Jesus), another was given two talents, and a third was given only one talent—each according to their ability. The one who was given five talents invested them and returned ten to his master when he returned from his journey; the one who was given two talents returned four, while the servant who had been given only one had buried it and simply returned it to his master. I learned from this that it is better to receive five and return ten than to save the one and give back the one; that is, if you are given some gifts, you have to make them grow, to multiply them. That is your duty in life.'

This parable of the talents, just like the prayer as to 'giving without counting' has, at a deeper, more subtle level, affected Hélène Ploix ever since. Her business leadership deals to a great extent with being a caretaker of other people's investments. The idea of giving without counting, and of the duty to 'make them grow, to multiply them' have been guiding lights for Hélène Ploix throughout her career.

Madame Ploix went on to tell us how her spiritual view of life is integrated into daily leadership practices. 'What is also important for me in the idea of spirituality is the concept of values. You have to be conscious about the values, and you have to be guided by the values, and these values can encompass a lot of things. One has to have wider values, values about the universe, values about what is right and what is wrong, values about balance. And integrity, of course, that is the key. All the team members share the same values; we have developed an ethos based on trust, responsibility, involvement and teamwork.'

'In our management company, we believe that values have to fill your life all the time, at work and at home. I often discuss with my husband matters about business life, ethics, values, the purpose of business, and how to behave as a leader,' she told us. 'He is very wise and intellectually very inspiring.'

When asked if she could succinctly express her perspectives on spiritual-based leadership as a spiritual theme, Madame Ploix replied: 'To contribute to society. And to try to be attentive to others and have a better understanding of them.'

Breaking the path for women

After receiving her MA from the Institut d'Etudes Politiques of Paris in 1965, Hélène Ploix did a master's degree in Public Administration at the University of California in the USA in 1966. 'I thought that what I studied at Berkeley would prepare me well for working in a consulting firm, so when I came back to France my father introduced me to a management consultant, and he told me two things: (1) "You never studied business—go to a business school", and (2) "I would never hire a woman!" He suggested that I go to INSEAD, which is a top international business school located in France.' Although INSEAD had never accepted women, she applied and, together with another young woman, became the first females ever to get an MBA there. In addition to her MAs from Institut d'Etudes Politiques and the University of California, and her MBA from INSEAD, Hélène Ploix also obtained a BA in Law and English Literature in Paris.

So she was now qualified for a position as consultant, and for eight years she was Senior Management Consultant at the highly respected McKinsey & Co. 'The reason why I left McKinsey was the fact that, although you have to cope with very interesting people, you are not responsible for implementing your recommendations, and you don't work with people who are very different from yourself. It was just like being in a cocoon. I thought that it was better to personally meet more difficulties, to be out in "real life".'

Leading at IMF, the World Bank and Caisse des Dépôts

Between 1986 and 1989, Hélène Ploix was Executive Director of the International Monetary Fund and the World Bank in Washington DC. 'I was the first woman Executive Director of the IMF, while there had already been at least one woman in a similar position before me at the World Bank. As I was not a civil servant there was no possibility of a further career in these organizations. The job I got afterwards as Deputy Chief Executive Officer at Caisse des Dépôts et Consignations in Paris (1989–95) was a perfect blend of public and private sector. At that time it was the largest institutional investor in France. It was state-owned and I was in charge of all the financial activities which were in the competitive sector—capital markets, asset management, custody, and we had our own proprietary trading. I was in charge of 4,000 people working there. I was, I think, the first non-civil servant in my position since the creation of Caisse des Dépôts in 1816.'

Reflecting on how she led from a spiritual basis at this major financial institution, Hélène Ploix told us: 'I don't have a spiritual practice. I don't go to church regularly; I don't like the rituals. But I try to integrate my values and my world view with my work. For example, when I developed the code of conduct at Caisse des Dépôts, I wanted people to start thinking about the way they behaved and why they behaved as they did.'

'In 1992 when I was at Caisse des Dépôts one of the people who was working with me had the good idea to start some research on ethics and finance. Although I was very, very, very busy, I wanted to keep some time for that programme. I started thinking more about ethics and finance; what did ethics mean? What did finance mean? Was "ethics and finance" an oxymoron or was it possible to meaningfully speak of "ethics and finance"? I started thinking that ethics was balance, not going beyond limits. That became clearer and clearer to me, and I started discussing it with research people in order to clarify my thoughts. We had no code of conduct at Caisse des Dépôts, so I created one. This was at the very beginning when different markets were trying to organize themselves in that respect and it was very difficult to have people share it. It was difficult to convince them that they had to think about these issues.'

From 4,000 to 4

'At the beginning of 1997 I was asked to be Chairman of Pechel, a holding company of non-listed companies, what is called private equity; neither Pechel nor the holdings were listed on the stock exchange. Private equity is an activity that I find very interesting, and I knew what it was all about. I was happy to go from leading 4,000 people to an organization with four people, because for a while we were only four at Pechel.

'Running a private equity investment firm is really about people. You have to get along with managers (in the companies invested in). You have to understand them to see if they will be good managers or not, you have to work alongside them, so you really have to have empathy with them. In addition, you have to understand the market, the products. You have to have a strategic vision.

'The companies we work with are mainly mid-market. These mid-market companies would want an outsider like us to come in, either because they need an increase in their capital, or because the founder or founding family wants to be able to cash in on some of his holdings, which until now have been tied up in the assets of the company, while still maintaining a significant influence over the future of the company. If we think they are doing well, that we will work well together, and they want us to come in for the good of the company, we are happy to help. We become minority shareholders ranging from a very small percentage to 49 per cent.

'In 2003 the shareholders of Pechel Industries decided they would like us to divest. We agreed to create a management company, Pechel Industries Partenaires, which is totally independent of Pechel Industries and which would divest Pechel Industries holdings. We have now roughly 25 investors in the new company's fund, not only from France but from many places in the world.'

The importance of creating wealth and contributing

'From my spiritual point of view, I think the purpose of business is to create wealth to the company and to create wealth for a larger number of people without harming the others. This should not be done just for yourself or for a few others, such as managers or owners. I think that the purpose of my own organization and for business in general is creating wealth for the largest number of people—to contribute! I feel it is also important to contribute to work environments where there are people who might be less clever, people who have less education. It is very good to be aware that you have to work with them and have a duty to help them develop.

'One of my ideas for the future is that one of our new funds also has a possibility of investing in Eastern Europe. I know they need minority investors in these countries, investors who come to help them develop their companies, who provide them with the wisdom they have accumulated, who provide them with insight as to good governance, and who can help them open themselves to the rest of the world. I want to choose small companies and help them to grow. Just as I also have to help the young people here to develop, to think of the future, to think of our role in the world.

'When I joined the World Bank and the International Monetary Fund as Executive Director, I did not only do it just to have a career, I wanted to understand better the developing world, and to see what we could do. When I was working as a member of the Cabinet of the Prime Minister for the French Government, it was for the same reasons—to contribute to the best possible management of our country. I have always had an attraction to doing work which contributes to society. Even now through my work with private equity, because you help smaller companies to develop. My life has been directed towards contributing to society.

'Private equity is more and more seen as an activity where people are very greedy. I reject that sense of greediness that has been more associated with, for example, some large leveraged takeovers. I would like for my organization to avoid greed—and that wealth should be for the many beyond the top managers and owners—for the benefit of the many.'

Success as a spiritual-based leader

'I consider myself as having two responsibilities at present. The main one is here in Paris, leading the investment company Pechel Industries and the management company, Pechel Industries Partenaires. But, in addition, I am

---

3 BNP Paribas is rated as the No. 1 French company (Forbes) and is the world's 16th largest company overall, operating in over 85 countries with 110,000 employees.

4 Lafarge is a world leader in building materials and cement with sales of roughly US$20 billion in 2005 and 80,000 employees in 76 countries.

5 Publicis Groupe is the world's fourth largest communications group, operating in 104 countries with over 38,000 employees. In 2005, revenues exceeded US$5 billion.

also a non-executive director of five rather big companies, three of these, BNP Paribas,[3] Lafarge[4] and Publicis Groupe,[5] are among the 40 largest companies in France. The other two major companies are the Boots Group[6] in the UK and Ferring Pharmaceuticals.'[7] In all of these companies Hélène Ploix is either a member of or chairman of the audit committee. 'Being on these five boards makes me see things a little differently and broadens my perspectives,' she says.

'Success for me personally is achieving the goals I have set for myself, both in business and in my private life. I can feel that I have been successful when I have been called upon to sit on the board of such major organizations because they think I can contribute and I will speak out my own views— when I am called upon to do something which is important for the business world or the world of which I am a part.

'Success for me is also related to duty. At my present work at Pechel, the problem with private equity is that we have a duty to the investors. I am trying to do my best for the companies we have invested in and for the long-term benefit of all the people involved. In life you are not always able to do what you want to do from your spiritual perspective; there may be a conflict of interests.

'Success for me is also to have people within the company grow so that they feel it is their company, and afterwards they are able to take over and ensure that there is a good future for the company.

'I would like to be remembered as a person who contributed—to our employees and investors, to the firms we work with, to society as a whole.'

Listening to your conscience

Asked about what advice she would give to aspiring spiritual-based leaders, Hélène Ploix told us: 'I would advise them about their behaviour; one's character is most important. This also means listening to your conscience. It is important to develop good reflexes, good reactions. I try to instil this in my team. There were several times in my earlier career when I didn't have the right reflexes. When you are a top manager in a large company, you don't have much time, so your reflexes, your spontaneous reactions, are most important. A priest once told me that morals is about creating right reflec-

---

6 Boots is the United Kingdom's leading health and beauty retailer, with revenues of roughly £5 billion/US$9 billion in 2005 and 63,000 employees.

7 Ferring Pharmaceuticals is a privately owned, Swiss based, research-driven bio-pharmaceutical company with offices in over 40 countries and revenues in 2003 of roughly US$750 million.

tions and the right reactions; I think that he was very right. You develop right reactions by being more and more conscious about that necessity.

'But you must also learn; if you don't do something right, you must think about it, you have to really become very conscious about it. I also believe you learn by being with people who are good examples; this is critical. If you are joining forces with others who have the same motivations as you, you are stronger. I would tell aspiring spiritual-based leaders to be with people who share their own views and who want to discuss them, to share what is important for them.'

26

Federico Cuneo
Chairman, American Glass Products, Peru

Federico Cuneo was partner and Chairman of American Glass Products (the world's largest producer of bullet-proof glass for vehicles) in Peru at the time of the interview. Prior to his active leadership of American Glass Products he held leadership positions in the Peruvian operations of several multinational corporations, including Price-Waterhouse, Anderson Consulting, and Bank of Boston. He has also been CEO at a large domestic brewery, run a family-owned business producing alcoholic beverages, and chaired a professional soccer team. He has a degree in Accounting from Eastern Michigan University in the USA.

'I think my spiritual journey is really the essence of my life,' he told us. 'I now find that my life has a purpose. Since I began my spiritual journey, I have always included spirituality in my conversations, whether it was with a boss, or a partner, or people who reported to me, or my kids. I just had an excellent conversation about spirituality with my partner that we had never had in 16 years.'

As of summer 2006, Federico Cuneo is Senior Partner at the Peruvian branch of Ernst & Young, the international accounting, auditing and consulting company. He also chairs Peru 2021, an NGO comprised of business executives in Peru promoting sustainable development and corporate social responsibility for the country; 'I truly believe that CSR is the language of the Spirit that can be understood by the corporation,' he told us. He is also an active board member of the international organization, Spirit in Business.

Sharing spirituality in business

I know that spirituality can help me as an individual. However, I want to be involved in something much bigger that has to do with the well-being of the world. I think that business is a good platform for doing this, because people respect successful businessmen. If we can set examples as leaders, then I think we can change the world. I don't think our major challenge is to have the biggest corporation. I think our major challenge is to have less poor people in the world.

Federico Cuneo was 50 years old at the time of the interview. After university studies in Michigan, USA, he returned to his native country Peru and began his career. 'Andersen Consulting in Peru was a good school for my learning,' he explains. 'After that I worked for a couple of years as a Financial Manager for a development bank. In 1985, I went on my own for a year as a consultant and that's when I made an investment in a glass manufacturing company in Peru, American Glass Products (AGP), where I am today a shareholder and Chairman of the Board.

'While I was consulting, a large brewery was a client and they asked me to join them as their CFO. I was the CFO for the first four years and then became the General Manager of their trading company. While I was doing this, I was also the Chairman of a professional soccer team that was owned by the brewery.

'In 1994, I left the brewery and managing the soccer team and tried to recuperate a family business where we made alcoholic beverages. I had had a lot of prestige and even coverage in the newspapers, and found myself really floundering in my family business. Things were not going well and I felt bad about producing alcoholic beverages. So we sold the company. But something had happened within me; while I was doing this I began to read about spirituality.'

'One day, a good friend of mine contacted me. He had decided to retire from Citibank where he had been a banker for 15 years. He told me that the Bank of Boston had looked him up and asked him to run their operations in Peru, and that he was looking for a Corporate Director. He wanted me to do it. I tried to tell him that I really didn't know anything about banking. He told me not to worry. He wanted my leadership capabilities and sent me to Boston in the USA to learn the business. We started the operation in Peru and it was very successful. I was the head of their corporate banking in Peru and had business relationships with all of the large local and multinational corporations. I did this for the last five years and left them at the end of last year.'

Considering eternity

'Today I think my spiritual journey is really the essence of my life. Unity with the rest of the world, love, eternal life and light—those would be words I would use as my spiritual theme. When I managed people at the bank, I told them that I didn't want them to work over eight hours a day because I respected their personal life. I told them not to give me excuses, if they needed to go and take care of a family matter, then they should go. To me this was more important than the work we were doing. If I found people who were working overtime, I told them we should look more closely at why they had to do that. Maybe we were asking them to do too much and we needed to adjust that. This way of being has also allowed me to enjoy my life more.

'There is a saying in Peru that your problems go up enormously at night. So if your life is a nightmare, then your problems are there all the time. I try to help people see their problems from a more spiritual perspective. Sometimes I tell them, "We've come from eternity and we'll return to eternity. Don't lose your perspective of what is most important." I don't mind saying this even in our management meetings; it helps them to see things differently. Sometimes they even say that they need more of this kind of attitude.'

Federico Cuneo reflected on what he said about eternity: 'One of the things that really struck me the most in one of the books I read was, "Remember that you are a spiritual being, temporarily in flesh and bone that will go back to eternity. Yet we need to experience being flesh and bone in order to grow as a spirit." So if we come from eternity and we go back to eternity where there is no time, where there's no space, then our time as flesh and bone is a mere fraction. This is what has now shaped my perspective of life. I now understand that the most important thing is my soul, or my spirit, or my being. Whatever happens to me while I am in this flesh and bone is really a minor thing in my existence. In one way, this is good because I can look back at the bad things that have happened and say that it gave me some experience. However, I feel bad sometimes because I love my kids, my mother, my wife such that I want them to last in my life for eternity.'

Synchronicity

'I think that Joseph Jaworski's book *Synchronicity* really helped me understand that there is a collective mind and that you can access it and influence things and then things can start to happen. I believe in synchronicities and that there is a reason for why things happen.'

Federico Cuneo explained his thoughts about synchronicity: 'I had begun to feel that it was time for me to leave the bank. But before I resigned, they came to me and offered me a very good package to leave the company! So now I am helping to direct the corporation I had invested in back in 1985, American Glass Products (AGP).'

'We had initially started AGP in Peru and then sold the technology to a company in Colombia. That company went under and so they sold 80 per cent of their shares to a French company. This French company looked down on us because we didn't have a manufacturing plant in Brazil or Mexico. We took note of that and decided to buy a company in Mexico. We shaped up this company and then we found an investment firm in Brazil to help us build a plant in Brazil.

'My partner wanted to go into the international markets and become the leading bullet-proof glass manufacturer in the world. I initially thought he was crazy; I told him, "Who is going to believe this group of Peruvians who want to sell glass to the Germans?" We were just a small Peruvian company and yet today we are the largest manufacturing company of bullet-proof glass for automobiles in the world. We are also working to supply sophisticated, difficult-to-make glass. We sell to Mitsubishi and Toyota in Japan and to the secret service agencies all over the world. It has taken the company 16 years to grow to this stage.

'My partner has been quite overwhelmed with all of the growth and there are some challenges we have to work out due to the enormous capital investments we have made. But we have good sound technology and are considered top class in the world, so I am confident we will work through everything.'

New perspectives on life

Federico Cuneo spoke of how his spiritual journey began relatively late in his life: 'It began around 1994. I had just left the large multinational corporation I worked for in Peru, and found myself really floundering in my family business. I felt very weak at that time and our third child was about to be born. Since I couldn't sleep at night, I was taking sleeping pills. I was so worried about how we would make it financially.' By chance Cuneo started reading books about spirituality.

'This really enriched my life,' he says. 'I was raised as a Roman Catholic and all of my understanding of God came from that perspective. Since I began to read many books on spirituality, I respect Christ more, I respect the Bible more, I pray more, and I feel that God lives inside me; however, I do not go to church.

'Spirituality and religion do meld somewhere, but to me religion is a set of rules. Spirituality is more of a feeling that you are a free soul—it is feeling my inner essence. When I began to feel tolerance, patience and no hatred toward others, this to me was spirituality. In other words, spirituality is being able to connect with the collective soul, the collective intelligence that is fused with God. I know that I can obtain the things I need and can give the things that all people need. I think the Catholic Church is very good and, using business terms, it is a very good product for a certain market. However, it is not for me even though I thank God that it is there.

'After starting on my spiritual journey, my perspectives of life have changed. I now understand that the most important thing is my soul, or my spirit, or my being. Another concept that is important to me is the concept of light, the concept of working for the light, receiving the light, and reflecting the light. This is an energetic awareness that is starting to appear in my life now and it is very meaningful to me.

'Out of reading one of the books by the Vietnamese Buddhist monk Thich Na Hahn, the most important thing I retained is that, when we pray, God is inside of us rather than out there in Heaven as I learned from the Lord's Prayer—"Our Father who art in Heaven". This has really changed my life. God is not out there; therefore I cannot hide. I feel that I let God down when I do things that I am not supposed to do. God is the light that I have inside and is always there.

'People in my life have noticed a continuous change to be more selfless, relaxed, tolerant and patient in my life and have appreciated it. I do still lose my temper every once in a while, but mainly I feel relaxed and can help people understand that it's not personal.

'One of the difficult things I have had to deal with is how to mix spirituality with the pleasures I want in life. I like to have my house well decorated; I like to have a good car and good clothes. This is something I have not been able to resolve yet. I don't feel good with myself about all of this, but I'm not ready to give it up. To me this is part of the process and it is natural, so this is something I still have to work out.'

Talking about spirituality

'Around 1996 or 1997, I was in a business meeting where a consultant mentioned something and I responded by saying, "I really don't want to get into this, because if I start talking about spirituality it could take another hour to discuss." She thought that was interesting and wanted to talk further in another meeting.

'At that subsequent meeting I told her how I felt about spirituality. She then told me about the man who wrote the book *Re-engineering Yourself* and asked me if I would come and give a presentation at the same meeting where he would be talking to businessmen. I told her that I didn't want to do that because many of those businessmen would know me and they would think that I had started living a hippie life. She said, "No, you need to come and break the ice. There are so many people who are lost and things like this are so important."

'So I attended this meeting and I told them what had happened to me. I told them about a crisis in my life that brought me to spirituality. I told them about reading spiritual books and the comfort I had found in meditation. During the hour that I spoke I noticed that the audience kept intense attention on what I was saying. The day after the meeting, the consultant called me and told me that she had reviewed the written feedback and that the favourite topic from the whole meeting was my presentation, even more than the author of the book.

'One day I was asked by a mining company to go and speak at their annual meeting. This was still quite uncomfortable because they were not up to the topic of spirituality. So I am well aware that for companies to include spirituality into their success pattern is a new thing. But I think we need to jump to that stage. After attending the "Spirit in Business" conference (in New York City in 2002) I told the people in Peru that 500 people were there to talk about spirituality in their business. I told them that the large corporations were there. This helps the sceptical people to accept it easier.

'I think the world needs the business segment to be concerned about the good of the whole. I know this may be difficult, but it must start from within. We must all start to look within at our spiritual nature and change from the inside. I cannot imagine all of the good things that business could do for the world if this were to happen. If the people who run the highly successful companies would look inside, I know that they could do a lot more for the world.'

Have fun and feel good in business

'To me business is like a game, I always hope to be more profitable of course, but most of all I want the people to have fun and to feel good about what they are doing. Inside AGP, I think of the company as a whole—as a consolidation of the expectations of every one who is there—whether those expectations are for the environment they work in, or their salary, or a dividend.

'I can remember one of my secretaries who worked with my cheque book asking me why I was giving so much of my money away. I told her not to worry, that it will continue to come to me, and it has always been like that . . . when you give more, then you get more. To me this also applies to friendship, to love, to everything. Giving for me is such a pleasure; it is a concept I like very much.

'When I talk to others about spirituality, I use myself as an example to show them how things are going so much better for me. I talk about the peace of mind I now have and how I feel relaxed in life. About four months ago, we were having a very difficult time with some of our regional partners and investors. I approached the upcoming meeting by meditating and imagining their faces as being happy. I imagined telling them at the start of the meeting how I would be straight with what I had to say, and that I wanted the good for all of us. You must realize this meeting was like a battlefield. We had brought in two lawyers, and they brought in three lawyers who loved to fight. As it turned out, both groups came to a place where they could see that through me we could find a solution to our problem. I think that people who have this spiritual philosophy of life or this discipline can solve these problems, because both sides can trust them.

'I have attended meetings where everyone is so stressed. There isn't enough money to buy supplies, customers are not paying, our bank is reducing our line of credit, these types of things. Being the Chairman of the Board, I ask them, "Why are you so uptight about all this? We are mainly spiritual beings. Don't let all of this kill you."

'The General Manager of our plant in Peru is an artist and he loves to paint, even though he now runs the company. I said to him, "I would love for you to stay here, but you are an artist, why don't you go and paint and leave the company if this is what you would rather do?" This attitude helps him to step out of his problems.

'I also try to use familiar examples that they can understand. One I like very much is the story of a powerful man in Brazil who said that the most important decision he made in his life was to stop working. Another one is that I remind people that no one dies saying that they wished they had worked more, or that they had made more money.'

27

Parantha Narendran

Strategy Director, Eurotel Telecom, Czech Republic

Parantha Narendran, aged 34 at the time of the interview, was Director of Strategy at Eurotel, the highly profitable and largest mobile telephone operator in the Czech Republic. He is one of the youngest leaders we have had the pleasure of interviewing, but in spite of his young age he has already had considerable international experience; he was born and raised in Sri Lanka, educated in Holland and the UK, received spiritual inspiration in India, and worked in several parts of Europe.

Prior to his top-leadership position in the Czech Republic, he had left a hi-tech consulting company due to his high ethical principles and then co-founded Boon Consulting in London. There he had raised US$40 million for a start-up company to be based on his own patented technology for improving the performance of the Internet when the 'IT bubble' burst and the market crashed in the beginning of this century. This brought an abrupt end to his plans of collecting the final $20 million that was necessary to establish the start-up and led him to accept his top-management position in Eurotel in early 2002.

Parantha Narendran told us about how being a leader helps him to grow spiritually: 'I used to meditate as a child of about 10 or 11 and continued to do this until I was 16. After that I studied a lot of books dealing with spiritual matters. Recently I have felt that I don't really need to do all of that; I just need to be open to myself. I've learned a lot about my spirituality and myself in the commercial world by having to make hard decisions. In these everyday challenges that I come across, I find that I grow and learn much more than if I were to read about spirituality or meditate.'

Some time after we interviewed him, Parantha Narendran left Eurotel, and from the end of 2004 he has been involved in private equity investments in so-called CDMA 450 projects in a number of European markets.[1] He is also an investor and shareholder in several new mobile operators in the central European market. Although he now works all over Europe in the telecom sector, he still maintains his base in Prague.

The demands of this private equity work seriously challenge his ability to lead from a spiritual basis. As he told us recently: 'The main thing I have found, as I have moved on in my projects, is that it is very hard to keep one's perspective on the work one is doing, because private equity deals are very much driven by a strong desire to reach a goal with single-minded focus, which can—and does—push out other aspects of one's life into second place from time to time.'

Pushing beyond limits and fear

I think the world needs spiritual-based leaders. I don't openly talk with people about my spirituality, but I think they respect me as someone who is ethical, someone they can trust, and someone who works hard in a selfless way. I don't have to talk about it. I just live it and people appreciate it, partly because in companies there are always political camps and I am seen as a neutral. Often when I talk, I do not say that this is the right thing to do. I will say, 'It is in Eurotel's best interest if we do this or do that.' I think this helps me, and people respect this.

At the time of the interview, Parantha Narendran is Strategy Director at Eurotel Telecom in Prague, the capital of the Czech Republic. He has a degree in physics from Imperial College in London, an MSc in Technology Management from Manchester School of Management, and has started, but not com-

---

1   CDMA 450 is a 3G technology that operates in the 450 MHz frequency band and is part of the broader CDMA 2000 group of technologies currently being deployed worldwide.

pleted, a PhD programme in Innovation Management at the United Nations University in Maastricht, the Netherlands.

'If I think of how spirituality affects me at work, it would be that spirituality challenges me and makes me grow. For me, spirituality is how you live your life. When you view your life as spiritual, you do start to make certain choices. For example, I choose to be a vegetarian because I respect life. I am aware of violence when it appears in my thoughts, words and deeds and I try to control that. There are certain positive values that I have accepted, and I try to be aware of all of those values in everything that I do.

'I've learned a lot about my spirituality and myself in the commercial world by having to make hard decisions. I feel I have been forced to become a leader, something I had always wanted to avoid in my life. In these everyday challenges that I come across, I find that I grow and learn much more than if I were to read about spirituality or meditate.'

'I started by studying physics so as to understand and find a theoretical explanation for how the universe was created. This was one of the spiritual questions that I was hoping physics would answer. But I became quite disillusioned with physics after three years and instead wanted to do something where I would be more involved with society. So I went on to study economics and technology management, primarily because I felt there were two things I could do with it: First, I could help understand how technology could be used in society to contribute to a better way of living; second, I could help understand how technology could be used in developing countries. I thought that technology and economic development were keys to enabling and enriching people's lives. So I thought there was a role that I might possibly play with all of this.

'When I was 26 years old I went to India and visited a spiritual teacher there. I was changed quite a lot by that encounter. I felt a very strong message to stop my doctoral work and get a job. As a result of my insights from this trip, I began to look for jobs. I ended up taking one as a telecom consultant in a company. Following this I worked for a consultancy for about a year. At the end of that year I became involved with a colleague of mine, an accountant, who was trying to expose some fraudulent behaviour in the company being perpetrated by the CEO. None of our colleagues wanted to support the accountant, nor did they really understand the issues at the time. I got involved in supporting him—advising him on what he should do. He did get fired. Once he was fired, I felt strong enough to resign from the company based on my principles.

'I started my own consulting firm with a colleague who had also left my former employer. This was quite a difficult period, but I believed that it would test my belief in myself and that I might not have another chance to test myself in this way again. Some months we made money and some months we didn't. We knew that we could easily go and get another job with a very nice salary, but it was a good test of faith to see if we could hang on to our original visions despite the challenging financial situations. During that period, I faced one of my biggest challenges.'

Pushing myself beyond my limits

'I had this idea about how the Internet could be made more efficient by using a special technology in a particular way. So I spent a lot of time convincing my partner that we should patent this technology and we spent a lot of money doing this. I also spent a lot of time on the technical design and putting together a group of people to push it through, like team managers, marketing executives and high-profile people. After a while we took the project to the Cisco incubator programme.[2] We tried to raise US$60 million, and they offered us US$40 million. This was really a test for me as I was dealing with bankers and investors and technology experts. I would have to talk with them, to make presentations for them. It was a test of my confidence, since I didn't really believe in my capability to make such things happen. But here I was pushed into a situation where I had to do it. I knew that other people's hopes of making money were dependent on me. I myself wasn't interested in making money; I just wanted to see this idea happen. I was forced to try and make this thing happen, knowing that they were all expecting me to do it.

'Despite all of the rejections we had over a period of a year, we kept picking ourselves up and went on. After a year, we finally hired a guy to be the CEO who was a founder and marketing director of a successful company, so he had a lot of credibility. He came on board, and we were just about to get the US$60 million when the market collapsed. For the first month after the market crashed, it was incredibly depressing. This disappointment of what looked like a huge business success did have some immediate effect on me, even though I myself was well aware that money comes and goes. It was the best learning experience I ever had. I saw that I could push myself beyond what I thought were my limits and could achieve what I wanted.

'In the larger perspective, I didn't actually see it as a failure. I saw it as a failure only in the sense that I didn't succeed in helping others who had hopes and dreams. But I also felt like I had succeeded in that I pushed myself to the limit and even beyond my limits in some ways. To get that far I had to have

---

2   Cisco, based in the USA, is a leading supplier of networking equipment and network management for the Internet. Its so-called incubator programme has for many years provided support for innovative students and entrepreneurs working in networking for the Internet.

faith and do the right thing. I had to listen to myself and not be worried about anything else. And at the same time, I had the awareness that it was all kind of a game. I have learned as much from it as I possibly could. Succeeding wouldn't have made the things I've learned any more beneficial.'

Parantha Narendran reflected on his spiritual theme that 'spirituality challenges me and makes me grow,' and said: 'Having left a company due to ethical principles and having been through this demanding attempt of a start-up, I had really experienced some tests. Through experience I have noticed that as I've become more aware of myself, I have learned things about other people and life that have just seemed to come to me, and I have become more content and happy with myself.'

Responsibilities of a strong ethical position

'My consulting firm was offered a contract with Eurotel in the Czech Republic and I went there. The CEO was impressed by my work, so they kept me for about ten months, and then they offered me a job as a Strategy Director. Eurotel is the largest of three mobile operators in the Czech Republic and it is considered as the premier company in the country, having the same brand recognition as Coca Cola. It is also one of the best-run mobile operators in the world and has a very good reputation. It has an EBITDA [earnings before interest, taxes, depreciation and amortization] margin that is reaching 50 per cent and is one of the top three operators in Europe, so it has a very high profile. Eurotel has about 2,000 employees and is valued at roughly 2.50 billion US dollars.

'I am addressing questions as to how Eurotel should go from being a successful mobile business mainly built on voice to being a mobile operator which also collects revenues from data traffic (video downloads, games, etc.). I sponsored a project through the company to implement a highly controversial new network, which will bring mobile broadband Internet access to the Czech market at cost-effective levels. It will be the first such network in Europe and will help increase the valuation of Eurotel by around 20 per cent. It should also set the trend for the rest of Europe to follow—and forms the first part of Eurotel's data strategy.

'In some ways, I feel like I have moved around a lot in my career. I don't think it is bad at a junior level, but when you get to the senior level you recognize the impact that it has on the organization as a whole. For example, when I left my first company after the accountant had been fired, I was a reasonably high-profile consultant. There were 60 consultants within that company in the UK. Because I left for my own personal reasons, others started to leave for a variety of reasons—some of them also because the accountant had been fired. Within a period of six months, that company collapsed! This made me recognize that if you do take a strong ethical position, it puts a lot of responsibilities on your shoulders.'

Conquering fears and empowering employees

Parantha Narendran continued his reflections on responsibilities and success: 'I would say that success in my life would be learning to conquer my fears,' adding that what he seeks is 'awareness and contentment'.

'When I do not have an active ego, I am able to help get things done far more effectively. Essentially, it is like a game, and I am actually benefiting the most from the whole exercise. If my ego is active, then I tend to think, "I can't do this and I can't do that"—a bit like when I was trying to raise money and didn't have faith in myself. In that case I was forced into a position where I had to do what I thought I couldn't do. I had to make something happen for the benefit of everybody. I had no time to step back and say, "I can't do this" because my ego was afraid of failure. I just had to get it done. And I've done this and realized that I was a lot more capable than I gave myself credit for.

'I want others to learn the same thing. So I try to pass these lessons about ego and fear on to others when I speak to them. And I do this in a straight-forward, down-to-earth manner. I look to see why they are motivated to achieve the goals they are speaking about and what inhibits them in achieving their goals—it makes them think more about their life.

'Now that I am in this company as a leader and not as a consultant, a principle I have is to try to help the people I work with to achieve their best potential. This is an area where I think that spirituality and the objectives of an organization happily coincide. I think that when a leader believes in empowering individuals, he has the best interests of the company at heart, and can use the empowerment as a vehicle to this end. Having the individual realize his potentials along with the spiritual aspects, and having the organization develop itself at the same time, are my primary and secondary goals.'

An expanded concept of purpose and success

'In a company, there is nothing wrong with making money; what really matters is how you use it. Companies have to make money because they have to look after their employees. And they have to give some return to their owners. But there are a number of things which companies can do within this framework to help their employees to empower themselves and to give them a stable quality of life.

'A company can also be a good citizen within society. I think the long-term winners in a corporate environment will be companies that do take on some broader stakeholder-value orientation, rather than just being a profit-oriented company. So it is also in the interest of the company to have an expanded concept of purpose and success even though it may mean taking some harder decisions regarding profits.

'I don't have great expectations of what Eurotel can achieve within the Czech Republic in the future, since it's already a flagship company here. But my aspirations are twofold. First, that people can come to Eurotel and learn new skills, learn more about their own capabilities, and use Eurotel as a springboard to move on. Second, that Eurotel is a place where people can have regular jobs and some stability which can give them and their families a quality of life that allows them to pursue other interests that they might have. A third thing I aim at is to deliver value to Eurotel's owners and to cultivate our being a representative ethical company within the Czech Republic, and set the standard for other companies to follow.'

Love and appreciate all

'My advice to an aspiring spiritual-based leader is that he or she should not only try and lead by example in a practical way, but also make careful use of their language, of what they say and do not say. This can help them to transform their own spiritual aspirations into the creation of a healthy and helpful working environment. From a spiritual point of view, the approach towards all individuals should be one without fear—I should be able to love and appreciate all people regardless of their capability or attitudes.

'I am not sure whether there is a grand meaning to life. But the more experience I have, the more I think there is. And I am sure that, if there is a meaning to life, it is to get to an understanding where you can see all of life and yourself as united, as integral, as unity. I've seen glimpses of that every now and then. I try to carry this through into my work—I try to rise above the politics of the organization and meet people on an individual level—and I try to build relationships, which are based on honesty and openness.'

28

Deependra Moitra

Former General Manager, Engineering, Lucent Technologies, India

Deependra Moitra is General Manager—Engineering, in the Indian operations of Lucent Technologies, a major hi-tech organization with 70,000 employees worldwide and revenues of US$19 billion.[1] At the time of the interview he was 32 years old. Not only is he the youngest person interviewed for the Spiritual-based Leadership Research Programme; at the age of 29 he was also the youngest person ever to be appointed General Manager at Lucent Technologies. While carrying out his leadership role at Lucent Technologies, he is also very active at the industry–academia interface, working towards a doctoral degree as a PhD candidate in the Netherlands, being on the editorial board of 13 international journals and lecturing throughout the world. 'I do a lot of speaking both here in India and abroad. Other than Australia, Africa and Antarctica, I have spoken in every continent in the world,' he told us. As will be clear from his interview, he faces a major challenge of maintaining a balance between these demanding professional and academic activities and his family life.

---

1 Lucent Technologies, supported by Bell Labs, which is the research arm of Lucent Technologies, delivers systems, services and software for communications networks throughout the world. Since 1988 it has had a presence in India, where it has grown dramatically in the last few years; it has nine offices and more than 1,200 employees. It is also a major hub for Lucent Technologies' research and development activities worldwide.

He is a most dynamic and passionate person—so engaged in what he does that his spiritual focus is on subduing his ego and obtaining equanimity. He says: 'This is where spirituality comes into the picture for me. I look to spirituality to help me find inner peace and calm. I have a personality where I cannot sit quietly. I actually resist sleeping because my mind is so dynamic and active, and full of new possibilities and dreams. So my immediate focus is on developing peace of mind and staying calm.'

Deependra Moitra has a bachelor's degree in engineering from Calicut University in India. Before joining Lucent Technologies he worked for the prestigious Space Applications Centre and for Siemens Communications Software in India. Early on, however, he discovered that he was not interested in a career in engineering and switched to the profession of management. He is no longer with Lucent Technologies: as of summer 2006, he is Associate Vice President with Infosys Technologies Ltd, in Bangalore, India.

An approach to fulfilment

Even though I have only lived a short 32 years, my experiences with ego have been very revealing. I have seen that the root cause of all difficulties is ego. There is a spiritual scripture that says, 'Renounce ego is the Lord's request. You shall become God is the Lord's promise.' This is a very powerful statement and I am trying to live this. I do feel that I help people without a selfish motive; however, I still have room to grow.

Deependra Moitra grew up in villages and small towns. 'My father was a veterinarian surgeon, and he was working with a lot of United Nations projects; that is why most of the time we lived in villages,' he explains. 'I did not actually attend a proper school until I started my 11th standard. It was only when I came to my 12th standard that I actually moved to a somewhat bigger town.

'I then moved to the state of Kerala to do my engineering. I graduated with a degree in Instrumentation and Control Engineering. I was actually the first rank holder in the entire university in 1992. My dream was to become a scientist and so in 1993 I joined ISRO, the Indian Space Research Organization in Ahmedabad [a major city in north-west India]. I was a part of the organization for three years. It was a rewarding experience because I had a chance to be exposed to a lot of facilities and equipment, which I would never have seen elsewhere. At the same time, I was feeling bad because of the bureaucracy, since it was a governmental agency. I didn't have a free hand to work with an entrepreneurial mind-set.'

Concentrating on focus and purpose

Deependra Moitra got married shortly before leaving ISRO. He and his wife, who was in the process of finishing her doctoral work, decided to move to a place where both of them would have opportunities—'and particularly a place where I could contribute more meaningfully,' he told us. 'We moved to Bangalore and I came to work for Siemens here.' The part of the organization he worked for was responsible for project and quality management for the company's software operations. 'I think I did good work,' he said, 'because six months later I was elevated to lead that function.'

After another seven months at Siemens, he came to know that Lucent Technologies was setting up its operations in India. 'I approached the people in Lucent and they first told me that I was too young to work with a start-up team; I was 27 at the time. There was an American gentleman who came to set up the basic structure and hire the initial management team. I persuaded him by telling him that I was confident that he would need someone with my kind of background somewhere down the line.'

'Bell Labs and Lucent had a very strong brand name. I had read about them since my schooldays. I joined Lucent in September 1997, so I have now completed five years with them. In Lucent I have played various roles. For the first one and a half years, I spent my time strategizing the research and development operations and their growth in India. To give you an idea of how we grew, we grew to 1,200 people in three years. We had to go around the country interviewing people. Our hiring ratio was to hire about two people from every 100 that we interviewed, so it was a very tough hiring process.

'In Lucent we were a research and development cost centre. After one and a half years, I was asked to get the operation formally certified as Bell Laboratories. Now, not every entity in Lucent can be a Bell Laboratory. You have to be able to demonstrate that you can perform work that is technically excellent and that you have the basics in place to innovate.

'Typically, quality programmes are all about change. The orders are usually handed down from the top without really explaining the purpose and context for why they want this change. I feel that most people who have to implement these quality programmes are not clear about their purpose or how the programmes help the business.

'I have found a way to address this. I help them understand the role of process in this whole chain of technology and customers. I help them understand the need for processes and how they play a meaningful role in translating their technological products into customer delight. I also help them to realize how all of this will contribute to their own growth first, before we talk about the growth of the organization. Focus and purpose were very much present here—and that's how it links to my way of defining spirituality as an approach to fulfilment.

'As a result of all of this, we were able to become certified as a Bell Laboratory in just one year's time, which is the only time this has happened in the history of Lucent Technologies.

'This was also a time where I became the youngest General Manager in the whole of Lucent worldwide; I was then 29. So this was very good for me, because it kept prompting me to do more and more.

'I was then asked to set up a new organization in India, which is called Bell Labs Advanced Technologies. I was asked to work with Bell Labs in the USA and see what kind of work could be done in India that could be supported by the talent pool here. Unfortunately, that is when Lucent's financial situation began to deteriorate. Eight months into this job we had to stop it, because we didn't have funding anymore.

'For the last one and a half years, I have been on an assignment where I work with teams in China, Germany and the UK. We are a collaborative product development team that is spread across geographical locations. My current organization is about 250 people.'

Fulfilment and self-mastery

Deependra Moitra defines spirituality as 'an approach to fulfilment'. 'Now what fulfilment is to one individual will differ from what fulfilment is to me. It is important to me how I achieve fulfilment. It is a path. That is why I say that spirituality is "an approach to fulfilment".

'Ultimately, what is most important to me is: joy, satisfaction, peace and fulfilment. Now how do I get this? I have a four-pronged approach. Here is society, here is my family, here is my professional life and here is my personal life. Since joy, satisfaction, peace and fulfilment are what are most important to me, I look to see how I can achieve these in each of the four areas of my life. I do not want to say that I am able to do all of this in the manner that I would like to do, but this is an approach that I am trying to take.

'Let's take my professional life. I want to contribute something that has an impact on the way people think and do work. I do not merely want to be a player; I want to be someone who really has an impact on people and on businesses. A goal is to become a most sought-after leader. Now, here my intention is not to become famous or popular. It is more like being a coach that people feel comfortable coming to talk to and feel that they will benefit by their interactions.

'The personal side is what I call "self-mastery". This is what I want to achieve, even though I feel that I am far away from it now. But my ultimate goal is having control over my mind, body and thoughts. I have shared the concepts of "forgetting that you are somebody" and "striving to be a nobody" with many people and it has generated a lot of interest in some of them. However, there are other people who just brush it aside as if I am saying something they cannot comprehend.

'The third aspect is family. Here are the things that are important to me, such as peace and the education of my child. Wealth is important to the extent that I can live a peaceful, comfortable life, but not so much wealth that it takes away my peace of mind.

'The fourth aspect is society. I grew up in rural areas. One of the things I saw that was absolutely lacking was good education, even at the primary level, and good primary health care. Therefore, with my own money, I have started two organizations in a rural area where primary health care and primary education are provided. It is still in its embryonic stage, but I would say that I have put in 75 per cent of my savings on that project.

'All of this is a framework for me to operate in life. Perhaps I am doing well in some of these dimensions and not so well in others. That is my challenge as an individual: to balance and take an integrated perspective of all four. I do not want to do one thing at the cost of another. For example, I do not want to excel in my professional circles at the cost of my family life. So there is a need for me to balance and that is where I am struggling right now.'

His focus on 'balance' finds expression in his spiritual practice: 'My most current spiritual practice is to have peace of mind. This is an art that I need to develop. How do I insulate my mind, heart and body from external disturbances? The last two years have been extremely hectic for me, both on the personal front and on the work front. My involvement with editorial boards of journals has also put a tremendous amount of pressure on me. I am in a stage where juggling all of these balls is becoming difficult for me. I feel that as I develop more and more of this inner peace, then I can really serve others. Unless I do this, I cannot give my mind and heart to others. Therefore, my current focus is to come to a state where I am at peace. I am affiliated with a spiritual society[2] and am looking to their guidance to help me find this inner peace.'

---

2 He refers here to the Yogoda Satsanga Society (Self-realization Fellowship in the USA). He also follows writings from the Himalayan Institute (in the USA) and Sri Aurobindo Ashram, Chinmaya Mission, and Sri Ramakrishna Mission in India.

Living with a purpose

Having reflected on his definition of spirituality as 'an approach to fulfil-ment', Deependra Moitra defined his spiritual theme as 'living with a pur-pose' where 'true fulfilment is then the outcome'. He told us: 'Here's an exam-ple of what that means to me. There are millions and millions of people on this earth and yet there are names of people who stand out—names like Mother Teresa and Mahatma Gandhi. What is the reason that these names stand out from among the millions of other people who live on this earth? The fundamental reason that comes to my mind is that they all lived with a purpose. So, living with a purpose is something that is very important to me and I am making my best attempts to live in this way—it is an issue of passion and emotion.'

'I do not want to live with a purpose so that my name can stand out, just as none of these people focused on having their names stand out. I am trying to practise being someone who has no ego, who is a "nobody". I have seen that when we think we are important, it puts a lot of pressure on us. For example, if I am giving a talk somewhere and I think that I must give a great talk, then I feel a lot of pressure. I want to operate without an ego, as if I am no one spe-cial. This is still difficult for me to practise. I still have struggles from time to time between my own self-interest and a larger purpose that I should focus on.'

Creating joy all around you

Deependra Moitra tells of how his spiritual path is 'associated with a set of values or traits that a person will demonstrate. In business, here are the ones that are important to me. First of all, it is very important to me that I deliver comfort to people around me, so I place a lot of emphasis on emotional val-ues. If you look at some schools of spirituality, they will say that you should not be emotional. But the way I look at it, and what I practise in my work life, is that as human beings we all have sentiments and emotions. And, therefore, we all have an emotional reservoir.

'For me to be really successful in relationships and in doing productive work with others, I must tap into that emotional reservoir within myself and within others. When I tap into the emotional reservoirs of others, it basically makes people feel comfortable around me. I think that understanding and respecting people's emotions is very, very fundamental to both my work life and my private life, and I place a lot of emphasis on this. When I talk about spirituality in business I think it really boils down to taking care of people's emotions and being truthful.

'My fundamental goal is to help others succeed, so I am willing to sacrifice a lot to do that. I am willing to let others grow, blossom and achieve things at the cost of my own time and effort. I help a lot of people without feeling any selfish motive. When I see someone succeed, I do feel joyful, and this is important to me. Today I do have joy, but it is more momentary, more situation-driven. I think that peace and joy are different and yet they work together. I think that if my joy were constant, then I would have peace.

'I think that peace and joy are a form of wealth that businesses can create. I don't think there is anything wrong with creating wealth financially in a business, as long as the experience you deliver is rich to all of the stakeholders, which includes the society. Wealth does not just have to do with money. It is about protecting everyone's interest, along with creating joy and growing. This is how I would describe being spiritual: it is creating joy all around you and expanding the circle of joy and prosperity. But one thing I feel we need to realize is that we are in business to make money; there is no doubt about it. What is most important, however, is that we generate wealth through ethical means.

'Generally, within Lucent, there is a tremendous amount of respect for people. The amount of freedom it gives to its people, the amount of training and development it provides to its people, and the way people are treated, makes it certainly a great corporation. That is the reason I have worked here for the last five years.'

29

Ananth Raman
Chairman, Graphtex, Inc., USA

Dr Raman is another of the spiritual-based leaders presented in this book who has a multicultural professional background. He is of Indian origin and has held leadership positions in General Electric Company in India and Carborundum Company in the USA and India. Later he became Group Chief Executive in the USA of the Swiss-based holding company Catisa, with manufacturing operations in the USA, Europe, Asia and Africa. He has also been advisor to the United Nations Industrial Development Organization, UNIDO, as well as to several West African governments on industrial development. He was 55 years at the time of the interview.

He is a true product of this multicultural background, moving with equal ease in the globalized world of big business and the villages in his native India. Both of these environments have exerted a strong influence on his spiritual development. As he told us, 'I was taught by my mother that ethical values were the way to maintain order in society, so I naturally used them in my working experience over the last 30 years. The ethical guidelines that my corporation set up guided me in the right direction. Once I started thinking along the lines of spirituality, these kinds of ethical policies became a part of me. I discovered deeper values within each one of them. I realized that it is not just a good business practice to be ethical. We all have a duty, a role to perform, that has been given to us by God.'

Ananth Raman received his bachelor's degree in Mechanical Engineering in India and worked in the UK and India before getting his MBA from the Harvard Business School and later on a PhD from Columbia University in the USA. Throughout his professional career he has continued his ties with academia and has been an Adjunct Professor at several business schools in Europe and the USA.

He is now semi-retired and spends much of his time in his native India, where he has recently built a home in Bangalore, and where he currently is Honorary Professor at Sri Sathya Sai University.

~

Adding value

My spiritual development has helped me to institutionalize the principles of having a purpose, adding value, and setting an example. As a business leader I must set an example which others can follow. There is no point in me trying to get my organization to be truthful, unless I am truthful.

After he received his MBA from the Harvard Business School, USA, Dr Ananth Raman worked at the Carborundum Company in the USA and India for about ten years until the mid-1970s, eventually becoming Corporate Vice President of Corporate Planning and Diversification. 'I left them,' he told us, 'to join a Swiss group called Catisa, which is a holding company owning manufacturing units in different parts of the world. They typically manufacture things like aluminium and packaging materials—medium-technology kinds of products. They operate in about 30 countries around the world.'

He started working for them in Nigeria, and ended up overseeing the company's entire operations in nine countries in Africa. In 1993 he asked to be transferred to the USA, where his son was studying. 'At this time, there was a recession in the USA. My first challenge was to diversify and modify our operations and that challenge has continued over the years. While all of this has been happening, I wanted to continue my learning, so I started doing some teaching at Columbia University in New York. I also decided to go for a doctorate programme in international business. Thus, over a period of eight years, I was a student and teacher at the same time.

'For the past ten years, I have looked after three different operations in the USA. One, Graphtex, Inc., manufactures membrane switches for electronic input equipment, while the other two, which are subsidiaries, manufacture aluminium products. In one of the companies I am the Chairman and CEO; in the other two, I am the President as well as General Manager overseeing the operations.'

Spirituality and a sense of values

'I think my shift to looking more deeply into spirituality came about around ten years ago, and it was a gradual process. I felt that there was something more to this world. There were some things that did trigger this. One of these was when I was reading the book *Parable of a Sadhu*, where the author is climbing Mount Everest and somewhere around 20,000 feet he meets a sadhu (holy man). This was a defining moment for him and he decides to give up his climb. Then he starts pondering about the meaning and existence of life. So that also prompted this same inquiry in me, "What are we here for?"

'Little incidences like this continued to have me want to read more; it has been a quest for knowledge that has me wanting to continue to learn more. Thus, for me, spirituality is mainly a matter of self-inquiry. I don't think that practices always help. I think that different people must take different routes. Some people do a lot of service to foster their spiritual growth. I prefer the path of knowledge; to learn more and to read more has always been my path.

'Until now, I have never formally attempted to define spirituality. For a long time, spirituality was just a cliché, a word that all of us bandied around without any real understanding. My definition of spirituality would be "the awareness of myself" as part of supreme consciousness, that feeling of "I", and then to extend that to mean that "I" and the Divine are the same. The Divine is in all of us. Spirituality is knowing the true core of being within you, and realizing it is the same within everyone. Then you are able to de-link the "I" from the body.

'What I care to know is that there is a Being; there is awareness. It reminds me of a teacher who once asked his student, "What is it, knowing which, everything else is known?" To me this is awareness and this answers everything. As long as I know I am, then everything else is known.' Reflecting on this, Ananth Raman says that his spiritual theme can best be expressed as 'Awareness' and 'Realizing Divinity'.

He reflects on how his focus on spirituality affects his behaviour as a leader: 'Today, I may still need to discipline an employee by reprimanding him. But I can see that it is just an act, whereas five years ago I would have really gotten angry. Some of the words I say are just the same, and the decibel level is just the same, but now I do it because I believe it is my role to do it. There is absolutely no malice or anger at all in this for me. I think that the question of ego and malice is because of body consciousness, once you release this notion that the "I" is not the body, then this will naturally go.'

'I basically associate spirituality with a sense of values. The values that we learned at our grandmother's lap, the values we learned in school, and the values we use to live in the community. The values are simple, like self-respect, dignity and love. To me these are all values that are a part of you and should arise out of a feeling of union with all others. If you realize this, I think that a lot of life's problems will be solved.

'My spiritual purpose of life would be imparting knowledge and education, and enhancing shareholder wealth, which is also adding value somehow. I am not necessarily talking about increasing your personal assets here. It has got to add value somewhere in living life. I believe that everyone's life has a purpose and that that purpose must add some value. Even if it is a simple matter like soothing a fevered brow or wiping a tear from a child's eye. For this you must first set a personal example. As a business leader I must set an example which others can follow.'

Spirituality, religion and a spiritual teacher

'I think there is a distinction between spirituality and religion. I tend to consider religion more as formal, more as ritualistic, more as concentrating on a set of belief systems, like karma, death and rebirth. These are not the ultimate Truth; they are belief systems. Does karma exist? I don't know. Is there rebirth? I don't know. These are all belief systems that help us answer a lot of questions about life's mysteries, but they are not the ultimate Truth.

'I used to run in two parallel worlds: religious rituals and spirituality. The way we learn spirituality as Hindus is through the rituals. You do the rituals and most of the time you do not understand them; at some point, you try linking the rituals with the spirituality.

'All of the different religions have their own belief systems and at some point they do cross over with each other. While in spirituality there is no belief system. Spirituality talks about ultimate Truth, there is nothing to question. You must realize it, you must understand it, you must feel it. This is where I draw the line between spirituality and religion.'

'I have been coming to India from the USA and have been devoted to a spiritual teacher for the last 20–25 years. Being a devotee of this teacher is largely responsible for my thinking in this way. In all activities, in all actions, whatever happens—whether I am successful or not—I can sit back and realize God's guiding hand through all of it. Even when I feel He is pushing me into despair or into problems, I can see He is guiding me.'

Repaying debts in a responsible way

'There was an instance where I was not the decision-maker; my boss was the one who had to make a very important decision. However, I was able to see the basis of this decision from a spiritual perspective only after it had happened.

'We had borrowed a large sum of money from a banker who wanted to pull out of their operations in the USA, and we had a large multi-million-dollar loan due to them. I went to the lender and told them that, since they were the ones who were leaving, we would like to pay them less than the total amount. I proposed a certain reduction in what we owed them, and we had an extensive discussion about this. With hesitation, they agreed to a reduction, but it was a smaller reduction than what I had proposed. Since we couldn't finalize the actual amount of the reduction, they had the head person from their London organization come to the USA to meet with our principal shareholder from Switzerland, and we decided to let those two people work it out.

'I had briefed our principal shareholder, who was actually my immediate boss, on what had taken place up to that point. I suggested that he offer an amount for the reduction that was a little more than they had agreed to. I went into the discussions feeling very proud that I had negotiated this loan reduction, and had gained this extra income for the company.

'As we moved toward this critical point during the talks, my boss suddenly said, "I have not come here to ask for this reduction, I will not do it." We had negotiated so hard for this reduction, and now this man was saying that he would not ask for this! He told them that we would in due time pay back the entire amount of the loan.

'I was totally shocked. Here we had a huge gift of money available, and my boss was giving it away. Afterwards I asked him why he had done this, and he said, "As a businessman we have a responsibility. We are responsible not only to our shareholders, but also to our bankers. We have borrowed this money from them; we must repay it to them. There is absolutely no reason why we should take advantage of this situation just because they want to pull their operations out of the USA. This is no way to do business."

'I felt this was a deep spiritual lesson for me. The lesson was that *all obligations must be honoured*. They must be paid back in the right way, not by arguing like this. I saw that all obligations, whether they are in cash, such as this, or in some other form, must be repaid in some way or another. This is my duty and I must honour that duty. I saw that this was the only way to do business in this world.

'If I had not looked at this from a spiritual perspective, I would have thought, "I did all of this hard work for this man, and he is not even appreciating it." My financial controller was with me, and he is still not convinced today that what my boss did was right. He still calls it a stupid decision, and I continue to tell him why it was not a stupid decision.'

Unity of thought, word and action

'There was a time when we were introducing ISO 9000, which was a system of quality control measures for our company. One of our companies was a job shop where we do specialty items for our customers. Since these products are made for specific applications, it is extremely difficult to standardize things and is a very complicated process. This made it a difficult environment in which to introduce these types of quality measures, since they involve a lot of rigid procedures.

'The expert said, "This is all very simple. All you need to do is write down each of the procedures that you are already doing. You don't have to make any improvement; you don't have to say anything else except exactly the way you are doing it. This has nothing to do with right or wrong; you simply say what you are doing and do what you say." Even after he said all of this, my fellows were still completely worried.

'One evening I was thinking about this while attending a study circle with my spiritual group. I saw that all of this was simply talking about unity of thought, word, and action. So, I called in my employees and told them, "This is nothing but the concept of having what you feel, what you write and how you act be the same. This is all that ISO 9000 is about."

'So we went all over the company and said, "The company's objective with ISO 9000 is to have unity of thought, word and action." If I had used the word spiritual to describe the basis of this concept, I would have probably gotten some negative reaction. To me it was truth and honesty. When I explained what unity of word, thought and action meant, they understood the concept very easily.

'They started raising all kinds of questions throughout the departments; I was amazed at the chain reaction that began. So I told them, "Let's have a monthly meeting where we can discuss these problems where you find it difficult to be totally truthful." I tried to help them see the difference between telling a customer, "No, it won't go tomorrow, we are having difficulties", which is the truth, versus "It will go the day after tomorrow", which is a lie. In this way they could still buy some time without promising something which was not going to happen. We continue to have these monthly meetings where we examine these difficult situations and look to see how we can solve them with a unity of thought, word and action.'

Unanswered questions

'In a business sense, I like to talk about spirituality as ethical values. Initially the ethical guidelines that my corporation set up guided me in the right direction. When I was in one of the West African countries, the country was full of corruption, and you couldn't do anything without bribing someone. We were losing contracts and losing business. But the policy in my corporation was that you could not give bribes. At first, I wondered how I was going to get along without giving bribes. Ultimately, I chose to stay with the ethical values that the company ascribed to. Initially, I followed these ethical values because this was what I was taught. When I began thinking more spiritually, it gave me the reasons for why to behave this way.

'Values such as justice, truth, respect for others, equanimity, ability to take decisions, honesty and integrity are the core values that became very strong for me when I went into business. These are more on the ethical side, rather than on the spiritual side. Somewhere along the line, however, these two kinds of values began to link. Now I think of ethical values as nothing but a reflection of my spiritual values. For instance, in business you must respect yourself, your feelings, your customers, your employees. But then when you go deeper into spirituality, your self-respect begins to include respecting the inner Self. Then you try to understand: "What is meant by Self?" Self means "I", it means awareness.

'From this perspective, then, self-respect takes on a new kind of meaning. When we talk about self-respect in an ethical sense, we are talking about being respectful to your colleagues, shareholders and customers because it is a good business practice. But when you go a little deeper and look at it from a spiritual point of view, you realize that it is really about respecting the inner Self. You need to think about this, but when you do think about it you realize there is a linkage between the two. Then I think it brings about a whole new dimension. While ethics originally became something to maintain order in society, order in business, now it also gives you a level of equality with your Self and everything else. This is how I like to link spirituality with ethics and values in business.

'The best way to look at success is to look at the quality of your effort. Have I followed my inner conscience? Have I given my best effort? What was my underlining motivation? Have I done what was right? Have I learned from my effort? Have I used all of my senses and values that I am conscious and aware of? This is what is most important.

'I have questions constantly about spiritual practices in business. One of the most important questions I have is: what can business do to enhance values? Some others are: where does ethics end and spirituality begin, or *is* there a dividing line at all? Do we talk about spirituality in business, or just stay with ethics and not bother about spirituality at all? Businesses are a community of people from many cultures and different religious practices. Does business therefore have a role in attempting to ensure the unity of all religions? Does business have any role beyond just ensuring the rights of people and ethical values? Does it have to go the extra mile and cross the line to go into the arena of elevating spirituality in people? How do you do this without touching the sensitivities of the people? I haven't found the answers to these questions yet.'

30

Magnus Vrethammar

President, Finess, Switzerland, and Pergo, UK

Magnus Vrethammar was 52 years old at the time of the interview and has had 22 years' experience as a business leader. After a long business career as leader in major international manufacturing corporations, he was back in his native country Sweden as the President of the business development consulting company Cauldron AB,[1] a company that he founded some years ago. In this capacity he mainly works as a board member on behalf of the Swedish Industrial Development Council, which is a state-owned venture capital company. He told us about how he sees this new field of work with respect to his spirituality: 'My next focus as a leader is the "board power games", where greed, mergers and acquisitions flow freely and where interest in start-ups and new ventures by the emission of new shares are diluting the ownership position of the original founders. My challenge now is to take my spiritual approach and apply it to a new arena.'

In the profile presented here, however, we mainly focus on his leadership activities in major international manufacturing companies in Switzerland and the UK. In Switzerland he was the President of the Consumer Division of Finess, a subsidiary of a Sweden-based multinational, manufacturing paper products, with sales of 2.5 billion Swedish crowns (roughly US$300 million, given the

---

1   As of January 2007, Cauldron AB has changed its name to Creability AB. Magnus Vrethammar is President of this executive coaching and business development firm.

exchange rate at the time of the interview) and about 3,000 employees. In the UK he was President of the European activities of Pergo, a world leader in the production of laminated floors, with sales of roughly US$500 million, given the exchange rate at the time of the interview, and about 900 employees. He had previously been on its board for five years during the early 1990s, and he left the company at the end of 2001.

Magnus Vrethammar has a degree from the Stockholm School of Economics in Sweden.

We have known Magnus Vrethammar for a number of years. As should be clear from his profile, he is a deep and creative thinker, who has for many years reflected on the role of spirituality in business. He says, 'I want to have a life with an active consciousness. I want to be aware of my thoughts, I want to be aware of my actions, and I want to be aware of the consequences of those thoughts and actions. I also want to be aware of my feelings. I actively work towards such a state of conscious awareness. To do so is a decision I have made. This means that I regard myself as totally responsible for everything that happens in my life, irrespective of the external source of what is happening.'

In contrast to most of the other leaders portrayed in this book, Magnus Vrethammar's emphasis is on *implicitly* leading from a spiritual basis: he provides a number of rather critical comments about leading *explicitly,* which he says can make people 'look at me as an organizational priest . . . This will crystallize spirituality and make it a religion. Then you will have to start defending spirituality.'

Opening up

If I look at business as if it were a playground, then asking if it can be done more simply, if it can be done with more fun, and if I can avoid a bad conscience, then these are all spiritual questions . . . I feel that business is one of the best playgrounds you can have in life for your spiritual development.

In our interview with him, Magnus Vrethammar continually returned to the idea of 'opening up': 'Spirituality is an opening process. And then the question is, "What are you opening up to?" I would say love, as long as I am very careful in how I define love. Love can be, on an energy level, a very encompassing and still impersonal energy.

'Spirituality is man's quest into his innate divinity. It's more like a road than a state of affairs, a quest more than an arrival,' he explains. 'Spirituality for me is a universal context; it is limitless. Religion for me is limit; it is content, it is dogma.

'Building on my definition, I would say that spirituality is a state of mind and a feeling of a universal divine presence. This state of mind and this feeling are benevolently, urgently and continuously waiting for me to open up. Spirituality, to me, also describes the goal for every thing and every being in the universe, from a stone to an insect to a human being to an angel. From this point of view, there is no difference; everything in the universe is seeking to return to its source of being.

'I used to make a separation between my spiritual life and my worldly life, quite definitely. I used to meditate intensively; my wife felt it was too much, as I didn't need to sleep much. Then I had a long period where I didn't meditate at all. I would say now that I have merged my spiritual life with my worldly life. I cannot say that I have arrived at the point where everything is spiritual, but it is more so now.'

When asked about whether he still carries out spiritual practices, Magnus Vrethammar gave us a rather unconventional reply: 'I do a lot of work and experimentation with sound. It started because I used to sing a lot of religious songs and noticed the impact of sound. I started to work with sound at the chakras or energy level of the body. This included working with a research institute on the influence of sound on consciousness. This has had an opening impact on me. I should also mention that my wife is very spiritually inclined.'

From Sweden to Switzerland to England

Magnus Vrethammar went to the Stockholm School of Economics and, after receiving his degree, stayed there for a year as a research assistant. 'After finding that I would not like to be an academic, I went into business. I worked for the Nobel Group in their Consumer Goods division for close to ten years. This was a normal marketing career path: from product manager to senior product manager to marketing manager of new products to export director. I then joined Swedish Match (roughly 25,000 employees at that time) in their offices in Switzerland in 1984. So my family and I moved from Sweden to a place outside of Geneva, where we spent the next 12 years of our life.

'In 1988, a company named Stora, a very large Swedish forestry company, acquired Swedish Match and changed our operations. They put together a new division from bits and pieces in the consumer-oriented paper industry—

and this became the Finess Group. I worked there up to 1991. I was President of the Consumer Division; our turnover was about 80 per cent of the Finess Group.

'We sold Finess to a Swedish competitor, and I went on my own and ran a consultancy for the next eight years, operating from Switzerland and Sweden. I also owned 25 per cent of the largest Swedish BPR (Business Process Re-engineering) consultancy, mostly working in traditional mechanical industry. During my consultancy period, I did a lot of business development and reorganization work, as well as mergers and acquisitions with large business groups like my former employer, Swedish Match.

'I went back into regular business again as an executive in 1999 when I joined Pergo, a world leader in laminated floors. I was stationed in London being president of the European organization. It had a turnover of about US$500 million and about 900 employees in Europe. I left the company at the end of 2001.'

'Opening up' to one's own potential

Magnus Vrethammar expanded on his spiritual theme of 'opening up': 'I have often thought about how I can contribute to the process of "opening up" in others. When you first open yourself up to spirituality, you can very easily find yourself becoming a missionary of one kind or another. You feel that your experience is good, and you want the whole world to experience specifically what you have experienced—not necessarily the good that *others* have experienced, but what *you* have experienced.'

'Over time I feel that that missionary attitude does become more and more balanced and attuned to circumstances and other minds. You begin to realize that there is far more than just your own self-imposed importance. Then, hopefully, I think it turns to being an inspiration to others for their opening up. This would be more an implicit, rather than explicit inspiration; it takes place without having to say anything about it.

'One way I have experienced this process of opening up in others was with a very traditional business, like the paper mill business. It had a very traditional, production-oriented, corporate culture that was formed way back in the 1920s, and we turned it into a process-oriented organization.

'We gave a lot of responsibility down the lines to the machine operators, sales representatives, customer service and so on. There was much less control from above. People can accept such responsibilities because today they do a lot of work privately that qualifies them for much more sophisticated and independent work professionally. So during this process, we had a lot of opportunity to have the attention of the people, and that included the opportunity for spiritual development, because people felt they were opening up. This is the key word for me to the whole thing: they were "opening up" to their own potentials. They were "opening up" to their own self.'

If it is implicit, it stays; if it is explicit, it goes

'Since the business world is changing so rapidly, it's very seldom you can have that stability and safety for the roughly ten years that is required to turn the organization fully towards spirituality. Because what you are bringing out in people is their belief in themselves, and that is a very fragile thing to start with; it has to be pampered, in particular in the beginning, for the process to continue. But whatever shorter time is available can enable the organization to cope with some circumstantial pressure and still stay spiritual—because surely it will be seriously challenged under way and management changes can delimit the process. This is also the reason I want to be implicit because, if I work implicitly with spirituality, a lot of individual changes happen and that stays. If it is implicit, it stays; if it is explicit, it goes.

'There are a number of performance indicators that use the word "sustainable". In these, you can probably find support for a spiritual approach to management. But organizations also go through periods where they may have to flip-flop values completely, like at war. This is due to the creative process. It is creativity that creates more business, creates the advances in the culture; and, sometimes, different creative forces are at odds with each other—leading to "success" at one company and "failure" at another. At other times there can develop intense wars with various stakeholders—for example, with unions, competitors or owners, and in such situations values can flip-flop.

'What I mean is that to be sustainable—and to live up to being spiritually based in your leadership—you have to maintain your values through all the shifting climates, and this may not be possible. When you are explicit and you say that this organization has a spiritual purpose, or that you have policies that are specifically spiritual, what you do then is that you throw spirituality out the window when you have to flip-flop the preferences. This is why I want to stay implicit, because this is how spirituality will survive.

'The minute I put spirituality as the explicit part, people will look at me as an organizational priest and they will focus on the deviation of what I do as compared to the "textbook", rather than looking at my good deeds as a business leader. This will kill spirituality. This will crystallize spirituality and make it a religion. Then you will have to start defending spirituality.

'I used to be more explicit in how I led by my spirituality. I did that through company values and mission statements and through education and development programmes. However, looking back, I gradually became more implicit: less programme-oriented and more doing-oriented. This is how I lead now.

'Some of the most profoundly spiritual persons I have met are business leaders, but many of them would never consider themselves as spiritual or even reason in spiritual terms. I value those persons highly and consider them examples for anyone to follow. There are quite a few of them and they thrive in the business society because their approach creates trust and success.'

Economics as the explicit; spirituality as the implicit

To make his point on the need for being implicit with one's spirituality, Magnus Vrethammar digressed on the purpose of an organization. In contrast to most of the spiritual-based leaders we have interviewed, he focuses on economics as an/the end, not as a means: 'The organization is created for the purpose of effectively and efficiently utilizing resources—for creating economic value, what I refer to as "house-holding". The explicit and outward motive for house-holding an operation is simply house-holding an operation, nothing else. It is economics. To me, this makes life very simple and what you have to do as a spiritual-based leader is very clear too: it is house-holding. Now the implicit part is: "How do I live my life while doing this?" "How does this way of living affect my professional situation and the organization?"

'As an example, Pergo was the most implicitly value-oriented company I managed. At Pergo, I was faced with a severe decline in turnover. We were compelled to reduce the workforce by 30 per cent. Circumstances were such that Pergo had not put out new products and had not changed technology for the last five to eight years. So the first thing that I did was to convince the board of the strategy of how to change the whole thing. I came with plans for a wave of new investments and provided a lot of positive thinking. Then, in the next meeting, I had to announce that there must be a reduction in workforce by 30 per cent in order for the rest to survive. First the strategy came, then came the tough news.

'If I had been explicit about spirituality prior to this I would have been looked upon as a "smiling Boston strangler". Nobody would have believed me, and I feel that credibility is important.

'If you have developed a shared expectation in the organization that it is a spiritually oriented organization, this can lead to rules and expectations.

Then new members, who have not participated in the creation of this spiritual orientation, only have the choice of acceptance or defiance. It is very complicated to keep spirituality alive in such an organization because it can very quickly be turned into a survival game for the spirituality. Then the underlying spirituality becomes materialized into content, with rules, like a religion. It is no longer a quest.

'While I now take a more cynical approach to having explicit rules, to having explicit systems of value-based leadership and to auditing corporate responsibility—since my experience tells me these will crystallize the values and will have a diminishing potential—they are better than other kinds of rules. And while people do not become spiritual because of these types of rules, since spirituality is not rules, on the whole, it may be better to have such rules than not to have them.

'For example, the most explicitly value-oriented organization I managed was Finess. At Finess we had a lot of written policies and we also explained the policies. This helps people to reflect on things like "me and them", "me and my work" and so on. It was very interesting that, when the company was sold, all of this *apparently* went out the window. Later, when I came back to work with them as a consultant, I wanted to see if any of it had been left. To my surprise, a lot of these values stayed within the individuals, more than I could have expected. They *internalized* these values and now relate to this as a successful part of their lives.'

Success: ease and simplicity, contentment and joy

'For me success used to be about achievements of one kind or another, such as achieving a new culture in the company, achieving a quality programme that opens people up, achieving the process orientation. I do still believe in this process orientation, but otherwise success to me is all implicit now. Success for me now is a lasting, positive attitude towards an opening-up in the people, whose lives have touched me and that I have touched.

'The bottom-line question for me when considering a decision is: does this give me a bad conscience? If it does, then I don't do it. This is my guide. I very often ask whether something could be done with more fun. I have found that things can be done dramatically differently if you take this approach, and very often much more successfully. I also ask if something can be done more easily or more simply. Ease and simplicity are very much spiritual concepts.

'I feel a new value has developed in me to a larger degree than before and that value is contentment. So I measure my results by the level of contentment that I feel. This is different than feeling happy or sad in the face of success or failure; it is a more balanced feeling. I do feel joy, but it is a much lighter joy than before; it is not a huge laugh.

'I do feel that I have a balance between my professional life and my private life. Do I face questions or situations in my professional life that challenge my ethical and moral stance? Yes, definitely I do. I feel that the only way I can do this is to stay very firm on my own personal borderlines.'

Magnus Vrethammar told us of a learning experience—where he did not stay firm: 'Nothing kills an "opening-up" project and process orientation so much as having a person in a key position who is devoid of spirituality and does not understand anything else but self-interest. I have experienced this! You have to realize that, if you want to perform spiritual-based leadership and if you have this type of person close to the top, then you will have to remove him. My mistake was that I did not remove such a person, and I will never make that mistake again.'

'When I look at the world of business, I have never seen so much constructive work being done, so many open collaborations, and so much constructive opening-up. So I feel that business is one of the best playgrounds you can have in life for your spiritual development. Looking back on my own career path, I realize that it was also a highly spiritual exercise.'

In this section

This section of the book is unique; while in each of the previous six sections you met four to six spiritual-based leaders, in this section you will meet only one such leader—and you will meet her twice. When we first interviewed Amber Chand in 2002, she was able to tell an inspiring story of her experience as co-founder and VP of Vision at the rapidly growing firm Eziba, originally an Internet-based company selling high-quality crafts from artisans around the world. She told us, 'This is engaged spirituality—one which I find particularly meaningful as my spiritual practice.'

Amber Chand is a very poetic and exuberant person; she refers to her spirituality in metaphoric terms as 'a beautiful tapestry of compassion, balance, grace, and friendliness'. We have chosen two of these words, 'balance' and 'grace', as the title of this section, since these words so accurately and concisely portray the essence of how she deals with the challenges she faces when implementing her 'spiritual mission and vision'.

We next interviewed her in the spring of 2006—roughly a year after Eziba went bankrupt—and we were struck by how these qualities had enabled her to maintain peace of mind and courage in the face of Eziba's demise. She told us, 'Without the anchor of my spiritual practice, I could not have weathered this personal tsunami. For, at some level, I knew that Eziba's meteoric rise and fall were part of a larger archetypal story. That there were to be many lessons learned and that somehow I would find my way, guided by a sense of profound trust in Life and the truth of who I am and what I believe in.'

In this section, you will read about her entire journey, from the highs to the lows with Eziba, and her establishment of a new business that promises to be the fulfilment of her life.

Part I:

Amber Chand, Co-founder and VP of Vision, Eziba, USA

In *Caring for people, planet and profit,* Amber Chand speaks about the vision for Eziba, the company she co-founded: 'In the world as a spiritual woman, I see my purpose as trying to find a way to put love into action. The company I have created is very much an expression of my sense of service, allowing me to use business as an important and purposeful platform for my spiritual practice, knowing that our work with artisans around the globe—many of whom are talented craftswomen—helps to support, sustain and strengthen their lives.'

Part II:

Amber Chand, Founder, The Amber Chand Collection, USA

In *Balancing success and failure—the fall of Eziba and the rise of Amber Chand's spirit*, she reflects on her experiences with Eziba and her new endeavour: 'I am grateful to Eziba for teaching me important lessons and in illuminating for me that one can indeed create successful businesses that are spiritually inspired—only when this becomes one's singular mission and clear intent. I have no doubt that armed with patience, trust, focused clear effort and humility, the "Amber Chand Collection" will grow successfully.'

31

Part I

Amber Chand

Co-founder and VP of Vision, Eziba, USA

Amber Chand was born in Uganda in Africa of Indian parentage. As an adolescent she was sent to boarding school in the UK and then returned to Uganda to take her bachelor's degree in anthropology from the University of Uganda. Soon after, during a time of volatile political turmoil in 1971–72 under the regime of Idi Amin, she was expelled from her country along with all others of Indian origin, and her family lost all their belongings. She then received a full scholarship to the University of Michigan in the USA, where she completed a master's degree in social anthropology. At the time of the first interview, she was 51 years old.

Amber Chand has a very clear sense of the meaning of spirituality in her life. She told us, 'Spirituality for me is the essence of being, a space where the heart resides; it is soul. What comes to mind when I think about my overall spiritual perspective is a tapestry—a woven tapestry that has many threads weaving through it with a central thread that runs throughout. My spirituality feels like a beautiful, powerful central thread in this tapestry. Compassion, balance, grace and friendliness are words that ring as a spiritual theme for me.' She added, 'My spiritual practice is the context for my entire existence—and it offers me deep and rich support as I navigate through life. Service is the cornerstone of this practice and I see my entire life as an offering to serve this sense of higher calling or purpose.'

As an expression of this sense of service to a higher calling, in 1999 she co-founded Eziba, a multi-channel retailer of handcrafted objects from around the world. She was its Vice President of Vision, active in creating and growing a socially responsible enterprise that directly contributed to the economic and cultural viability of artisan communities worldwide. She travelled globally to identify talented artisan groups with whom she worked on product development and design. And she became Eziba's recognizable 'face' via her regular interviews in the media, her public speaking engagements, and her 'Letter from Amber' column prominently featured in Eziba catalogues that were read by over 2 million American households. She was highlighted as 'The Social Entrepreneur of the Month' in *INC Magazine*, July 2004 issue.

Following dramatic and extremely demanding events toward the end of 2004, Eziba faced bankruptcy proceedings and was sold in 2005. This provided Amber Chand with great professional and personal challenges, as well as with the opportunity to reflect on the purpose of business and her role as a spiritual-based leader. The story of the demise of Eziba and Amber Chand's reflections are related in the second half of this section.

We have known Amber Chand while she was on her roller-coaster ride, first up at high speed, then down at even higher speed, at no time with a safety belt. She told us that through all of the ups and downs it was her deeply rooted spiritual view of life that enabled her to remain a calm, generous and loving person, both at home and at work.

~

Caring for people, planet and profit

It seems as if people are beginning to look at Eziba as a case model of what business can look like if it is truly steeped in a mission that focuses on its impact on the people and the planet, as well as profits. If we are going to go out into the world and ask people to look at us as an organization that cares deeply about the planet, then we must care deeply about our people right here in our own home. I sincerely believe that in order to do this there must be a spiritual source to it.

At the time of the first interview, Amber Chand—anthropologist with a profound interest in issues affecting global exchange, artisan enterprise and peace-building strategies—was co-founder of Eziba, and its Vice President of Vision. She told us: 'A big part of my work is to cultivate relationships with all of the different constituencies that we have, which includes the artisans we work with.

'My co-founder, Dick Sabot, had created a very successful Internet company, which was then subsequently sold. We brought together our talents to bring beautiful handcrafted objects to the world using the Internet as our major vehicle. So my long-time fascination with cross-cultural studies, bringing worlds together, and finding beautiful things from artisans around the world, all came together with Eziba.

' "Ziba" is derived from the Persian word for beautiful. Since we started as an e-commerce company, we called the company Eziba.

'We were very clear from the beginning that we wanted to be a profitable company. This was unusual, because this area has typically been covered by non-profit groups or international organizations. This was one of the first times an entrepreneurial company was coming along with the aim of being a profitable, sustainable company. At the same time we are a company whose mission is absolutely embedded in the art of giving back.

'So, this is a very spiritual mission and vision of contributing to the well-being of artisan communities worldwide by stimulating demand for their products. Because this was such an ambitious goal, we realized after one year that we could not sustain our growth by being just purely e-commerce. So we then added a catalogue, and now we send out catalogues to nine million Americans. Last month we opened up our first retail stores, one here in our own community in North Adams, Massachusetts, and one in New York City. We have plans now to expand this retail presence around the country. So we are now a multi-channel retailer.'

Cross-cultural perspective

Amber Chand explained, 'I was born in Uganda of Indian parents and I was sent to a boarding school in England as an adolescent. This cross-cultural perspective guided me into my subsequent training as an anthropologist.

'After my first child was born in the USA, I took a part-time job with a local museum of art where they asked me to take a very tiny shelf of postcards and recreate it into a profitable, viable museum shop. For the next ten years I worked at this museum shop and became very interested in merchandising projects that were based on travelling exhibitions at the museum—products such as: American quilts, Japanese folk art, African masks, Indian textiles. My job was to basically create a wonderful display of products to sell alongside the show.

'This is where I began to develop a real instinct and passion for handcrafted objects. This is also when I realized there was such an abundance of exquisite products that were coming from some of the poorest regions of the world. While it made sense that they could be sold in this museum setting, I began to wonder how we could make these products more accessible to a larger market.' This wonderment found expression in 1999 when Amber Chand and her brother-in-law Dick Sabot co-founded the privately held, equity-based company Eziba—he as its Chairman, she as its VP of Vision.

Tea with Amber

'As a co-founder of Eziba, I have a tremendous amount of influence. I know when I walk through this company that employees look to me sort of like a mother, a nurturing spirit. So I try to continually find ways to be that nurturing, reassuring, loving spirit for them.

'About a year ago, I created a new initiative and called it "Tea with Amber". I was inspired to do this when, one day, my heart sank when I realized that the company had grown to such a degree that I no longer knew everybody. I could not see how I could be in the nurturer role if I didn't know everyone by name. I began to search for a way that I could connect with everyone in the company.

'So the idea came to me to just begin to have a cup of tea with every person. I rearranged my office completely, I created a little sitting area where I have some lamps and plants, I got out my lovely Mexican tea set and then I began to invite people to tea. Some people were very nervous because they were sitting with the co-founder. I would make them a cup of tea and what I noticed was that once they began to sip their tea, they would start to relax physically. Once we could both relax with each other, then we could actually open ourselves up to the "art of conversation".

'This is definitely something that the employees look forward to. It has become seen as a very important part of my work and as a way for us to continue to highlight Eziba as a company with a social conscience.'

The customer is God

Another initiative Amber Chand started early on at Eziba was to speak to the customers who were unhappy. This was inspired by her spiritual background. She grew up in a Hindu household, went to the Church of England while in boarding school, and has a strong interest in Buddhism. 'In my childhood my mother and father taught me to treat a guest who came to our house as God. You do everything you can to make their time with you happy and satisfying and comfortable. During our first customer training, I told our people that at Eziba I like to feel that the customer is God.

'We have a fabulous customer service group and yet I still want to speak with all of the unhappy customers. I pick up the phone and call them. I begin by apologizing to them: "I am so sorry that we have dissatisfied you in some way." The customers are amazed; they cannot believe that one of the founders is taking the time to call them. From this call, I always end up with a happy customer; we usually end up feeling a lot of joy and laugh together. I tell them to call me if they ever have any problems and I give them my direct line.'

A vision for the company

'What sustains us is that we know that the vision of this company comes from a spiritual source. It has been a challenging process, and yet from the very beginning we had a tremendous amount of interest from private funding. Our vision seemed very resonant with whomever we spoke to and in our first round of funding we raised US$40 million. We have grown exponentially and are now a multi-million dollar company. We have been in existence now for three years and we hope to become profitable within the next year.

'To me, being productive means that you are producing something for someone else. So, yes, everyone must work very hard in order to be productive so the company can be profitable. But I like to use the word "creativity" instead of "productivity". I feel that creativity allows each individual to feel a sense of meaning and connection to the deeper part of their lives. I have found that the more employees are encouraged to be creative, the more it gives them both a sense of ownership and a feeling that they are contributing to the company.

'I want this company to honour and celebrate the creative spirit and to applaud cultural diversity through its crafts. We find the best craftspeople all over the world and showcase their beautiful objects to the consumer who appreciates this type of culture. We are active in over 70 countries. We go directly to some of the countries and get directly involved in some of the villages and cooperatives. We meet with the artisans and create objects that are relevant to the global marketplace while at the same time being authentic to the techniques of their tradition. Because a lot of our artisans are women, our work empowers women to continue their craft traditions.'

Downsizing with humility

'One of the most painful periods for me as a leader in this company was the end of 2001. We were restructuring the company and looking seriously at our goal of being a profitable organization. As a result we had to let some people go. This was very painful for me. Here was a company that had promoted itself to be a kind, thoughtful, compassionate company and people came to work here because they had a sense of alignment with our mission of doing good for the planet.

'And yet I had to be realistic about the start-up phase that we were in. We were not a solidly profitable company yet. Once we had communicated to everyone about who would be laid off, we had an open forum meeting with everyone in the company. We clearly expected people to express their distress, unhappiness, frustration and anger.

'Even though some people did become quite angry, I could feel my heart accepting all of this. When one of our senior members became defensive, it sparked a battle between two wills; it was awful. Everyone looked so sad and devastated. I then very quietly went and stood in the centre of the room and said, "I am so sorry. I apologize for the way this has turned out." At that moment the faces of the people began to soften and a space was created that let them know that this was not about us versus them. It was simply all part of the journey of this company. The apology felt like a quiet, but powerful flame within me.

'Humility would be the word I would use to describe that moment. It was in this humility that I found my greatest courage. In that moment I literally redefined what a leader was meant to be. I have always known that I was here to serve and, anytime I forget this, I lose my way. Without this faith, this spiritual source, I do not feel it would be possible to be an exemplary leader. If we are going to go out into the world and ask people to look at us as an organization that cares deeply about the planet, then we have to start in our own home; we must care deeply about our people right here.'

Mindfully walking in balance

'I believe our success can only be measured by these three factors: the degree with which we impact people, internally and externally; the degree that we are stewards for the planet; and the degree we are profitable. Many of our senior people have come from traditional organizations and so our way of looking at people, planet and profits is new to them. For some it is still uncomfortable: it sounds good, but they don't yet believe that it will really work. I think our challenge is to show that we can purposefully and mind-fully walk in balance among the three components. I sincerely believe that in order to do this there must be a spiritual source to it. Otherwise, it just becomes another ideology or philosophy. It must be rooted in your being, and that's what I am seriously considering now. I wonder what it will take for people to experience this deep, deep belief and I wonder whether it is the role of business to help people find their spiritual source.

'I come to this whole experience of being a spiritual-based leader in business from the perspective of a seeker, rather than a knower. It is a very humble process and journey for me, and I do not feel that I have the expertise to tell the world how to do it.

'I like the idea that business can become a spokesperson in very legitimate ways for compassionate action in the world. Yes, we can be profitable and, yes, we can create wealth, and as we do that we can make sure that we are helping the people in our companies, in our communities and societies, and all around the world. And we can find ways to stop extracting and devouring and exploiting the resources of our planet. I think this is a very poignant time for businesses and I am very hopeful that business leaders will take on this kind of leadership.'

Part II

Amber Chand

Founder, The Amber Chand Collection, USA

Balancing success and failure— the fall of Eziba and the rise of Amber Chand's spirit

There is a particular story that each of us will tell about the collapse of the company—each bringing our own nuances and perspectives to the tale. My story ultimately rests on the importance of balance, sobriety, sufficiency, and patient and sustainable growth—as fundamentals in business practice, especially for a company that is founded on a strong mission to support impoverished people around the globe.

In mid-2002, looking back on the rapid growth of Eziba, Amber Chand told us, 'I think that this is a matter of balance. The attitude of greed and excess has really undermined most businesses. Here at Eziba, we know that a larger company could buy us or that we could go public and sell our stock on the stock exchange, but the question to us is: "How large do we really want to get?" I think that sometimes the idea of becoming a multi-billion-dollar company is so tantalizing that people forget what that really means in the lives of the employees. I think that finances must be discussed in this larger context.'

However, two and a half years later her thoughts were not on how large Eziba should be, as she faced perhaps the most daunting challenge of her career: the demise of the company, and the dream she had helped to bring forth in the world. It was a time that tested her ability to stay in touch with her spiritual purpose—which she describes as 'being in a reflective place of inner calm and divine connection' from which she can 'connect courageously with her life experiences'.

What happened? Here, in her own words from summer 2006, is a brief synopsis of the events, after which we will hear from Amber Chand how she responded and drew from her spiritual view of life to deal with, grow and learn from this difficult period of time—and to create a new structure for her vision.

The ups and downs

'Eziba's collapse in January 2005 was breathtaking! I remember leaving the company offices, with two cardboard boxes of belongings in my hands, numbed by the certain reality that the company had imploded and closed its doors to the world and equally frightened by what the future held for me and my family! Without my spiritual core, I would not have been able to navigate through this tumultuous time.

'From the outset, I had envisioned a company that would incorporate the values of service through enterprise—I termed it "compassionate commerce". My co-founder, Dick Sabot, was a well-regarded development economist and, more recently, a successful Internet entrepreneur. Dick was ambitious, interested in creating a fast-growth multi-million-dollar company that would rise to become a profitable leader in the global crafts arena. Both of us shared a commitment to creating a socially responsible foundation for the business.

'As Chairman, he quickly and skilfully raised $40 million in private equity funds within the first year. I, on the other hand, was much more sober in my ambitions, seeking a model for business that would be inspired by spiritual values and grow organically over time. Whilst Dick focused on structuring the company and putting together a powerful and influential board of venture capitalists, I focused my attention on assembling a collection of distinctive artisan-made products and on becoming the company spokesperson, forging relationships with editors, customers and artisan producers alike.

'There was a tremendous sense of excitement and enthusiasm from all our stakeholders when we launched in 1999—for what we all collectively experienced as an innovative, Internet-based, socially responsible model for business. By the time the company launched, it was valued at $100 million without having sold one object; Forrester Research, an influential research organization, touted Eziba as one of the most influential Internet companies to watch besides Amazon and eBay. *Forbes* magazine voted ours as one of the best websites around. The accolades were overwhelming—and based on what we aspired to accomplish and not on any particular reality of accomplishment.

'Armed with a profusion of cash, Eziba was quickly able to build itself into a marketing phenomenon, with billboards on buses in San Francisco and New York, advertisements in major national publications and a management team of heavyweights from companies such as FAO Schwartz, L.L. Bean, etc. And the promise to grow into the world's leading retailer of global crafts supporting millions of artisans continued to be projected. But therein lay the seeds of the company's ultimate demise.

'I have come to believe that an overcapitalized company can be just as vulnerable as an undercapitalized company—for, unless an organization is already firmly rooted in its unique mission, confident in its innovative and visionary leadership and willing to grow through its own merits and performance, it will not be able to create an enterprise of lasting change. Just as you cannot force a plant to grow quicker than it can, no matter how much fertilizer you throw on it, you cannot force a business to grow quickly, no matter how much cash you throw its way. Excessive money can breed arrogance and a false illusion of stability. Because Eziba already had $40 million in investments in its early days, it felt compelled to spend it, and to build a large operational infrastructure. "Big is Beautiful" became the aspirational vision.

'Even though Eziba's socially responsible mission supported responsible and reasonable growth, its financial infrastructure necessitated a different model—one based on fast growth supported by venture capitalists seeking sizeable returns and an exit strategy.'

This was in great contrast to Amber Chand's view: 'This was my life work, so there were no exit strategies for me.

'The internal pressure to grow the business into a profitable venture within a few years informed all of the decisions the company made, often to the detriment of its underlying mission. I remember the first time this happened. It was within a year from its launch, and Eziba sent out a small test catalogue during the holiday season. It was an attractive catalogue, maybe 14–15 pages, and it did fairly well. Based on that one-time experience, our management team shifted the business model entirely—now actively pursuing the inherently expensive and capital-intensive path of direct marketing through print catalogues. This shook up the roots of our entrepreneurial, Internet-based foundation. Suddenly, expensive mailing lists were purchased, a slew of catalogue experts and consultants hired, a new office in a major metropolitan city established, a large call centre and warehouse created. The shift was radical and ultimately hurt us.

'Like many businesses, Eziba had numerous ups and downs in the course of its six years. And some of these challenges proved ultimately fatal. From once being a company of great promise and vision, with $7 million in net sales in its last holiday season, a strong, exciting brand, stores in Boston, Chicago, New York, 60 employees, thousands of artisans supported, it was now required to close its doors in January 2005, at the instigation of its board. Soon after, the company was put into bankruptcy and, by April 2005, the company was acquired by Overstock, the online retailer of clearance goods. A visionary dream had come to an end!

'In July 2005, only six months after the company closed, Dick's heart literally gave out, through a massive heart attack. He was barely 61 years old. In many ways, through Dick's painful and early death, I saw a certain tragic symbolism for what had happened to this company that had set out with such great promise. Perhaps its focus on rapid and frenzied growth, its abandonment of its core mission early on, and its culture of careless and frivolous expenditure, coupled with a lack of visionary and confident leadership, finally drove the company into its death.'

Earlier, two of Amber Chand's colleagues had suggested that she resign because her reputation would be tainted. She told us: 'Even though I wanted to walk away and separate myself from some of the decisions that were made which I did not agree with, I also felt it irresponsible for me to abandon the company in its dying moment. As one of its co-founders I felt a particular sense of responsibility—that of a mother wanting to protect her child! Were I to have walked away, I never would have forgiven myself.'

The dual culture

'Eziba had offered a remarkable platform to test out new innovative models of business. It also became somewhat schizophrenic as it tried to navigate and make sense of two distinct sets of values.

'On one hand, there was a culture of innovative entrepreneurship founded on socially responsible practices that highlighted performance and success from the perspective of the "triple bottom line"—its impact on people, planet and profits. Here there was a sense of creating a community rather than a company, highlighting the connections that were happening around us—especially between our customers (who were 80 per cent women) and artisan producers (who were similarly 80 per cent women). I was intrigued by this "feminine" conversation happening between people on either side of the world—through stories and handmade products.

'On the other hand, there was another structure of thought that we had to deal with. This followed a more traditional, patriarchal form of business culture where investor returns, fast "testosterone-driven" growth and heightened profitability were the company's priority and drove the company's decisions.

'In the end, we were not skilful enough as an organization to bring together these two distinctive cultures. Had we been able to find that necessary balance, weighing the costs of every decision in terms of our mission in the world as well as our financial health, I have no doubt that we would still exist!'

A greater gift

'The collapse of Eziba was catastrophic—to all its stakeholders! I do not pretend to understand all the minutiae of details that complicated the process, from vendor workouts, banks being paid out before the poorest artisans, legal haranguing, bankruptcy proceedings. But what I remember most was the shock and pain of seeing my colleagues at the company leave—one by one! Desks abandoned, products from all over the world left behind sitting tidily on shelves, offices emptied. We were exhausted and devastated. I was one of the last to leave the building!

'It was painful, terrifying and confusing to watch the company collapse at such a startling pace. I felt completely powerless to influence its course during this time—surrounded by legal experts, a disappointed but resolute board, devastated staff members, vendors clamouring to be paid, customers asking for their products, and the media ready to pounce.

'As a child, I was encouraged to see everything—the ups and downs of my young existence—as an expression of God, and to accept all of it—the full catastrophe of living, you might say! My spiritual practice is the context for my entire existence: it offers me deep and rich support as I navigate through life.

'Once before, I had experienced the solid structures of my life implode around me—as a young woman of 22 years old, my family was expelled from Uganda as refugees during Idi Amin's presidency. We lost everything—our financial assets, our beautiful home on the hill, our possessions, and our country. Through that devastation I had to pick myself up and find my way, trusting that within that experience was also a greater gift. My task was to discover it.'

The Amber Chand Collection

Enriched by her experiences, like a bird-Phoenix, Amber Chand rose out of the ashes of Eziba and founded 'The Amber Chand Collection: Global Gifts for Peace and Understanding' in 2005. The next year, she enthusiastically told us about its foundations.

'It took me many months to recuperate and heal from the company's demise. Beckoning me was the pleading gaze of the artisans I had met on my past travels around the world, who echoed a similar request "Please do not forget us". Even though the structure of Eziba had collapsed, I believed that its mission in the world was still intact. It was with this mind that I launched my own company, The Amber Chand Collection: Global Gifts for Peace and Understanding, an online company that was setting out to create a different model from Eziba's—one more truthfully and authentically in alignment with who I am in the world.

'To me, in order to be successful, I must embrace all three aspects of mind, body and spirit. My spiritual theme of "a God-being tapestry of compassion, balance, grace and friendliness" provides me with the inner guidance for what I do and how I do it. Today I sit here, at my home office, delighted in the enterprise I have now launched. Barely nine months old, The Amber Chand Collection: Global Gifts for Peace and Understanding is a mission-based social enterprise that supports talented craftswomen in regions of conflict and post-conflict. I work explicitly with women who are the inadvertent victims of war, genocide, civil strife, pandemics and natural disasters. Currently, I am working on projects in Israel/Palestine, Darfur/Sudan, Cambodia, Afghanistan, Iraq and Guatemala. The foundation of the company is informed by the lessons I learned at Eziba.

'In many ways, I am carrying on the vision that Dick and I had created for Eziba in the very beginning: to serve artisan communities around the world by offering them access to a sophisticated international market. But I chose a different business model for growth—and ultimately one that I hope will be sustainable and successful over time. The Amber Chand Collection is focused, offering lovely handmade gifts whose design aesthetic is guided by me. In this paradigm, Small is Beautiful! I work closely with non-profit organizations that have field operations in these vulnerable regions of the world and are able to offer me both operational and marketing support. All products are shipped from around the world to my warehouse in central Massachusetts, a facility which exclusively hires developmentally disabled adults to package and ship my products. At this time, I am choosing to finance the company solely through family/friends and "angel investors" who offer loans with a reasonable return.

'The Amber Chand Foundation has been created as a non-profit entity that will be able to support artisan communities more widely through grants and investments. Referring to itself as a social enterprise, the company will measure its success in terms of both its financial and social impacts on the artisan communities it serves. For instance, in Guatemala, The Amber Chand Scholarship Fund supports primary school children and is funded through purchases of the Mayan Harmony Necklace and Bracelet. In Cambodia, net proceeds from the purchase of the Silk Bag of Smiles is donated to the House of Smiles, an orphanage of disabled children set up in the cooperative that supports children who are victims of landmine accidents. In the Middle East, net proceeds from the sale of the Jerusalem Candle of Hope supports the work of the Parents Circle, an organization of bereaved family members on either side of the conflict who have lost a family member in the Intifada and seek reconciliation and healing. Each of the gifts in the collection is made by mothers, who through these lovely creative expressions offer us their gift of hope, strength and courage.

'At every juncture, I seek to be in alignment with my mission. I am more than ever convinced that, if we are to create businesses with healthy foundations at this urgent time in our planetary evolution, we need to create systems based on balance, wisdom and humility. As a social entrepreneur, my task is to create an enterprise that is fiscally responsible, grows thoughtfully, and impacts thousands of craftspeople in creating a dignified livelihood for themselves.

'At the heart of this work are the spiritual principles of "service" and "love in action". I have no doubt that armed with patience, trust, focused, clear effort and humility, The Amber Chand Collection will grow successfully.

'I am grateful to Eziba for teaching me important lessons and in illuminating for me that one can indeed create successful businesses that are spiritually inspired—only when this becomes one's singular mission and clear intent.'

Section 8

Harvesting the wisdom

In this section

You have now read the profiles of 31 spiritual-based business leaders from very different geographical and industrial contexts—executives we have chosen for being, in our view, both enlightening and inspiring. In this concluding section, we will not attempt to draw firm conclusions—which would be rather bold indeed, given the most varied nature of the data (the interviews we have drawn upon). Rather, we will first make a few brief comments about the role of spirituality in business, and then focus on harvesting the wisdom delivered by these leaders. This wisdom consists of the many 'fruits' that they have given to us, each from their own orchards of experience. We will gather and discuss ten such themes, looking at commonalities as well as differences.

Since the underlying idea of this book is to let the leaders speak for themselves, rather than our performing extensive interpretations and analyses the presentation here will primarily consist of reflections by the leaders in their interviews.

Although we will make certain broad generalizations based on the observations, the main motivation underlying this section is not to develop theory. Rather *it is to stimulate your reflections* and *to help you, the reader, to develop faith* that business can be successfully developed from a spiritual basis, and that *you* can be successful as a leader by founding your leadership on a spiritual basis . . . where success includes, but transcends, the dictates of traditional economic rationality.

As you read our comments about each theme, please note that we have been parsimonious; you may certainly find more quotes, and more themes throughout this book to stimulate your own reflections, and we encourage you to do that.

However, before harvesting the wisdom, we feel it important to present a context for what binds together the 31 leaders you have met, based on observations that both predate the research reported on here, and insights that were a by-product of the research itself.

The role of spirituality in business

Amongst those leaders who seriously consider the role of spirituality in business (and of business in spirituality), there is a tendency to structure their thinking in one of three ways.

With the *first* approach, people ask: *How does spirituality fit into the business world as we know it?* In this approach, business is a context for spirituality. Here, leaders are interested in whether spirituality can contribute to improved performance and bottom-line results. Very similar inquiries have characterized developments in the field now referred to as corporate social responsibility (CSR), where attempts at justifying responsible behaviour/ethical behaviour by an economic rationale have been referred to as 'the business case' for CSR.

While this approach is an important and intriguing line of inquiry, it implicitly assumes that 'the business of business is business', and that the sole measuring stick by which the value of spirituality is to be judged is its contribution to traditional measures of business success (profitability, productivity, and so on). This 'business case' perspective, which tends to dominate the thinking of many leaders, can be looked upon as the unconscious 'inheritance' from cultures dominated by materialism, from narrowly focused MBA programmes, and from appraisal/reward systems that emphasize growth while disregarding personal and societal well-being. Our experience indicates that many leaders are increasingly experiencing the shallowness of the business case and its 'it pays to do so' arguments. Many of them truly want to be able to respond in a more holistic, inclusive manner, but lack the vocabulary, role models, and courage to do so, dominated as they are by the logic of the market with its focus on growth, profit and stock prices, and the corresponding value norms of the 'old boys' club'.

This leads to the *second* approach, where people ask: *How can we integrate spirituality and business?* This gives spirituality and business a certain equality, with an attempt to bring a balance between them—that spirituality serves business performance and that business serves spiritual development. Often there is a focus on overcoming a split between work and personal life. Therefore this line of inquiry often focuses on integrating spirituality into values alignment, job enrichment and stress management programmes in business.

The focus on values alignment aims at increasing personal commitment at work by attempting to align corporate values and personal values. The focus on job enrichment bears in mind that personal fulfilment is found not so much in *what* the work is but *what spiritual meaning* a person finds in the work. The focus on stress management often includes meditation or yoga in corporate wellness programmes, provides access to religious or spiritual coaches, and encourages spiritual retreats. However, these different attempts to balance spirituality and business lack a spiritual foundation; spirituality is not the basis and is not, so to speak, 'in the driver's seat'.

Therefore, we now consider the *third* approach to the inquiry and dialogue about spirituality and business, where people ask: *How can we define and lead business from a spiritual basis?* Here, spirituality is the context for business, and not vice versa, as in the first approach. In this approach, spirituality is the foundation upon which the nature of business is defined and the profession of leadership is conducted. In this book we have focused on this third approach, whereby spirituality is the basis for business leadership. This meant seeking out and interviewing executives who have a spiritual view of life and who have led in accord with that view, so as to gain their insights, perspectives and experiences. This is what the 31 executives you met in this book have in common. Interestingly, in their reflections and stories, you may have noticed that they often naturally addressed the first two questions regarding the contribution of spirituality to business performance and the integration of personal and work life.

The harvest

These general observations lead to a more specific focus on the wisdom that can be harvested from our 31 profiles. Appendix A presents some methodological reservations as to our ability to generalize on the perspectives, beliefs and experiences of the spiritual-based leaders presented here.

We have grouped our observations in the form of selected quotes and comments about ten major themes. Many of these themes correspond directly to questions explicitly asked during the interviews; later, we became aware of several other such themes when going through the material in the knowledge-base. The website of the Spiritual-based Leadership Research Programme[1] provides all the underlying material as well as the interview guide employed while meeting with the leaders.

1. How do leaders define 'spirituality'?

Since 'spirituality' is the keyword that distinguishes this book from other books on leadership—and the key attribute that distinguishes these 31 leaders from most others—we will start by considering how the leaders we inter-

---

1 A full description of the purpose, context, scope, definitions and interview guide for this research programme can be found at www.globaldharma.org/sbl-research.htm.

viewed look upon this term. Here we expand on the Introduction, where we provided a very brief sample of the interviewees' definitions of 'spirituality'.

Spirituality is man's quest into his innate Divinity. It's more like a road than a state of affairs; a quest more than an arrival.

—Magnus Vrethammar

Like Magnus Vrethammar, some of the leaders focus more directly on spirituality as a 'search' they consciously participate in—most often a search for something that has considerable significance and meaning for them, such as unity with a transcendent Source or God, or for happiness. This search typically takes place both within one's self as well as in the outer world of business, as illustrated in these two statements:

To me, spirituality is the search for true happiness.

—Francisco Cañada

It's trying to see God in everyone and trying to interact with everyone on a very loving basis, seeing everything as being perfect, and not pointing your finger at anyone or anything.

—John R. Behner

For some, spirituality is an 'essence', a 'being' or a 'manifestation'—something that is simply *there*, often as something that is to be 'experienced' or 'realized' rather than sought after:

Spirituality is the manifestation of the perfection that is already there within you.

—A.K. Chattopadhyay

Spirituality talks about ultimate Truth—of myself as part of Supreme Consciousness. You must realize it.

—Ananth Raman

And, for others, spirituality is a sense of connection:

I conceptualize spirituality as the connection among myself, other people and the Divine. It is the common linkage between these three aspects of existence for me.

—Thomas Daugherty

The quotes are chosen to highlight commonalities and differences, while in fact the spiritual views of the leaders are often far more complex than any single quote can express. Thus, some of the leaders we interviewed, such as Ricardo Levy, fit into two or three 'categories'—searching, experiencing and connecting—at the same time:

> *Spirituality is the deep inner search for a fuller personal integration with a transcendent greater than our narrow self. It is a deep connection with a force greater than myself. It is a very individual, lived experience that includes both longing and belonging, expressed often and perhaps best through love and compassion.*
>
> —Ricardo B. Levy

No matter how a leader defined and spoke about spirituality, there appears to be a 'thread' that weaves through all the interviews; each of the leaders has an 'internal' perspective on the purpose of life in general and of leadership in particular, and this internal, spiritual perspective constitutes the context for their actions in the 'outer' world of business.

FOOD FOR THOUGHT
Before we continue, we suggest that you ask yourself: 'After considering this wide variety of perspectives, how would I define spirituality for myself?'

2. How does leadership contribute to one's own spiritual growth?

When we reflected on how the leaders we interviewed related leadership to spirituality, it surprised us that some of them had not aspired to be a leader. Instead, they had chosen to follow their career path due to their spiritual aspirations:

> *For me being a businessman has not always been easy, as I am a man of silence. All of my life, I have rejected the material world, and still I have become a big businessman. It is not easy for me to be the head of four companies as a member of their boards. It's difficult, it's a problem; it's not my nature. But I have been guided to do my work, so that I am able to live in the material world and combine work and doing business with spiritual growth.*
>
> —Francisco Cañada

> *I feel I have been forced to become a leader, something I had always wanted to avoid in my life. In these everyday challenges that I come across, I find that I grow and learn much more than if I were to read about spirituality or meditate.*
>
> —Parantha Narendran

This relationship between spirituality and leadership is something we feel would amaze 'traditional' business leaders and the authors of bestsellers on leadership! While the common assumption is that leaders use tools to achieve leadership aims, here leadership is a tool to attain spiritual aims.

Most of the executives we interviewed, however, appear to have a more symmetric perspective on leadership and spirituality: They see their work and their place of work as being important for their spiritual development—and they see their spirituality as being vital for their performance of good leadership:

> *Little did I know that this new path in my career as a banker would run hand in hand with my spiritual growth.*

> —Flordelis Aguenza

> *I feel that business is one of the best playgrounds you can have in life for your spiritual development. Looking back on my own career path, I realize that it was also a highly spiritual exercise.*

> —Magnus Vrethammar

So it appears that, from a spiritual perspective, the executives we have interviewed live up to the modern adage that leaders should be 'whole people', where there is harmony between their work life and their private life. They do not hang their 'clothing' of spirituality on a hanger before they cross the threshold to their office, and only put it on once again when they return to their homes; they are 'spiritually based', no matter whether at work or in their private lives.

FOOD FOR THOUGHT
Before continuing, ask yourself: 'How does leadership contribute to my own spiritual growth—and how does spirituality contribute to my leadership?'

3. What is the relationship between spirituality and personal success?

Building on the above reflections on the close association between spirituality and business leadership, we consider now the complex relationship between spiritual-based leadership and success—both *personal* success and *business* success.

Before letting the leaders 'speak for themselves', we note that all the executives we interviewed have achieved their leadership positions *while* being spiritual. In other words, this in itself provides strong evidence that spirituality and obtaining a leadership position do not have to be mutually exclusive, as some sceptics seem to fear.

The interviewees themselves present a rather nuanced picture of the concept of personal success as seen from a spiritual perspective. For some, the concept of one's own success is directly related to a concept of God:

> *It's so easy to think that success is about the work that's getting done, but to me it is not about that. To me, success means that I get a chance to use the gifts that God has given me every day. I get a chance to serve other people with those gifts and I help other people to feel heard and cared about and help them to use their gifts.*
>
> —Nilofer Merchant

For other leaders, the concept of personal success is more directly related to the concept of 'making a difference' and affecting others in a positive way:

> *Success to me is when the people I work with have become better because of their association with me. I want to give our employees a better life. I hope that I have moved people to become better, to become closer to God, and to be spiritually stronger.*
>
> —Flordelis Aguenza

> *For me, the real measure of my success is how my obituary will be written when I die. When I die, I want my success to be measured by how much positive impact I have created.*
>
> —Deependra Moitra

> *By most standards people would say that I have been very successful. I think the heart of success for me is to make a difference and to try to do it in a manner where I can stay connected with people, with myself and with the Divine.*
>
> —Thomas Daugherty

> *Success is getting the collective participation and the collective win of everybody who is responsible in the system.*
>
> —Anand Pillai

And, for other executives, the concept of 'success' is intimately related to the concept of 'contentment':

The most successful person is the person with the least desires. The successful individual is the contented individual.

—James E. Sinclair

As I have matured, I have started to realize that it is not management that decides my destiny, but rather God. Unfortunately, it is only when you get older that you see that everybody gets their just rewards, and the ones with principles and integrity are usually the happiest and most content, if not the richest.

—Rajan Govindan

FOOD FOR THOUGHT

Before continuing, ask yourself: 'Based on my spiritual view of life, what would I consider "personal success" to be?'

4. What is the relationship between spirituality and success in business?

We now consider the second perspective on success: how, based on their spiritual view of life, the leaders reflect on the success of their corporations and/or of business in general.[2] Based on our own experience with corporate leaders, the executives we interviewed present a far richer and more realistic perspective on business success than is provided by traditional economic rationality with its major focus on the bottom line and commercial growth. When leading from a spiritual basis, the concept 'success' becomes more complex, more demanding and potentially more satisfying. Leading from a spiritual basis necessitates simultaneously dealing with the outer world of business (rationality) and the inner world of conscience (spirituality), as André Delbecq states so eloquently:

I think a business exists to provide an innovative and compelling answer to a societal need in the form of a needed service or product. This is how we

---

2 In principle, this could be looked at from a more quantitative perspective. For example, one could attempt to demonstrate that companies are more successful if led from a spiritual basis. Such an approach could be based on comparing the performance of companies that are led from a spiritual basis with companies that are not so led, based on various criteria such as earnings/returns, market share, quality of products/services, reputation, employee turnover, etc. Similarly, one could attempt to demonstrate that leading from a spiritual basis results in a more successful business career (attainment of higher positions in shorter time, wealth accumulation, etc.). Both such approaches are outside the realm of the present investigation and would require very different data and analysis procedures.

should judge business organizations. When this purpose is approached through a spiritual lens, it will be shaped differently in many ways. The needs you start becoming attentive to shift. The transformational system you create to receive inputs and transform outputs will also shift, allowing greater attention to stewardship, justice and inclusiveness of the concerns of all stakeholders. The character of the organization's culture will shift. Your own willingness as a business leader to endure the mystery of suffering will shift. You will see all the elements of business challenges as part of a calling to service.

—André Delbecq

For some, there is an intimate relationship between business success and serving others, often considered as wealth creation on their behalf:

At an organizational level, success must be measured by the wealth that is created for all people.

—V.V. Ranganathan

I think that the purpose of my own organization and for business in general is creating wealth for the largest number of people without hurting others.

—Hélène Ploix

From an existential perspective, the raison d'être *of organizations is to serve human needs. Really, there is no other reason for their existence. Individuals and organizations grow when they give themselves to others. Relationships improve when there is a focus on serving the other, be it at the level of the individual, the family, the organization, the community, the society or all of humanity.*

—Stephen Covey

In particular, some of the leaders we interviewed highlighted that profits are no longer a fundamental measure of success; profits become a means for serving others:

Though being profitable is necessary for our development, success for the companies is not simply success in the traditional financial sense, but is tied to the principle of selfless service. As to our earnings, our aim is to use 25 per cent of our profits for paying taxes, 25 per cent for reinvestment, 25 per cent for us, and to give away 25 per cent in donations.

—Francisco Cañada

In Grundfos it has always been a part of our policies that profit is not a target in itself. Money and a good profitability are necessary for us to maintain a successful growing company, which is a good place for people to work in.

—Niels Due Jensen

Finally, for some of the leaders, the concept of success meant contributing to the happiness of others:

We are the market leader in every product that we are in, by huge margins. We are making huge profits, and in our debt–equity ratio there is no debt, only equity. How has all of this happened? It has happened because we are concerned about the human being and their happiness. We are helping them, through spiritual methods, to know their latent divinity and they are feeling much more happy with themselves, with their work, and with their life.

—Ashoke Maitra

I think the ultimate game of business is that we should have happiness for all stakeholders of the business: employees, customers, suppliers, and shareholders. The happiness I am talking about is the faith and commitment you must have to achieve something together.

—S.K. Welling

FOOD FOR THOUGHT
Before continuing, ask yourself: 'From my spiritual point of view, what is success for our business? How does *my* spiritual-based leadership contribute to *our* business success?'

5. What is the relationship between ethics and spirituality?

Ethics has in recent years become a word that has moved from the realm of philosophy into that of business. A simple explanation is to be found in the demands as to acceptable business behaviour that have followed in the wake of business scandals. Unfortunately, the emphasis has been almost exclusively on avoiding accusations of being unethical. When leaders have been asked to justify this new focus, the common answer has been that it pays to avoid being unethical. In this way, ethics has become an instrument, a management tool, for protecting a corporation's licence to operate and its earnings, rather than an expression of a fundamental aspiration that is important in its own right.

Strikingly, though not at all surprisingly, this was not the case with the executives we interviewed. In contrast to the instrumental focus, the leaders we interviewed considered ethics in business leadership as a bridge between the inner world of the soul and the outer world of business. Consider the following four longer, but most enlightening, statements:

Values such as justice, truth, respect for others, honesty and integrity are the core values that became very strong for me when I went into business. These are more on the ethical side, rather than on the spiritual side. Somewhere along the line, however, these two kinds of values began to link. Now I think of ethical values as nothing but a reflection of my spiritual values. When we talk about self-respect in an ethical sense, we are talking about being respectful to your colleagues, shareholders and customers because it is a good business practice. But, when you go a little deeper and look at it from a spiritual point of view, you realize that it is really about respecting the inner Self. This is how I like to link spirituality with ethics and values in business.

—Ananth Raman

I believe that God put us on earth to find joy and happiness and to become enlightened. I believe He will test us with a thousand episodes and it's our job to learn how to walk through them. I have had people that worked for me in the past come and tell me that I have the highest ethics of anyone they have worked for. This is always a surprise to me when people say these things because to me this way of operating in business is so natural.

—Janiece C. Webb

[Speaking about a lawsuit he filed against a company that was cheating and hurting poor people in Africa . . .] Do you know what hell is like? Hell is having 21 lawyers working for you. I put every cent I had in the world into it. No one paid me anything to do this. I did this because following God through my spiritual teacher and my sense of ethics had made me a warrior.

—James E. Sinclair

As an auditor of large multinational companies, I have been confronted on almost a daily basis with situations where I have to pass transactions through my internal 'ethics' system and see if they pass my litmus test: the Lakshman Rekha. This is the imaginary boundary line that every individual has that he will not cross . . . the invisible line that is within everyone's system that is driven by consciousness. This is a consciousness that has its own existence. It comes into the mind; it is not a product of the mind or societal influences. It is like a direct knowing, rather than a belief system.

—V.V. Ranganathan

FOOD FOR THOUGHT
Now ask yourself: 'What does it mean to me to be ethical? What is the relationship between spiritual-based leadership and ethics to me?'

6. What is 'power' from a spiritual perspective?
While there are many understandings of the word 'power', perhaps the most widely accepted definition within an organizational setting is that *A* has power over *B* to the extent that *A* can get *B* to do something that *B* otherwise would not do. Within the world of business, this concept of power over people is rapidly becoming transformed due, in part, to developments in effective communications technology in 'flatter' and more transparent organizations, and an increased reliance on independent, self-organizing and creative 'knowledge' workers. A shift is taking place from power as coercive control over others to what we might call 'spiritual power': the ability to control one's self and to serve others.

Personally, I believe that the source of all the principles that give your life its integrity, and its power and its meaning, all of them link up to the Divine. To be a spiritual-based leader is to have these universal principles integrated in your inner life and to be true to them in your actions, even when it's dark—when you have power over people and can do things and not be found out.

—Stephen R. Covey

My spirituality brought to this exciting project a true respect for and feeling of equality on the soul level with everybody in the small team; nobody was afraid of opening up. We were passionate. We had a strong curiosity, which I see as spirituality, as a life force. We got connected to a universal power, and we all felt a great commitment. This is why we succeeded.

—Niran Jiang

I am only powerful when my energy is connected with other people's energy and we do things as a team . . . In truth, I believe that a position of power is a position of serving the people around you. I believe that you can create

*giants out of ordinary people when you act in balance and harmony with
people.*

—Janiece C. Webb

FOOD FOR THOUGHT
Reflecting on these statements, as well as others you might have met in this
book, ask yourself: 'How do I look upon the relationship between my spirituality and my power as a leader? What is the source of my power?'

7. How easy is it to speak about spirituality and leadership?
A number of the leaders we interviewed found it difficult to speak of their
spirituality—not because of a lack of reflection on what they mean by this
term, but perhaps just the opposite:

*When we try to define spirituality we are actually attempting to articulate
something that cannot be articulated. We are trying to do our best, but we
are trying to define the Infinite, which by definition is a contradiction. Yet
we need to try.*

—Ricardo B. Levy

For some, reservations in speaking about spirituality are due to concerns
about being misunderstood:

*It is easy for people to misunderstand what you mean. In today's language
we seem to avoid strong words, and spirituality is a strong word.*

—Niran Jiang

And, for others, the interview was one of the first times they had ever
attempted to explicitly communicate what they mean by spirituality.

*Until now, I have never formally attempted to define spirituality. For a long
time, spirituality was just a cliché, a word that all of us bandied around
without any real understanding.*

—Ananth Raman

We also note that there appears to be a considerable difference in how interviewees express their thoughts dependent on where they come from. In particular, it appears that people working in Europe are more reserved, more
reluctant to openly speak of their spirituality.

I think it is typically European not to use big words or to talk about God, although people from a lot of different cultures do that.

—Carol Franklin

I don't openly talk with people about my spirituality, but I think they respect me as someone who is ethical, someone they can trust, and someone who works hard in a selfless way. I don't have to talk about it. I just live it and people appreciate it.

—Parantha Narendran

On the other hand, there are also those who, while recognizing this tendency not to be open about one's spirituality, are bold in their own communication about spirituality.

Today so many people seem to be very proud to say that they are, for example, atheist; it seems to be a sign of liberation. Unfortunately, it seems easier to talk about wealth or sex or not believing than to talk about your values, about faith, and even about God. I am a spiritual person and I speak openly about these things.

—Ramon Ollé

Some of the leaders also remarked that there are many executives who lead from a spiritual basis, but do not describe themselves in this way. This coincides closely with our own experiences, particularly in Europe.

Today a major share of managers in both private and public organizations would not admit if they were managing their organization from a background of spirituality—although many would in fact do so unconsciously.

—Niels Due Jensen

A final observation regarding the role of language in spiritual-based leadership has to do with whether a leader should explicitly refer to his or her spirituality. Consider these provoking reflections:

I believe that you can be totally spiritual without having to use the word 'spiritual'.

—Ananth Raman

The minute I put spirituality as the explicit part, people will look at me as an organizational priest and they will focus on the deviation of what I do as compared to the 'textbook', rather than looking at my good deeds as a busi-

ness leader. Then you will have to start defending spirituality. I want to stay implicit, because this is how spirituality will survive.

—Magnus Vrethammar

It is possible to speak openly about spirituality at work . . . When I know that someone can handle the subject of spirituality, I talk and discuss it openly. When I know someone cannot handle it, then I just 'be' my spirituality and I don't talk about it openly. I can be it, I can show it, and I can exhibit it in my behaviour and attitudes, and I don't have to label it.

—Janiece C. Webb

At the other end of the spectrum, we have also seen that the organizations represented by four leaders in this book have been honoured with the *International Spirit at Work Award* for having 'implemented explicit spiritual practices, policies or programmes inside their organizations'. As one of them comments:

My work is about cultivating a holistic, comprehensive spiritual environment where caring can take place . . . and cultivate that environment through a process we call 'values integration' . . . connecting the world of spirit with the world of productivity in such a way that there is a blending, a 'wholeness' that emerges.

—Thomas Daugherty

FOOD FOR THOUGHT
Reflect now upon the following questions: 'Do I have difficulty in expressing myself about my spirituality and about spiritual-based leadership? If so, why? Do I think that it is wise to speak openly about such matters—is it best to be "implicit" or "explicit"?'

8. How does spirituality relate to peace of mind and a balanced life?
A few of the leaders we interviewed mentioned two problems that appear to characterize many, especially younger, leaders: how to calm their minds, and how to achieve a better balance between their work life and their private life.

I do not want to excel in my professional circles at the cost of my family life. So there is a need for me to balance and that is where I am struggling right now . . . I look to spirituality to help me find inner peace.

—Deependra Moitra

Be the same person at work as you are in your family life. You have to be able to live with the values that you have as an individual in your work life, because otherwise things won't work. You have to have your thoughts, words and deeds work together.

—Carol Franklin

Others referred to the relationship between inner peace and 'following your conscience'.

To be a spiritual-based leader is to have universal principles integrated in your inner life and to be true to them in your actions. Following your conscience means that you are true to that which you have internalized as being right, and this gives you tremendous tranquillity and courage. Peace of conscience is much greater than peace of mind.

—Stephen R. Covey

Start listening to the inner voice inside and stop rationalizing. When you stop rationalizing, your inner voice will tell you right away when you have done something that was not correct. Instantly you will feel it.

—Rajan Govindan

FOOD FOR THOUGHT
Consider now the following questions: 'Do I feel that I have peace of mind and "peace of conscience"? How might leading from a spiritual basis contribute to my realizing greater tranquillity? How do I listen to my conscience when performing my leadership?'

9. What are the spiritual practices of spiritual-based leaders?
Most, but not all, of the executives we interviewed had some kind of systematic spiritual practice. These included physical exercises (e.g. yoga, t'ai chi, walking in nature), reading literature on spirituality, seeking the company of spiritually inclined people, singing uplifting songs, meditation, prayer, attending religious services and performing religious rituals, and visiting a spiritual master.

A number of those we interviewed referred to the fundamental notion of 'service' as important in their spiritual practice—just as it is important in their concept of personal and organizational success. Here is just one example:

My spiritual practice is the context for my entire existence—it offers me deep and rich support as I navigate through life. Service is the cornerstone of this practice and I see my entire life as an offering to serve this sense of higher calling or purpose.

—Amber Chand

Prayer was one of the most widely referred-to personal spiritual practices.

Prayer is a part of everyday life. I may pray at certain times during the day, such as at a meal or when I feel thankful for the day, and I also pray in difficult situations. There are difficult situations where I think it is a great strength to be able to express yourself via prayer and to feel that you are in dialogue with a higher being.

—Lars Kolind

Meditation was another practice mentioned by a large number of the leaders.

I go to meditation retreats, and I practice chi gong which is the physical dimension of meditation, practising the heart power . . . Meditation for me is throughout the day. It is being mindful; staying connected with what is around me: people and the universe. When I am out of place—being busy, shutting my door—I know that I am also out of place with my spirituality. When I am connected, I am practising spirituality.

—Niran Jiang

FOOD FOR THOUGHT
Ask yourself: 'Which spiritual practices would be beneficial for my growth as a person and as a leader?'

10. What is sound advice to aspiring spiritual-based leaders?
The final question we asked of all the leaders we interviewed was: 'What advice do you have for others who want to lead from their spiritual point of view?' We received a wealth of answers. Therefore, the following can only be an 'appetizer': a 'bite of a juicy, newly harvested apple' that hopefully makes your mouth water and inspires you to delve deeper into your own spiritual yearnings and longings, and to reflect upon how best you can be a spiritual-based leader.

A number of those we interviewed focused on actively loving:

Above anything, I would stress non-attachment to the material results and rewards of one's deeds and the practice of love: love for oneself and love for others.

—Alvaro Cruz

There were also leaders who focused on leading by example:

The power of example is important; you must practise what you preach. You must express what you believe, with your deeds, as best you can . . . to practise what you preach is the key to personal and organizational success.

—Lars Kolind

Amongst these, some underlined the importance of doing before telling:

I would tell someone that they must live their spirituality first and not speak about it till they can practise it. I would also talk to them of the importance of trust and how to build that trust in an organization.

—N.S. Raghavan

You should lead by example, and then you can explain why you have done what you did . . . Do first and tell afterwards!

—Carol Franklin

And there were leaders who noted the importance of choosing 'good company':

The first response that comes to me is that leaders must deepen their own spirituality; this is key. The second one is to find a community to support that deepening . . . one that has compassion for others. There is something that happens when you are in a community that goes beyond the mental thoughts and words. It can be so powerful.

—Ricardo B. Levy

Not unexpectedly there were a number of leaders who focused their advice on 'listening within' and 'going inside':

People who want to be spiritual-based leaders sometimes face conflict when they try to listen to their inner self. They are sometimes afraid to follow their conscience because they do not want to lose money. However, the more that aspiring spiritual-based leaders do so, the more they will be successful. As there are successes, then they will grow in their courage to continue in this way.

—A.K. Chattopadhyay

I think the problem with leaders in our Western business is that we are not aware of the need to go inside. And, because the decisions we make can impact many people and can even impact them in dramatic ways, we have an even greater responsibility to make sure that this process is much more than an initial gut feeling. We have to connect with a much more human universe and be willing to take the time that is needed to make our decisions from this deeply felt inner guidance.

—Ricardo B. Levy

And there was a leader who gave a very down-to-earth practical bit of advice regarding potential conflicts of values:

My advice would be: Sometimes there will be conflict between your spiritual values and the values of the organization or the values of top management. When you get into any of these conflicts, you don't really have to consider it your life's mission to try and win this battle. Find a compromise solution and get on with your work . . . unless you believe that something is against your core values, and then you can go at it and fight it out.

—Ananth Raman

Finally, there were leaders who would not give advice—but would seek to create the atmosphere that would help others to find their own answers.

If someone were to come to me and seek my guidance on how to live their spirituality in their work, I would tell them, 'How courageous, how beautiful, how wonderful it is that you have come to me with this concern. Let us sit and have a cup of tea.' Then I would ask them to tell me more about themselves. I believe the guidance would come naturally out of creating the space for the person to begin to unravel their own truth. All I can really give them is the space in which to have this happen.

—Amber Chand

I would first want to listen and ask them: 'What does spirituality mean to you? What does leadership mean to you? What are you aware of, right now, about the disconnection between leadership as you now provide it and the spirituality that you've just described?' I would then encourage them to think about which places of disconnection are most important for them to deal with right now.

—Thomas Daugherty

For us, G. Narayana put together many of these pieces of advice when he spoke about the inspirational qualities of spiritual-based leadership:

Spirituality is inspired responsibility towards people, other living beings, and the world . . . seeing and relating with divinity in every aspect. Self-improvement plus world service equals spirituality. To grow spiritually, I follow and give the following advice: Never say 'no'. Offer, offer, offer. Work is worship beyond the time limits. Be available and assist always. If you love, you give time. If you do not love, you will not give time. If you look at the Divinity in the other man, then you can inspire. That is inspiring leadership.

—G. Narayana

FOOD FOR THOUGHT

Ask yourself: 'What advice given here do I find most helpful to me as a spiritual-based leader? What advice would I give others?'

The 'harvest feast'

It has not been our intention here, or elsewhere, to draw conclusions. The whole book has been structured around the words of wisdom of spiritual-based leaders. In this section we have attempted to 'harvest' some of this wisdom and to structure it. Now it is time for you to celebrate the harvest—to reap the inspiration and meet the challenges it offers.

Each of the leaders you have met is a product of their own unique experiences. Each has developed their own unique spiritual perspective on life and, in particular, on leadership. Each has their own unique way of expressing this spirituality in words and in deeds. And each has developed their own way of leading from their spiritual basis.

Although until now we have abstained from giving advice, we would nevertheless like to conclude by synthesizing their experiences and our own personal experiences in the form of six simple maxims:

1. Be aware of and embrace your own spirituality, your own spiritual view of life.

2. Seek the company of uplifting and inspiring colleagues who lead from a spiritual basis—and learn from their experiences.

3. Develop your own approach to spiritual-based leadership based upon your spiritual view of life. Don't try to copy how others have led; spiritual-based leadership is a very personal matter.

4. Integrate your spiritual principles and values in all your life, not just at home, not just in your temple/church/mosque, not just in your place of work. Spiritual-based leadership is for life.

5. Don't just think about it and talk about it; practise your spiritual-based leadership. But remember: you cannot lead others if you cannot lead yourself. As Mahatma Gandhi said, 'Be the change you want to see in the world.'

6. If it feels correct and wise to do so, strengthen the culture of your organization through your leadership, so that spirituality is the basis of its identity/self-reference, reputation, values, sense of responsibility, success criteria and vision.

Above all: have faith that business can be successfully developed from a spiritual basis, and that *you* can be successful when you found your leadership on a spiritual basis.

Epilogue

Spiritual-based leadership beyond business

A.P.J. Abdul Kalam

President of India

Although this book is about spiritual-based leaders in business, we have chosen to end it with the profile of a spiritual-based leader who has spent much of his life leading major research projects, and who is now the leader of more than a billion people—the Honourable A.P.J. Abdul Kalam, President of India. We do this both to underscore that spiritual-based leaders are to be found in all walks of life, and because the story of Dr Kalam is so inspiring, particularly in these times characterized by religious strife and tension between scientific and humanitarian world views. What initially inspired us was this unusual quote from President Kalam in his book *Wings of Fire*:

> *Each individual creature on this beautiful planet is created by God to fulfil a particular role. Whatever I have achieved in life is through His help, and an expression of His will. He showered His grace on me through some outstanding teachers and colleagues, and when I pay my tributes to these fine persons, I am merely praising His glory. All these rockets and missiles are His work through a small person called Kalam, in order to tell the several-million mass of India to never feel small or helpless. We are all born with a divine fire in us. Our efforts should be to give wings to this fire and fill the world with the glow of its goodness.*

President Kalam is a Muslim in a predominantly Hindu society. He is a rocket scientist with a deeply spiritual message. Throughout his career he has held highly responsible technical and scientific positions. This, however, did not shake his spiritual foundation—just the opposite. He told us: 'The path of science can always wind through the heart. For me, science has always been the path to spiritual enrichment and self-realization.'

Dr Avul Pakir Jainulabdeen Abdul Kalam is the eleventh President of India. At the time of the interview in 2004, he was 72 years old. For the past two years, his home had been the majestic Indian 'White House', the Rashtrapati Bhavan in New Delhi, an address that has been receiving more visitors and more letters and emails during his presidency than ever before. Why? Because President Kalam continually communicates in a personal and down-to-earth manner with his people, especially the young people, about the future of India. He never misses an opportunity to ignite young minds to champion the cause of national development. Millions of them!

As a matter of fact, this bachelor, internationally respected space technologist, and the biggest role model ever to occupy the Indian presidency, has lent a new buzz to the top job: he is the first President who has made himself accessible to the common people. Hardly a day goes by without his picture being prominently placed in the major newspapers and the TV news. He is shown giving a talk to high-school students, opening a new highway, visiting HIV patients or the stock exchange, entering a submarine, receiving heads of state. Every time he uses the opportunity to encourage and speak words of wisdom to his constituents. No other leader in India receives as much attention and respect as President Kalam.

Few people in the world, no matter what their origin, have had as impressive and impacting a career as this spiritual-based leader of research and of a nation—who was born in a remote Indian village without electricity or telephone in the southern state of Tamil Nadu.

Wise mentors saw to it that the young, bright Abdul Kalam received the necessary support to be able to get a degree in Aeronautical Engineering from Madras Institute of Technology. Later this humble but yet ambitious and unusually visionary young man became the Project Director responsible for developing India's first indigenous Satellite Launch Vehicle. No matter what high position Abdul Kalam has held since then, his focus has always been on taking India into the world of the powerful, developed and independent nations.

Before being elected President of India, Abdul Kalam was piloting the India Millennium Mission 2020, which is an ambitious plan for making India a developed nation by 2020. During our interview with the President in Rashtrapati Bhavan, he told us that out of more than a billion people in India, nearly 260 million people are living below the poverty line. He spoke of his mission of lifting these people out of poverty: 'At present I am the President of India, and naturally I want to see the billion people smile. We have a Parliament and a Cabinet here, so the President is some sort of an integrator of the management system and the leadership of the country.'

As a predominantly Hindu country, India also has the world's second largest Muslim population and a minority of Christians, Buddhists, Jains, Sikhs and Parsis. President Kalam is an inspiring leader of this amazingly heterogeneous multi-religious, multi-cultural, multi-lingual democratic nation. When asked about the relationship between religion and spirituality in such a complex society, he provided us with a clear and concise reply: 'When religion transforms into a spiritual force, the people become enlightened citizens with a value system. It is therefore most important for the happiness, peace and prosperity of the mankind that we transform our religious forces into spiritual forces.'

Four books by or about President Kalam have become household names in India, and among Indian nationals abroad.[1] Not surprisingly, Dr Kalam has received honorary doctorates from more than 30 universities and academic institutions. Prior to becoming President of India he was for a short time Professor of Technology and Societal Transformation at Anna University, Chennai, Tamil Nadu. In an article paying homage to him upon being elected President, a friend and former colleague, Dr M. Vidyasagar, Executive Vice President of the major Indian company, Tata Consultancy Services, reminisced: 'Unlike many persons who consciously cultivate a public persona, Professor Kalam is exactly what he appears to be: Truly humble, polite and, above all, patriotic and idealistic. He inspires everyone around him to give just that little bit extra . . . Though it sounds odd, I cannot help feeling that "merely" being the President of India is somehow beneath him. Here is truly a case where the position is honoured by the person occupying it, not the other way around.'

Giving wings to the divine fire

I learnt in my life that, if you don't do anything, you won't have any problems. But, if you do something, suddenly something will pull off. Problems should not become your master. You have to become the master of the problems. God gives us the opportunity to grow through problems. You have to concentrate on what can be done, not what you think cannot be done. If I could, I would remove the word 'impossible' from the dictionary. Defeat your problems and succeed.

---

1   *Wings of Fire; India 2020: A Vision for the New Millennium; My Journey;* and *Ignited Minds: Unleashing the Power within India.* The books have also been translated into many Indian languages.

'Basically, I come from a rural area, Rameswaram in Tamil Nadu, with a dream injected in me by my teacher. I wanted to know: *How do the birds fly?* His explanation about the bird flight and a practical demonstration on a beach inspired me to take up a profession in aeronautics. My career began as an aeronautical engineer with a love for mathematical physics. This led me to become a rocket engineer, space technologist and missile scientist. I started building rockets, missiles and similar things. Wherever I worked, I worked with a mission.

'Out of a billion people in India, nearly 260 million people are below the poverty line. My new mission is "How to make our people come out of poverty". A developed nation has two components: one is the economic growth and prosperity, which is what the Western societies normally look for. The second component is the preservation of civilizational heritage. In India basically we have a heritage of values, of the joint family system, being good human beings, having respect for gurus [teachers] and respect for elders. We want to couple the economic prosperity and the human values, which are drawn from this civilizational heritage. This heritage was the basis on which my own life started.'

Learning from elevated minds

'I am going to tell you a practical case so that you can understand what spirituality means to me. I am going to give you a seed, and from that seed you will understand what spirituality is.

'I had a guru, Professor Vikram Sarabhai. He was the leader of the space programme in the 1960s, visualizing the space programme for this country. As a young fellow I worked with him. He was interested in cosmic ray studies, in particular how cosmic rays originate. He had a laboratory in the city of Ahmedabad where he had also taken up space research. He was interested in carrying out this research very close to the earth's equatorial region. The south-western Indian state of Kerala was suitable for this mission as it is very close to the earth's magnetic equator and could be a good site for launching rockets. He identified a site near the city of Trivandrum, in a place called Thumba. Professor Sarabhai wanted the area, about 600 acres of land near the sea coast. He wanted the land to start the space programme, for building the Space Technology Centre.

'First, he went to the bureaucracy. They said that the area he wanted housed a large church, a bishop's house, a school building, and was used by a large number of people for fishing and marketing of the fish. The administrators said it was a very difficult proposition. How can you displace the people whose livelihood is fishing? Second, their families have lived in that area for hundreds of years. Third, a church is there. How is it possible to dislocate all of them?

'Professor Sarabhai approached the Chief Minister, a politician, instead of the bureaucracy. The Chief Minister said, "Professor Vikram, you are asking a difficult thing. We cannot vacate the area. A church is there; fishing industry is there; the people are there. It is very difficult. You may ask for any other land and I will give it to you."

'You know, once he made up his mind, my guru, Professor Vikram Sarabhai, always worked for it with a smile, a big smile. The Chief Minister then suggested that he should meet the Bishop of Trivandrum, the Reverend Father Dr Peter Dereira. He went to the bishop on one Saturday evening and told him, "I am doing scientific research; I am studying the cosmic rays' structure, and also the ionosphere. I need your help. I want this land since it is scientifically suitable for my work. I will provide an alternate land and rebuild whatever facilities you require." The Reverend Father Dr Dereira said, "Vikram, you are asking for God's abode, the church; you are asking for my abode, the bishop's house; and, above all, for my children's abodes; you are asking for their livelihood. You say you will replace all of them—how is that possible? What you are asking for, I cannot give you. But you seem to be a good human being. Tomorrow is Sunday; you come to church during the congregation time. Okay?"

'Professor Sarabhai went to the St Mary Magdalene church on Sunday at 8 o'clock. Some of us accompanied him. The Reverend Father Peter Dereira was reading from the Bible, the book of Matthew. When he finished, he noticed that Professor Sarabhai was there. He called him in front of the congregation and introduced him to the people, who had come for the Sunday mass.

' "Here is Professor Vikram Sarabhai. He does space research, my children. What I do as a priest, he does for science. What does science do? There is electricity; there is the telephone; when I talk to you, the congregation, I talk to you through a mike system. Science helps human beings in many ways. We get increased agricultural yield by the use of fertilizers. It continuously contributes to the prosperity of the individual, the family and the nation. What do I do as a preacher? I pray: may the Almighty be with you, so you can live in peace. Money alone is not sufficient; you need peace. So both of us are doing the same job for mankind. You need both. You need economic well-being and the well-being of mind. So both of us are doing the same job."

' "Oh, my dear children; this Professor is a good scientist and he wants your abode, our abode, my abode, and God's abode. Can we give him that, my children?"

'There was a pin-drop silence for a while. Then all the people got up and said, "*Amen! Amen!*"

'For me, the spirituality is visible there. The Christian Father with an understanding of science and what it can do, and a scientist who can understand what the Christian Father can do. Here I find a spiritual force operating between two good human beings. All around us the congregation was agreeing. That is real spirituality.

'What these two minds had done was that they built a bridge of compassion and love for humanity. Both these minds were elevated minds. The Reverend Father Dr Dereira and Professor Sarabhai elevated themselves to the state of good spiritual leaders.'

The challenge of a spiritual-based leader

'Real spirituality is when you go beyond your religion. Your religion is what it teaches. One part of it is a religious code; the other part is the moral values. You take any religion; moral values will be the same. But the religious structure, the theology, is different. When religion transforms into a spiritual force, the people become enlightened citizens with a value system. It is, therefore, most important for the happiness, peace and prosperity of the mankind that we transform our religious forces into spiritual forces.

'I have visited all the religious chiefs here in India: Christianity, Islam, Hinduism, Buddhism, Jainism and Sikhism. I have met all the religious groups. Whenever I go into the religious places they preside over, when I am with them, I feel as though I am in an oasis. I am in a beautiful orchard, music is there, birds are chirping, deer are dancing, and the human beings are peaceful and broad-minded. Every religion looks like that. But when I come out from their place, every religion appears to be an island. How do you connect these islands? They are all good people. Every religion has got a good message, but they are giving the message to individual groups of people. How do we connect them? You can connect them with compassion and love; that is the bridge. Can we do that? That is a challenge I have taken.'

Fundamental truths revealed by my father

'One person who kept my spiritual background continuously operating for me was my father. He lived for 103 years. I have tried to understand the fundamental truths he revealed to me, and got convinced that there exists a divine power that can guide one to one's true place.

'When I was a 12-year-old boy, my father was elected as a member of the *panchayat*, the county council, by the villagers. He was also elected as the

President of the *panchayat* council, not because of his richness, not because he was famous, but because he was a good human being. In spite of his belonging to the Muslim community, a large number of members of other religious communities voted for him. He got the position because he was a good human being.

'The following event occurred on the day he was elected. At that time we didn't have electricity. I am talking about 1941. On that evening, he had gone to the mosque for prayer. I was reading aloud my homework in history and geography. I was in the habit of reading aloud in my sixth class days.

'Normally we never used to close the doors of our house. When I was reading, somebody opened the door and asked me, "Where is your father?" He had a big packet with him. I told him, "My father has gone to the mosque for prayer." He asked me, "Can you please give this to him?" Then I called my mother to get her permission to accept it. My mother was also praying, as it was 6 o'clock. She didn't respond to me. So, what could I do? I asked him to keep it and go. [But] he left the packet with me, and went away.

'After the prayer in the mosque, my father came home. "What is this?" he asked me. I said, "Somebody came. He has put a slip with it and given it to me." My father opened the packet. There was a silver plate, some nice, costly *dhotis* (men's clothing), lot of fruits and other very attractive things. Then my father got up, and for the first time in my life he beat me. I started weeping, and my mother came to my rescue. Then my father stopped, and he read a *Hasid*, a saying of the prophet Mohammed. He read, "God says, when you are given a position, he has given us everything, you don't need to seek anything from others." My father explained the *Hasid* to me: "You should not receive any gift. The gift itself has got an intention. Don't ever do that, my son." And I have never done that from that day. This teaching nobody has taught me, except my father. All the spiritual background comes from the family.'

Spiritual happiness

'When I was recently addressing the assembly of about 300 legislators in the state of Andhra Pradesh, a young lady, a member of the assembly, asked me: "Mr President, we know you have done so many things in your life; can you tell us which of these gave you immense happiness?" '

President Kalam told us that he gave the woman who questioned him many examples of what had given him happiness, and then asked her: 'Is there anything beyond happiness? In the Indian language, we speak of *Ananda*. You may call it bliss, but bliss is not the correct meaning of this word. *Ananda* means spiritual happiness. How do you get spiritual happiness?'

To exemplify what he meant by 'spiritual happiness' he then told her the following story: 'For some airborne structures, I developed a very light material, one-tenth of the weight of materials with the same strength. It is called carbon-carbon material. This material was needed for a particular missile. One day a doctor friend of mine, an orthopaedic surgeon, Professor Prasad, came to my laboratory in Hyderabad, and I explained to him about this material. He then lifted that whole thing and said: "So light!"

'He was wonderstruck. "Oh, Kalam, what are you doing? You are doing missiles and various things, why not remove the pain of the people," he said. Then he took me to the hospital and showed me the ward where there were 15 young physically challenged children, polio patients. After having been operated on, they were carrying a calliper to support their legs. Each calliper weighed about 3 kg. My friend said, "Can you lighten them? Nobody wants to wear them, because they are so heavy."

'I took it as a challenge and made a mould out of a composite structure. The resultant calliper weighed only 30 grams, 1 per cent of the previous weight. When the children wore them, they started running. When the parents, fathers and mothers, saw this, tears of joy came from their eyes. That was *Ananda* for me. That was spiritual happiness.'

Core competence of India . . .

'A Stanford professor asked me the other day, "Mr President, tell me, what is the core competence of India?" I thought of it and said, "The core competence of India is to choose a leadership for leading a multi-religious, multi-cultural, multi-lingual democratic nation of a billion people."

'I believe that every country has spiritual people in important positions in society. As long as the person comes from a family with a background in the joint family system—that is, with the father, mother and grandparents together—the traditional value system gets embedded. Family background influences nobility, and nobility comes from the way the children are brought up.'

. . . and of business

When we then asked him about the core competence of business, President Kalam poetically replied: 'The most important thing is righteousness, *dharma*. When there is righteousness in the heart, there is beauty in the character. When there is beauty in the character, there is harmony in the home. When there is harmony in the home, there is order in the nation. When there is order in the nation, there is peace in the world. You see the beautiful connectivity between these. The question before all of us today is: how do we get righteousness in the heart?'

If God is with me, who can be against?

'One thing I have found is that I am influenced by a certain belief. It's something like this: "If God is there, who can be against?" It's very simple, biblical. It's beautiful, isn't it?

'I met HIV patients in a sanatorium. I saw them; I talked to them. Finally I told them, "My dear friends, can you recite the following poem? If you recite it to yourself, you'll get the strength." I felt I had to help them to strengthen their minds. They wrote it down and made thousands of copies and sent it to everybody.' President Kalam then recited for us the poem he had read to the patients:

> *If God is with me, who can be against?*
> *I sought the Lord; he heard me;*
> *he delivered me from fear.*
> *The Divine Light enters into me, penetrates into me,*
> *and cures my pain in body and soul.*
> *Divine beauty and peace enter into me,*
> *blossoms happiness in body and soul.*

'They were in pain. The pain felt by people who are losing their life. How do you help them? Divine cure! The Unseen Hand. They should be aware that God is with them. I created this poem in the course of time of my life. Of course, I was inspired by sayings from the Koran, from the Bible, from Buddhism, but the message is mine.

'After becoming the President in 2002, I have visited almost all parts of the country and met over 500,000 young people. Every day I meet at least a hundred or two hundred students. They have their problems. I share their pains, and, when I come back, I try to do something good for them. Whether the child is from Nagaland or Kerala or Puttaparthi or from Delhi, every child wants to live in a prosperous, happy, safe world. As the President of India, my feeling is that I have to work for my nation to bring this prosperity, happiness and safety. I give students, the young people of India, this message: "Dear friends: Learning gives creativity, creativity leads to thinking, thinking provides knowledge, knowledge makes you great!" '

Appendix A
Research methodology

This section supplements the introductory section, 'Spirituality as the basis for leadership', where we briefly considered some of the most important methodological aspects of the research programme.

The purpose

As stated in the description of the Spiritual-based Leadership Research Programme, 'the overall purpose of this research is to contribute to the emerging field of and the consciousness about spiritual-based leadership in work organizations worldwide, by making high-quality and reliable data, information, knowledge and development methodologies about spiritual-based leadership easily accessible.'

The primary emphasis of the programme so far has been on interviewing executives in business who (1) have a consciously held spiritual view of life, (2) who have led their business from that basis, and (3) who are willing to share their perspectives on spirituality as the basis for their business leadership with us and with others.

The process

In order to be able to conduct the interviews, we drew upon two sources: executives we knew personally who were spiritually inclined; and our network of colleagues and friends whom we trusted to refer us to executives who were spiritually inclined.

Prior to the interview, a detailed letter and the interview guide that we would employ during the interview were sent to the interviewee to explain how the interview would be carried out; this was accompanied by a questionnaire to collect quantitative data. The interview itself typically took 1½–2 hours. On a few occasions the interview was followed up by a second, shorter interview. This was, for example, the case when the interviewee contacted us and told us that he or she had more to say. In some cases, after an interview was transcribed, we contacted the leader in writing to obtain further information or regarding any apparent inconsistencies (e.g. as to dates for events). In all cases, the final transcribed interviews were sent to the interviewee for approval.

Almost all the interviews were face to face, most often in the executive's office or home. In a few cases the interviews were made via telephone; except for one situation, these telephone interviews were with leaders whom we had previously met in person. In all cases, and with the explicit permission of the interviewee, the interview was recorded, and handwritten notes were taken to complement the recordings. Aside from two interviews that were conducted in English through a Spanish interpreter, all the interviews were directly carried out in English.

Each interview followed an interview guide that was developed, tested and modified during the early stages of the research programme. This template was built up around four major themes:

1. *Your career.* Provides relevant background information on the leader.

2. *Your spirituality.* Provides the leader's definition of spirituality and reflections on its relationship to religion, the leader's spiritual perspectives (view of life, purposes for life and work, principles and values), the leader's 'spiritual theme', and how the leader has evolved and continues to 'grow' spiritually.

3. *Leading a business from a spiritual basis.* Provides stories of how the leader has embodied spirituality in his or her leadership. Also focuses on the leader's spiritual perspective on such matters as the purpose of business and of one's own organization, success in one's career and organization, and the development of the organization's culture and of how it, and business in general, can contribute to society.

4. *Being a spiritual-based leader.* From the leader's spiritual point of view, treats such matters as the leader's relationships with other executives and major stakeholders, what the leader feels he or she needs to learn

about being a spiritual-based leader, internal questions to guide decision-making, and advice to aspiring spiritual-based leaders.

The interviews were 'semi-structured', meaning that the guide was simply that: a template, where, depending on the specific situation, the amount of time spent on certain questions or themes might differ from one interview to another. This also permitted posing exploratory questions as required in order to better understand the interviewee's replies.

Some of the leaders we spoke to were no longer associated with the company they spoke of; in such cases, we refer to the leader as 'former CEO' or 'former Senior Vice President' and the like. Some of those we spoke to have since moved on to new positions; in such cases, we have supplemented the profiles with the latest information we have been able to obtain on their new business affiliations.

Since *Leading with Wisdom* contains profiles of leaders from many parts of the world, a comment is called for regarding the word 'from'. In this epoch of globalization, leaders may be born and raised in one country,[1] carry out studies in another country, have their home in another country, and work in still other countries. The following are a few examples: Amber Chand was born in an Indian family in Uganda, attended boarding school in England, received her university education in Uganda, before going to the USA for graduate studies, where she finally settled down and led her business. John R. Behner is another example, this time in 'the opposite direction', so to speak. He was born in the USA, where he was also educated and spent the first few years of his business career. He later moved to El Salvador where he still resides. Niran Jiang was born and raised in Mongolia, university-educated in China and the USA, and has her business in Australia. Ramon Ollé was born and has his home and family in Spain, has his office in the Netherlands (Holland) and is the leader of the European, Middle Eastern and African operations of a transnational company that has its headquarters in Japan.

In this regard, when we refer in the text to a leader as coming *from* a particular country, this ordinarily refers to the country where *she or he has carried out the leadership activities* presented in the profile, and not to, for example, the country of the person's birth, citizenship or the like.

Most of the interviews were conducted by two members of the research group. One of the interviewers then transcribed the interview. Because the flow of the interview may not have perfectly followed the interview guide, the transcription was then reorganized to fit it, in order to make for easier

---

1   The executives were born in India, Sri Lanka, Mongolia, the Philippines, France, UK, Denmark, Sweden, Spain, USA, Colombia, Peru, Ecuador, Argentina and Uganda. Ten of the leaders work in a country different from their country of birth.

reading, interpretations, and comparisons among interviews. The resulting edited transcript was then reviewed and discussed by all four members of the research team, making minor adjustments and ensuring that the language (grammar, use of English words, etc.) would be understandable to an international audience. Following this, it was submitted to the person interviewed for approval, comments and suggestions. In some cases, this led to a number of modifications and changes by the interviewee.

The final approved version of the transcribed interviews were abridged and edited by us to form the profiles included in this book. All four members of the research team discussed the resulting profiles. We note in this connection that we have avoided personal remarks (except in the profile introductions in those cases where we have known the executive for some years) and subjective evaluations; our emphasis has been on simply presenting the leaders' own words in a well structured, easy-to-read manner.

Limitations/reservations

Our presentation of the 31 spiritual-based leaders does not correspond to what you would ordinarily find in a traditional academic book. There are very few references and footnotes, and there is only a minimal attempt to present a historical framework or overview of the development in spiritual-based leadership.

Furthermore, and most significantly, we do not base our interviews and analyses on existing, well-established theories as to spiritual-based leadership; such well-established theories do not exist! In addition, no attempt has been made to formulate concrete hypotheses that can be tested by other researchers. Rather, the book has been designed to let the leaders speak for themselves. This qualitative research approach is more like 'storytelling' than traditional scientific analysis.

A reservation concerns the leaders who agreed to participate in the investigation. Based upon their demographic characteristics, the 31 spiritual-based leaders in business who have been presented here appear to be a most heterogeneous group. For example, the age span of the leaders at the time of the interview was from 32 to 73 years and, of course, the profiles include both men and women. They perform their leadership in 15 nations (India, Australia, the Philippines, Czech Republic, Switzerland, France, UK, Denmark, the Netherlands, USA, Colombia, Peru, El Salvador, Argentina and Tanzania). The size of the companies as measured either by the number of employees or revenues varies by a factor of more than 1,000—from small start-ups with only a few employees, to major international companies with more than 100,000 employees. In fact, one could say that by categorizing the 31 leaders presented into seven groups, corresponding to the seven sections of the book, we have made the group appear to be even more heterogeneous.

Another way of looking at this heterogeneity is to consider whether the sample is representative of the total population of spiritual-based leaders. When researchers attempt to generalize from their observations, they tend to refer to the sample they have observed as being 'representative' of some overall population. We make no such claim whatsoever. First of all, we do not know what this would mean, as there are so very many factors that could enter into determining the 'total population of spiritual-based leaders', and what would constitute a 'representative sample' of these leaders. Certainly, at the level of geography, the sample provided here cannot be said to be representative for leaders throughout the world—we do not have leaders working in such major countries or regions as Japan, China, Indonesia, Germany, Italy, Russia, Arab countries/Middle East and most of Africa. In other words, we cannot support whatever preliminary observations/generalizations we may draw by using an argument that our 'sample' is representative, as in a typical quantitative analysis.

For this reason we have not carried out and presented quantitative analyses based on the 'hard data' we received from many of the interviewees (the responses to the questionnaires). The data is not sufficiently 'representative' to permit testing any hypotheses or even presenting any tabulated results, though it may be of considerable interest for designing further investigations.

Another reservation or limitation of the study is that we have taken the leaders' responses to our interview questions at face value; we assume that the interviewees talk about their work and spirituality in an accurate manner. Thus, in contrast to a biography, where it is the responsibility of the biographer to check the reliability of the information one receives before making things public, we did not attempt to audit the accounts we received—for example, by interviewing people they worked with or by performing a '360 degree evaluation', or, for that matter, by speaking to members of their family or their friends. Of course, this assumption can be disputed; acceptance of their reflections, stories and self-evaluations may be said to lead to positive bias in the form of a more positive impression of their personal and professional success as spiritual-based leaders. The leaders we have interviewed, like all of us, may have a different way of looking at and interpreting their motives, actions and communications than others (such as their employees) may have. It would not be unreasonable to assume that these leaders, like leaders in general, may tend to have a more positive picture of their own thoughts, words and deeds than others have.

Related to the above is the reservation that we cannot claim to have been unbiased in a traditional sense of the word. We introduced the Preface with the following statement: 'From the very beginning of the project in 2002, it was our goal to demonstrate that business leaders can achieve success, recognition, peace of mind and happiness, while at the same time serving the needs of all those affected by their leadership, if they lead from a spiritual basis.' Furthermore, as stated in the programme description, the research group shared a particular perspective regarding spirituality. That is, the spiritual basis on which the programme is founded includes the basic assumptions:

- We are all spiritual beings, first and foremost; we exist beyond our bodies.

- Divinity is the very core of our humanity, so to be fully human is to be spiritual.

- Leadership, in business and all other work organizations, is therefore a spiritual activity to be conducted for the benefit of society.

- The goal of life is to experience spiritual fulfilment; therefore, work and business are means for spiritual growth.

We have been most aware of the possible biasing influences of these perspectives on the project when carrying out the research and in presenting the results. Therefore, we have consciously attempted to be as objective as possible in the interviewing process (by keeping to the interview guide and avoiding leading questions) and in our editing of the transcripts.

Choosing the profiles and structuring the book

We have *not* included profiles of all of the leaders we interviewed. In some cases this was simply because of the minor role that spirituality apparently played in the interviewee's leadership. In one case this was due to reservations by the interviewee about publicly revealing his spirituality after he had seen his transcribed interview. In another case, this was due to the interviewee's leadership experiences being primarily from other fields of work than business.

As we began to construct the framework for this book, we considered organizing it according to relatively objective criteria, such as the leader's age group, position, industry, nationality, business location, etc. We decided instead that the thematic criterion that would best structure the various profiles would be subjective: the leader's expression of his or her spiritual view of life, since that is what is unique to these profiles more than any other quality or criteria of leadership. The book is therefore organized into a number of sections containing profiles of leaders whose spiritual perspectives have a common focus. This enabled us to coordinate the profiles and to reap more subtle and focused insights—'harvesting the wisdom'—from the underlying diverse, extensive interviews.

Ultimately, we feel that the profiles included in this book are particularly relevant in today's business world, as well as encouraging and uplifting examples of what is possible in leading a business from a spiritual basis.

Appendix B

Business topics addressed in the profiles

The profiles in this book are from top-level executives who, from a spiritual basis, deal with practical, day-to-day business challenges, as well as strategic issues such as mergers, downsizing and building a corporate culture. This index describes the kinds of business situations dealt with in their profiles.

Topics

Purpose of business

- **Purpose of business related to 'creating wealth'**
  Leader profiles: Aguenza, Chand, Cruz, Daugherty, Franklin, Govindan, Kolind, Maitra, Moitra, Narendran, Ploix, Raghavan, Raman, Ranganathan, Sinclair, Vrethammar, Webb

- **Purpose of business related to 'serving and benefiting society'**
  Leader profiles: Aguenza, Behner, Cañada, Chand, Covey, Cruz, Cuneo, Delbecq, Franklin, Jensen, Jiang, Levy, Merchant, Narendran, Ploix, Raghavan, Raman, Sinclair, Ollé, Webb, Welling

Setting direction

- **Leading with mission and vision**
  Leader profiles: Chand, Covey, Kolind, Maitra, Moitra, Ploix

- **Developing strategy**
  Leader profiles: Chand, Franklin, Jiang, Merchant, Ploix, Welling

Business growth, success and failure

- **Starting a new business**
  Leader profiles: Behner, Chand, Cuneo, Levy, Merchant, Narayana, Narendran, Ploix, Sinclair

- **Building/growing an already-existing business/venture**
  Leader profiles: Aguenza, Behner, Govindan, Levy, Narayana, Ploix, Raman, Sinclair

- **Handling acquisitions and mergers**
  Leader profiles: Jiang, Levy, Maitra

- **Turning around a business**
  Leader profiles: Chattopadhyay, Kolind, Narayana, Welling

- **Dealing with business downturn or failure**
  Leader profiles: Chand, Narayana, Narendran

- **Selling assets (including a business)**
  Leader profiles: Chand, Levy, Narayana, Sinclair

- **Downsizing an organization**
  Leader profiles: Chand, Kolind, Levy, Welling

- **Improving quality and productivity**
  Leader profiles: Moitra, Raman

Relationship with stakeholders

- **'Doing what is right'—fulfilling duties to customers, suppliers, dealers and other stakeholders**
  Leader profiles: Behner, Chand, Chattopadhyay, Daugherty, Jensen, Pillai, Raman, Sinclair

- **Exercising social and environmental responsibility**
  Leader profiles: Cañada, Chand, Franklin, Jensen, Kolind, Raman

Organizational culture

- **Leading with values, ethics and integrity**
  Leader profiles: Behner, Cañada, Chand, Covey, Cruz, Delbecq, Franklin, Jensen, Jiang, Kolind, Levy, Moitra, Ollé, Pillai, Ploix, Raghavan, Raman, Ranganathan, Sinclair, Vrethammar

- **Creating a culture of empowerment**
  Leader profiles: Aguenza, Cañada, Chattopadhyay, Covey, Daugherty, Franklin, Jensen, Jiang, Merchant, Moitra, Narayana, Narendran, Raghavan, Raman, Vrethammar, Webb

- **Creating a culture of spirituality**
  Leader profiles: Aguenza, Cañada, Covey, Cuneo, Daugherty, Maitra, Narayana, Ranganathan, Sinclair, Vrethammar

- **Changing a culture**
  Leader profiles: Aguenza, Chattopadhyay, Covey, Daugherty, Franklin, Jiang, Ollé

- **Instituting appraisal/reward systems**
  Leader profiles: Covey, Franklin, Kolind, Ranganathan

Relationships with peers and employees

- **Influencing, coaching and building executive teams**
  Leader profiles: Daugherty, Franklin, Jensen, Jiang, Levy, Maitra, Merchant, Narayana, Ploix, Raghavan, Ranganathan

- **Treating employees with trust, honesty and love**
  Leader profiles: Behner, Chand, Covey, Cruz, Daugherty, Jensen, Kolind, Maitra, Moitra, Narendran, Ollé, Raghavan, Raman, Webb, Welling

- **Coaching, mentoring, developing skills and mind-set of employees**
  Leader profiles: Behner, Chand, Covey, Cuneo, Daugherty, Franklin, Govindan, Jensen, Maitra, Merchant, Moitra, Narendran, Pillai, Raghavan, Raman, Ranganathan, Sinclair, Vrethammar, Webb

- **Relating with unions**
  Leader profiles: Chattopadhyay, Welling

Conflicts, mistakes, crises and unethical behaviour

- **Resolving conflicts**
  Leader profiles: Covey, Cuneo, Maitra, Pillai

- **Addressing misbehaviour and employee mistakes**
  Leader profiles: Behner, Daugherty, Govindan, Narayana, Pillai, Raghavan, Ranganathan

- **Managing crises**
  Leader profiles: Aguenza, Behner, Chand, Chattopadhyay, Pillai

- **Dealing with unethical behaviour (including bribes)**
  Leader profiles: Govindan, Narendran, Raghavan, Raman, Ranganathan, Sinclair, Webb

About the authors

Dr Peter Pruzan is Professor Emeritus at the Department of Management, Politics and Philosophy, Copenhagen Business School, Denmark. He is internationally known for his work on business ethics, values-based leadership, corporate responsibility and spirituality in business. He has degrees from Princeton (BSc), Harvard (MBA), Case-Western Reserve (PhD) and the University of Copenhagen (Dr Polit.). He has been the president of a successful, international business and has authored 11 books and over 100 articles in international scientific journals. Together with his wife, Kirsten Pruzan Mikkelsen, he spends several months each year in India, where he is guest professor at leading business schools.

Leading.with.wisdom@gmail.com

Kirsten Pruzan Mikkelsen is an eminent journalist and former newspaper editor at *Berlingske Tidende,* a major daily national newspaper in Denmark. As a journalist she has worked on assignments in more than 50 countries reporting on the human aspects of development politics as well as interviewing politicians, presidents, kings, spiritual masters, authors and business executives.

. . . together with:

Debra and William Miller, residents of India and the co-founders of the USA-based Global Dharma Center, a non-sectarian, non-profit spiritual institution. Together they have dedicated their more than 50 years of combined corporate and consulting experience to inspire and empower people of all professions to live and work from a spiritual basis.